ROARING FORK VALLEY

02598

Hell Gate—above a 3,000-foot chasm—was touted by the Colorado Midland Railroad as, "The Gateway to the Pacific."

ROARING FORK VALLEY
By Len Shoemaker

Len Shoemaker

Produced By

SUNDANCE LTD.

DENVER

ROARING FORK VALLEY

An Illustrated Chronicle

By Len Shoemaker

This historical account of "my land of enchantment" is dedicated to all of its early pioneers, but more especially to Hiram C. and Elvira (Hurt) Shoemaker and George S. and Anna (Gerkin) Swigart, our forebears, who did their bit towards its settlement and development.

"So fleet the works of men, back to the earth again,
Ancient and holy things fade like a dream."

—Kingsley

SUNDANCE LTD. STAFF MEMBERS RESPONSIBLE FOR THE CREATION OF THIS BOOK . . .

Editor-in-Chief — Russ Collman

Production Editor — Dell A. McCoy

Editorial Assistant — Paula R. Erickson

Color Director — Peter E. Voorheis

Copy Staff — Carol Garcia, Eva Van Vors

Business Manager — Viva A. McCoy

Color Consultant — Tom Donner

PRINTED IN THE U.S.A. BY SUNDANCE LIMITED / DENVER.

THIRD EDITION (REVISED) PRINTED NOVEMBER 1973.
ISBN 0-913582-06-9.

Len Shoemaker posed in the first Forest Service
uniform for this photograph, taken in 1915.

It is indeed sad Len did not live to see his book, "Roaring
Fork Valley," printed for the third time in this new revised
edition. Len was born on April 22, 1881, at Rosita, Colorado,
and accompanied his parents to the Glenwood Springs area
in 1886. The Shoemakers were married at Carbondale,
December 2, 1906. He was a member of the Washington
Park Community Church, the Masonic and Elks lodges, and
the Eastern Star, all in Denver. Len was author of several
books during and after his long career with the Forest Service.
He retired in 1943, having served at posts in Boulder,
Carbondale, along the Frying Pan and in Denver, where he
remained for twenty years. He returned to Glenwood Springs
five years ago—where he died at the age of 92, July 18, 1973.

The publishers proudly present this book for your reading
pleasure—authored by an outstanding Western American
pioneer.

SUNDANCE BOOKS: DELL A. MC COY

Forgotten by the passage of time—rusty iron rails and rotting timbers slowly return to the Earth from which they came. Standing over a mine dump, these relics are all that remain of a miner's dream to get rich quick. Photographed on the south side of Cathedral Peak during the autumn of 1966, this view shows the Pearl Pass Trail zig-zagging upward between Star Peak, on the left, and Pearl Peak, on the right. This trail was traveled by many sourdough miners as they journeyed between Ashcroft and Crested Butte.

AUTHOR'S NOTE

A part of the material contained in this account of the Roaring Fork River Valley of western Colorado was obtained firsthand while I lived and worked there. Some of it was obtained from old-timers who lived there earlier than I did; some from people of my own age who remembered details more clearly than I.

Other parts of it were derived from old newspapers, bulletins, directories, and reports, and I am very grateful to Miss Ina Aulls and Mrs. Alys Freeze of the Denver Public Library, Miss Frances Shea and Mrs. Laura Ekstrom of the State Historical Library, and Mrs. Veda Burford of the State Coal Mine Inspector's office, for their help.

Miss Ruth Guest of the Colorado Fuel & Iron Corporation, N. K. Martin of its Colorado Supply Division, and Carleton Sills of the Denver & Rio Grande Western Railroad Company gave me some interesting items, which I greatly appreciate.

Many items were given to me by friends and acquaintances who were interested in what I was doing. To all who assisted, I give my sincere thanks; their contributions added much to the story.

I hope the few remaining pioneers of the valley and their descendants will find something of personal interest in the story, and that they will condone any errors that have crept into the text.

May the reader find in this review of its early settlement a bit of the magical allure that I found there as I played or labored among "its woods and templed hills."

Denver, Colorado
May 1, 1958

6

PHOTO BY DAVID S. DIGERNESS

Ashcroft was one of the earlier mining towns of the area. H.A.W. Tabor and his new wife, Baby Doe, arrived there in 1883 and bought drinks at all thirteen saloons in celebration of his smelter business there. During that year Ashcroft boasted of having a population of 2,000 souls.

TABLE OF CONTENTS

Chapter I
Introduction

1. Introduction. With the exception of a few Spanish colonists in the San Luis Valley in the early 1850's, settlement of Colorado began at a few points along the east side of the Rockies in 1858 and 1859. Then, for thirty years from those first settlements at Denver, Colorado Springs, Pueblo and other places the prospector migrants from the eastern states overran the so-called Pikes Peak region and other parts of our present state in search of gold.

To and fro over the Continental Divide they ran, leaving a countless number of prospect holes and dumps behind them. Whenever and wherever they found rich ore, towns sprang up, and for every town there were a hundred settlements on the arable lands nearby, as some of the wayfarers found favorable homestead location sites.

Almost the last part of the state to be reached by those tireless searchers for wealth, land or adventure was the Roaring Fork River Valley of Western Colorado (herein called *the valley).* But in 1878 and 1879 they at last found it. And straightway, they began to settle on the land and develop its resources. This is a tale of those immigrants and their activities in the new land.

Most of the valley was then inside the Ute Indian Reservation. The White River tribes lived at lower elevations during the winters, but came to the valley each summer to hunt and to bathe in the hot water of the springs. They called the Roaring Fork "Thunder River," or a name which translated meant Thunder River. They were awed by its mighty roar as it thundered by each June night. For in its roar they heard the angry voice of their god, Manitou, chiding them for their misdeeds and ordering them to make reparation for their wrongdoings.

The Shoemaker family came into the valley at Aspen in 1885 and I lived there with but one short exception until 1934. Beginning in 1896 I worked at many places throughout the area, and later, as a forest ranger, I helped to manage some 300,000 acres of its forested lands over a 20-year period. Consequently, I saw much of the development, know the country well and remember much that occurred. During that time I could have collected several volumes of historical material, but alas! I wasn't interested then and missed a great opportunity.

However, much has been written about Glenwood Springs, Aspen and other towns of that region, and much of the history of the valley has been preserved. Now to that record, this bit will be added. So, if the reader is further interested, he is invited to go back into those yesteryears and follow the Indian trails to and through the valleys of the Roaring Fork, the Crystal, the Frying Pan and their tributaries with me. If lucky, he may find the gold mine in that glamorous and enchanting land which those early prospectors and I overlooked.

The valley then lay in Summit and Gunnison Counties. Subsequently Pitkin, Garfield and Eagle Countries were organized, and the valley now lies mostly in those counties. There are many tributaries of the three main streams, and those of the Roaring Fork are Lost Man, Lincoln, Difficult, Hunter, Castle, Maroon, Woody, Brush, Snowmass, Capitol, Sopris, Cattle, Red Canon and Fourmile creeks. From its forested mountains and Alpine lakes those streams bring clear, cold water to the ranch lands below, where large crops of hay, grain, potatoes and vegetables are grown. And those forests harbor many elk, deer, bear and game birds. This wildlife makes it, to fishermen and hunters, a paradise where dreams come true.

Within the valley lie Aspen, with its marvelous ski runs and tows; Glenwood Springs, with its miraculous hot springs and pool; and Carbondale and Basalt, both lively agricultural towns. Other

This photo shows the D&RG trackage that circled around Aspen — serving the mines. The Smuggler Mine, located in the center, produced the largest nugget of pure silver ever mined in the U. S. This view looks toward the east.

be mined more cheaply and other materials which supplanted the use of marble eventually doomed the production of those resources there. After the gold, silver, lead, zinc and coal mines, and the marble quarries were closed, agricultural pursuits, stock-raising and other industries supplanted them and counterbalanced the loss.

Today, the valley rests securely on its own well-established foundation. Its residents may never know again the excitement of a silver stampede such as the one at Aspen in the 1880's, but they are unconcerned about it. They still have the beauty of the green-clad mountains or the snowy slopes, the lure of the trail or the ski run, the curative balm of the hot springs, the freshness of the air, the cool waters of the streams and the fertility of the soil.

Those blessings will last as long as they shall live to enjoy them. And their combined attractiveness will, throughout the coming years, cause thousands of vacationists to return again and again to that part of our beautiful, colorful Colorado. For it is a land where Nature is at her best, where the Great Creator of the Universe, in various ways, has made it everlastingly attractive—rich in allure, witchery and charm.

Most of those twenty-six towns thrived for a number of years, then sank into obscurity or oblivion, following the generally fatal decline caused by the panic of 1892 and 1893. A few thrived in the 1920's and early 1930's, then faded out when markets for their natural resources vanished. The abundance of those resources may be glimpsed in later statements concerning the quantities mined. Some of the minerals were partially exhausted, but large quantities of silver, lead, coal and marble still exist. For instance, the marble beds in the Crystal River Valley are large enough to keep a gigantic finishing mill going for a hundred years.

Although I was only four when our family migrated from Rosita (where I was born) to Aspen, I remember a few of the things I saw. For instance, when our cavalcade crossed Taylor Pass the snow-comb (recently cut through) was higher than the covered wagons. Mother and I alighted and we followed afoot until a more level road was reached. As we passed Ashcroft, which lay below the road, we saw throngs of people and all kinds of horse and mule-drawn vehicles on the streets, each seemingly in a hurry to get to some other place. However, there are many more interesting things than my recollections to relate, so I'll hurry along, too.

towns where a few people still dwell are Cardiff, Satank, Redstone, Marble, Crystal, Lenado, Ruedi, Meredith, Thomasville and Norrie. Towns which now lie silent and somnolent under the noonday sun, ghosts of their former glory and renown, are Sunshine, Marion, Spring Gulch, Janeway, Coal Basin, Placita, Clarence, Prospect, Elko, Schofield, Emma, Tourtelotte Park, Highland, Ashcroft, Ruby and Independence.

Mineral deposits outside the valley that could

This old map was originally printed in 1890 — showing the mining communities of the Roaring Fork Valley and in the surrounding territory.

Chapter II

2. **Indian Occupation.** The valley is a large area—some 1,500 square miles—but it was so isolated and inaccessible that the pioneer prospectors did not reach it until the regions to the east, north and south had been settled for several years. The high divides surrounding it were hard to surmount; the most natural one, the route from the east, was forty miles wide and over 12,000 feet high.

Of course, men afoot or on horseback could cross those barriers, but few men alone, or even in small groups, attempted it. For on the other side of the divide lay the Ute Indian Reservation, and the Utes were hostile. Harassed by the white settlers who treated with them and then ignored the treaties, they were, during the 1870's, jealously guarding the remainder of their land.

For many years prior to 1858, the Ute tribes had occupied most of the mountainous area of the state. They had held it by their superior strength and numbers from the plains tribes, but had been forced westward across the Continental Divide by the Pikes Peak invaders.

Then to acquire more of their domain, on October 7, 1863, Governor John Evans and his associates negotiated a treaty with them whereby, for certain considerations, they surrendered a large tract of land west of the Divide. The lands they continued to hold embraced the whole southwest corner of the Territory of Colorado as described by topographic features, one of which was the Roaring Fork River.

Still not satisfied, on March 2, 1868, Governor A. C. Hunt and his associates negotiated another treaty with them, which fixed the east and north boundaries of the reservation as the 107th meridian and a line fifteen miles north of the 40th parallel, respectively. The 107th meridian ran diagonally across the valley about ten miles west of present Aspen. That division line left the upper ends of the

Roaring Fork and Frying Pan valleys outside the reservation and the remainder of the valley inside. Therefore, the whites could legally enter the area around present Aspen, but were trespassing on Ute land if they advanced farther downstream.

However, this did not keep many of the prospectors from doing so, especially after the subjugation of the Utes following the Meeker massacre of September 29, 1879. This act of savage retaliation by the Utes for certain injustices imposed on them by the agent, N. C. Meeker, although sad to contemplate, was beneficial to the early settlers of the valley. For the Indians were somewhat subdued during the immigration to it in the 1880's.

As a result of that atrocity (for so it seemed to them) the new settlers west of the Divide demanded that the Utes be removed from the state. And, after considerable evasion of the issue, the government decided to do that. The U.S. Army then compelled the White River and Uncompahgre tribes to evacuate their reservation and move to another in Utah.

Following their removal, the government opened the lands to settlement about one year later—on September 4, 1881. By that time, settlers in sufficient numbers to have defied the Ute opposition had invaded much of the valley and had squatted on most of the arable land. And under so-called squatter's rights they held it until the government made it possible for them to file on and later secure patent title to their claims.

Those early settlers found many evidences of the former Indian occupancy of the land, for trails and campsites remained. Old-timers sometimes showed me trails that had been used by the Utes long before they had arrived in that country. And some of the Indian campgrounds showed the wear and tear of long use. Among these were the meadows at Ute Spring at present Aspen, those near Ruedi on the Frying Pan, those near present

Penny Hot Springs on the Crystal, those near the present Yampah Hot Springs at Glenwood Springs, and those on White Hill near present Carbondale.

In the 1890's a favorite form of recreation of the young folks (and sometimes the old) of Satank and Carbondale was a trip to White Hill or Red Hill, or both, north of the Roaring Fork. Colored beads, arrowheads and other artifacts left by the Indians could still be found. Also, at that time, there were many small poles which lay horizontally in the pinon trees. They had been burial litters for braves who had passed to their happy hunting grounds during a fight in that locality.

On Red Hill, directly north of present Satank, there was a stone barricade on its southern-most crest which had been built by the Utes. According to an unconfirmed rumor prevalent at that time, a small hunting party of Utes were attacked at the White Hill camp by a large number of Arapahoes. The Utes retreated to Red Hill, entrenched themselves and held the enemy at bay until help arrived, when the Arapahoes were defeated and put to flight.

If the tale be true (and it probably is), Colorow, the obnoxious subchief of the Utes, won his status as a "brave" in that battle. Be that as it may, he and Captain Jack and their followers ranged the several parts of the valley in 1879 and 1880, and drove out many of the prospectors who were over-anxious to secure good homesteads.

There were three branches of the confederated Ute tribes and they were termed the Southern, the Uncompahgre and the White River Utes. Ignacio, Ouray and Nevava were, respectively, their chiefs. Nevava and sub-chiefs Douglas, Captain Jack, Colorow, Antelope, Johnson, Bennett, Schivitz and Persune, and their followers occupied the region which included the Roaring Fork Valley.

Ouray represented the confederated tribes at the two treaties mentioned above and at another on September 13, 1873, and was thereafter recognized by government authorities as supreme chief of all the Utes. He was granted a salary of $1,000 per year, the agency was moved from its Los Pinos location to a site near present Montrose, and a house was built for his use and that of his wife, Chipeta.

Nevava and Ignacio were agreeable to the arrangement, but several of the sub-chiefs resented Ouray's authority and were continually stirring up trouble. Douglas, Johnson, Persune, Colorow and Jack led the revolt in 1879 which resulted in the battle at Milk Creek and the massacre at the White River Agency.

Nevava, Douglas and others were taken to Washington, D.C., and there on June 15, 1880, they agreed to release their lands in Colorado and move to Utah. Ouray died on August 24, 1880, thus avoiding the humiliation of having to see his people forcibly moved from their reservation. He was succeeded by Ignacio.

A Colorado Midland two-car passenger train rattled across the Maroon Creek viaduct on her way into Aspen in the early 1890's.

13

An early "Eighteen-Eightier" busily moved the Tourtelotte Pack Express out of Aspen in this scene from that era.

As evidenced in this 1880 scene, Aspen was showing a rapid rate of development—even though railroad connections were far away over the Great Divide at Granite. Goods were packed in on burro trains over the high mountain passes to the east and south.

Chapter III

3. Early Explorers. Following closely on the heels of the departing Utes, the horde of land-hungry immigrants gobbled up most of the cultivable lands and began to develop them. However, before we go into that further, some mention should be made of earlier visitors to the valley—those prior to 1879.

As far as can be determined, none of the early, recognized explorers reached the valley. The first white man known to enter the region was William Gant, a trapper. He claimed that he made a prospecting and trapping trip through the Crystal and part of the Roaring Fork valleys in 1859. He was able to authenticate his claim fairly well and it was generally accepted. He settled near New Castle in 1881 and built the first log cabin in that part of the country.

Other fur-trappers and mountain men possibly came into the area, but if so, the knowledge of it is dim. Their closest known approach was at Astor Flats in the Eagle River Valley, where they had some kind of a camp—undoubtedly a temporary one, as there is no record of it.

Probably the first exploring party to reach the valley was the one led by Richard Sopris, later a prominent figure as mayor of Denver. Sopris and fourteen other adventurous men decided to go on an exploring trip to western Colorado in the spring of 1860, and left Denver on July 1. They went through South Park to present Breckenridge, then down the Blue, crossed to the Eagle, thence to the Roaring Fork and the Crystal (then known as Rock Creek). There they prospected for awhile and incidentally named majestic Mount Sopris for their leader.

They didn't find any valuable ore, so soon turned down the Roaring Fork Valley. When they reached the site of present Glenwood Springs they cut trees, made a raft and crossed the Grand (now the Colorado) River to the hot springs, where they camped and rested for over a week. At that time there was an island in the river at that point. While there they bathed frequently in the pools of hot water, and one day—July 23, 1860—they blazed a large tree and inscribed their names and the date on it. The party then crossed to present Meeker and returned to Denver along the same route followed by Captain John W. Gunnison in 1853. Sopris kept a detailed record of the trip and of the area he traversed, and the data collected was used by William Gilpin, the first territorial governor, when he made his first map of Colorado Territory.

Prospecting parties occasionally ventured into the Ute Reservation, usually with sad results. One such was led by Benjamin Graham, who had prospected on the East River (Gunnison) side of the Elk Mountains as early as 1866. In 1870 he and six companions, James Brennen, C. M. Defouch, R. A. Kirker, Sam McMillan, Louis Brant and William Gant (previously mentioned), came into the East River Valley, thence across the divide to the head of Rock Creek (within the valley). They set up a camp and prospected, discovering many galena-bearing lodes and a seam of anthracite.

Although well within the reservation, they built a fort-like cabin and made other improvements. But in 1874 the Utes discovered their camp, drove them out and burned the buildings. They had to return to civilization over the same route by which they had come, subsisting on game they killed along the way.

Alvin Foote, in his booklet entitled, "The Fabulous Valley," misquoted me when he told about the Ben Graham incident. He had seen a previously written manuscript in which I had described it and he put this statement into the booklet: "Shoemaker goes on to say . . . Graham . . . reached the head of Rock Creek by *traveling up the Grand River . . . and turning up the Crystal at the present site of Carbondale.*" (My italics.)

I didn't say it and how Foote reached that conclusion is hard to determine. As the reader can easily see on any map of that area, they merely crossed the divide between the heads of East River and Rock Creek. Had they followed the route described by Foote, they would have had to make a 200-mile trip through the heart of the Indian Reservation—down the Gunnison, across to the Grand, and up the Grand, Roaring Fork and Crystal (Rock Creek).

It is the general concensus that the eviction of the Graham party was due to the activities of Dr. F. V. Hayden's surveying parties there in 1873 and 1874. Chief Ouray had granted the geological surveyors immunity, but had ordered his sub-chiefs to evict all prospectors. And this they had done to Graham's sorrow.

Dr. Hayden, U. S. geologist, and his associates crossed most of the valley during their survey of Colorado Territory. Although inside the reservation some of the time, they were seldom molested. They mapped and described the topographical and geographical features, and assigned names to many mountains and streams.

In 1873 J. T. Gardner directed the primary triangulation, Henry Gannett, the topographic work, and William H. Jackson, the photographic section. James Stevenson directed the quartermaster division which supplied all sections. Associated with them were: W. H. Holmes, artist and scientist; A. C. Peale, geologist; W. R. Taggert, assistant geologist; H. M. Stuckle, assistant topographer; J. H. Batty and W. D. Whitney, naturalists; W. L. Carpenter, entomologist; and John M. Coulter, botanist. "Potato John" Raymond was the cook, Tom Cooper and Harry Bishop, packers, and Tom Cole, a helper.

The present inhabitants of the valley are indebted to this hardy group for the first authentic maps of the region and some of the geographic names. For instance, Gannett reported that Mount Daly was named for Augustus Daly, the then president of the American Geographical Society. He described the Elk Mountain Range as being all the mountains that lie along the present Gunnison-Pitkin County line and those to Mount Sopris, northward, and Crested Butte, southward.

Dr. Hayden claimed that the Elk Mountain region presented the most complex geologic problem that he had encountered anywhere on the continent. He said the mountains had been lifted and tossed in several directions by some great force. That statement is readily understood when one looks them over from any of the peaks and sees some of the strata lying on their backs. Present travelers over the Buckskin Pass trail may note the red sandstone on the Maroon side and the gray granite on the Snowmass side. It is an unusual but beautiful spectacle not soon forgotten.

In his 1874 report Dr. Hayden said that one of his men became ill at the foot of Mount Sopris, and he had to stay with him for twenty days. Holmes, who took command during his absence, named the man as Assistant Topographer Shanks. He undoubtedly recovered as no mention was made of his death.

Jackson took many pictures of the area, sometimes climbing the peaks with his bulky equipment to get better shots of what he wanted. He had many mishaps and one of the most disastrous of these occurred in the Crystal River country; Gimlet, the mule that carried the exposed plates, fell and broke most of them. This caused Jackson and his helpers to do considerable back-tracking to retake the pictures.

After he and the others finished their work in the Elk Mountains, the whole party went on a search for the up-to-that-time, mystical Mount of the Holy Cross. They followed the Frying Pan River to its source, crossed and recrossed the Continental Divide to the Eagle River Valley, and eventually found the peak. On August 23, 1873, Jackson, assisted by Cooper and Coulter, climbed to the top of Notch Mountain, and Jackson photographed the peak (eight times) early the next morning.

For parts of two years those valiant surveyors traversed that wild unsettled region enduring many hardships, but to them it was just another job to be done which in itself was their reward. Today, the Elk peaks, towering and majestic, bear silent but everlasting testimony to their endeavor and accomplishment.

Having worked in the Elk Mountains for about eighteen years, I am closely acquainted with them. I know how difficult it is to get through them with saddle- and pack-animals where there are no trails, and hereby commend their courage, resourcefulness and endurance.

Chapter **IV**

4. **Independence, 1879.** The actual occupation of and residence in the valley began in 1879 at four prospector camps which later became towns. Actual settlement on the agricultural land did not come until later, because those early pioneers had but one thought in mind: they had to find gold. The four camps were Independence and Ute City on the Roaring Fork, Highland on Castle Creek, six miles south of Ute City, and Schofield on the head of Rock Creek, some twenty-five miles southwest of those towns.

Following the Leadville boom of 1877 and 1878, prospectors crossed the Continental Divide at Hunters (Independence) Pass and began their search near the head of the Roaring Fork River. And there they did find gold. Some of those prospectors were William Belden, John R. Williams, Theodore Ackermann, William Langstaff, Charles L. Moore and Robert Borsen.

Billy Belden and a partner found a good-looking vein in the spring, dug into it and on July 4 struck rich gold ore. They had called their claim Belden, but in honor of the day they renamed it Independence. When they broke the news of their strike, all work stopped and an all-night celebration was staged. And as soon as the news reached Leadville, many other men crossed the Divide and a tent-town sprang up. It naturally took the same name as the mine—Independence.

Bill Langstaff and Jack Williams built a log house—a place to eat and flop, as Williams later described it. Theodore Ackermann started a store in a tent with a small stock of goods that he packed in on jacks. He soon built a house and eventually expanded his store into a store-restaurant-boarding-house business. Langstaff also sold a few things, and both of the places handled liquor and cigars.

5. **Ute City, 1879.** In June, 1879, before the strike in the Independence Mine occurred,

three men—Phillip W. Pratt, William L. Hopkins, and Smith Steele—had by-passed that camp and gone on down the valley. When they reached the site of present Aspen, they pitched camp beside a large spring and started prospecting. They soon found outcroppings of good silver ore, and Pratt located the Spar claim, Hopkins the Pioneer and Steele the Galena. Pratt's Spar proved to be a bonanza.

On July 7, a group of four men—Charles Bennett, S. E. Haskins, A. C. Fellows and Walter S. Clark—arrived, and they, too, camped at the spring. They came in from the Gunnison country where they had seen the recently released reports of Dr. Hayden. Those reports showed that there was evidence of rich ores in the Roaring Fork country, so they had immediately started for that valley. Upon their arrival they were surprised to find the other group there, but welcomed their company. They started prospecting and also found good outcroppings. Within a few days they had staked the Monarch, Iron, Haskins, Steel and Mose claims.

Another group of five men—Warner A. Root, Henry Staats, Mitchell Lorenz, William Blodgett, and J. Warren Elliott—arrived shortly afterwards. They went up into the lower end of the Hunter Creek valley, set up a camp and prospected there. Later in the summer, Henry Tourtelotte came in alone and camped at the spring. He had whacked his jack across the Divide from Leadville and was prepared to spend the winter in this new country.

Other small groups of men arrived—a total of twenty-three: George Albert, John Carroll, James Cleaver, Little Evans, William Hillburn, Joe Lewis, Henry Parmeter, Frank Routt, William W. Amesbury, Mike Cavanaugh, Sam Creston, Thomas Fraier, F. McCandless, Charles H. Jacobs, Henry Reifstader, A. Schmidt, George Clarkson, Jim Egbert, Newton K. Hall, Henry Matheny, Dan

Independence had a toll road by 1881, providing access over the Divide to Pearl—in favor of the longer route over Taylor Pass and down to the Gunnison area. The once heavily-forested hillsides were stripped bare to provide fuel to feed the stamp mill at Independence.

McPherson, Jake and Matt Smith.

The entire group prepared to spend the winter there. They built dugout shelters, collected firewood and made other preparations. However, after the Meeker massacre on White River, Governor Frederick W. Pitkin, fearing that other whites would be slain, sent a fast courier to the Roaring Fork country to warn the men there of their danger. Heeding his warning, all the men except Pratt and Steele left for more secure locations. Those two decided to stay and as a precautionary measure moved to another camp on Aspen Mountain. As fear of an attack by the Indians decreased, they reoccupied their former camp, and soon afterwards some of the deserters returned and wintered with them.

In November three other men—Henry B. Gillespie, William C. E. Koch (pronounced Ko), and his son, of Leadville and Denver—crossed Hunters Pass on snowshoes to see and examine the new mines. Gillespie, an agent and co-partner of A. D. Breed, a Cincinnati capitalist, thought he might find a good investment. And he did, for after examining the Spar and Galena claims, he secured options on them from Pratt and Steele, and notified Breed.

Breed immediately took up the options, paying $25,000 for the two mines. This was a small fortune to the locators, but it was only a small fraction of the wealth which the purchasers realized from the highly productive Spar.

While at Ute Spring camp, Gillespie proposed

The Elk Mountain Lodge resides beside the road that earlier prospectors traveled while on their way over Taylor Pass through the notch to the left. The road over Pearl Pass turned off and crossed the peaks to the right.

that the camp be named. Phil Pratt suggested the name Ute City and that name was unanimously accepted. A rough survey was made and a rough plat drafted. Also, an agreement whereby each man present was allowed two lots was signed. However, Bennett and Hopkins were opposed to the plan and the agreement and soon thereafter filed homestead claims on the tract.

When the Indian scare occurred in September, William Hopkins went to Denver to look for money to develop the claims that he and his partners had located. He sought out B. Clark Wheeler and Charles A. Hallam, agents and co-partners of David M. Hyman, another Cincinnati capitalist, and told them what he had. They conferred with Hyman and made Hopkins an attractive offer.

Accordingly, in January 1880, Wheeler and Hallam procured a bond on the Smuggler, Durant, 1001, Monarch, Iron, Haskins, Mose and Steele lode claims, and the Bennett and Hopkins homestead claims, from Hopkins, et al. They paid Hopkins $5,000 down and agreed to pay an additional $160,000 under certain named conditions. Hopkins thought he had struck a good bargain and time proved that he was right. But the "good" applied not to him, but to Hyman who eventually realized several millions from the mines.

6. The Smuggler Mine. There is an old, oft-repeated tale about the Smuggler Mine (mentioned above) which, fittingly, should be related here. It goes thus:

One of the 1879 prospectors at Ute Spring shot at a deer near the camp. He missed it and the deer

19

Most of the residents of Aspen—including the school children—went to meet the first Denver & Rio Grande construction train to reach the town, hauled by engines 83 and 403. The date was October 13, 1887. The teachers and children were given a short ride on the occasion—while a local brewery took a wagonload of beer to the workers. Whistles tooted, bells rang, and according to one Judge Deane, "The miners set off enough giant powder to bore a mile of tunnel." The demonstration continued for several days, reaching a climax when the first 25-car passenger train arrived on November 1, with Governor Alva Adams, his staff, most of the top officials of the D&RG, and several-hundred visitors, as shown on the page opposite.

ran toward Smuggler Mountain. The prospector followed and shot again, this time killing the animal. As he was dressing out his kill, he saw a good-looking outcropping close by and staked it (put up a location notice).

Another prospector, riding a mule, came by. He stopped to chat and the hunter showed him the new claim. He examined it, and knowing it was a rich vein, he talked the hunter out of it by offering him $50 and the mule. As the Smuggler and other associated properties produced ores worth about $97,000,000, he also made a good bargain, provided, of course, that he got a fair share of that amount.

The tale may or may not be true, but it makes a piquant anecdote. It probably is true, for it has persisted down through the years. It was mentioned in one of the first editions of *The Aspen Times* (in 1881). Frank Henry (Frenchy) told it to me in 1915 at his camp on Rocky Fork Creek. He named the two prospectors, but unfortunately I didn't record their names. Later, I heard several men relate the tale and it was always told the same

way; none of them, however, knew the names of the prospectors. James and John Harrington first worked the Smuggler Mine, but I don't know whether either of them was one of the pair mentioned in the old tale.

The largest piece of silver ever mined was taken from the Smuggler. It had to be trimmed before it could be removed and then it weighed 1,840 pounds. While it was being locally displayed, someone facetiously remarked that he would like to have it for a paper weight.

The production figures quoted above were given to me in 1918 by Charles Anderson, who was superintendent of the Smuggler Leasing Company for many years.

7. **Highland, 1879.** During the summer of 1879 other prospectors from Tin Cup, Crested Butte, and other towns in the Gunnison country entered the valley over Taylor, Coffee Pot and Pearl Passes on the Taylor Range. One group from Crested Butte came over Coffee Pot and down West Castle (Conundrum) Creek, and started pros-

pecting on the Castle-Roaring Fork divide south of Ute City.

A group of town promoters, led by T. E. Ashcraft (pronounced Ashcroft) followed. They laid out a townsite which they called Highland east of the junction of West Castle with the main stream. It developed faster than Ute City did, due probably to the skillful promoting of Ashcraft. Woods Brothers, of Buena Vista, packed in merchandise and opened a tent-store. Other men from Ute City and elsewhere came in and the camp boomed.

Many lode claims were stalked on Carbonate and Copper Hills east of the town. A few of them—Mountain Elk, Iron, Little Russell, Opher, Hercules, Richmond and Ajax—are given to show the odd names used. Stevens and Leiter, Colonel Gray and Cree Brothers were among the first locators. A. W. Zern located the Eva Bell and was the first to strike ore of value. Soon afterward he bonded his mine to N. C. McAlpine and C. C. Harris for $30,000, but whether he ever got the money is questionable, for many bondholders reneged in those days.

Farther south on Fisher Hill, Frank P. Morgan and Dave Brainard of Denver located the Florence, Sheridan, Pittsburg and Silver King claims, and put a large force of men to work on them.

8. Castle Creek, 1879. In July, 1879, another group of prospectors from the Crested Butte country came over Pearl Pass into the head of Castle Creek, about twenty miles south of Ute City. They found rich pockets of gold ore and located many claims, but left no visible sign of a settlement. Some of the pockets of gold ore produced as much as $5,000.

Two of these men—Amos Kindt and Charles Culver—got down as far as the present site of Ashcroft and wintered there. They were among the group which started Castle Forks City in 1880. Kindt had been a buffalo hunter on the Texas plains; he was known locally as "Panhandle" Kindt, and he was active in mining affairs in that locality for about fifteen years.

9. Schofield, 1879. In June, 1879 a group of prospectors from Gothic came over present Schofield Pass into the head of Rock Creek Valley. They prospected the whole area around the place where the Ben Graham party had worked in the early 1870's and found several good silver veins.

A group of town promoters, led by B. F. Schofield, followed. With him were H. G. Ferris, Daniel Haines, G. Edwards, William Agee, S. H. and E. D. Baker, A. H. Slossen, and J. Evans, a surveyor. On August 24 they surveyed and platted a townsite on the south fork of the creek near timberline. They named their town Schofield and started to develop it.

According to rumor they sold every lot in the townsite, even selling one each to ex-President Grant and ex-Governor Routt when they visited the camp later. Several businesses were started, among the first being a hotel by Mrs. Buddee and a store by Charles Scheue (pronounced Shoe, or more often Shooey).

Thus it may be seen that Independence, Ute City, Highland and Schofield (in that order) were the earliest town settlements in the valley. Ute City, now Aspen, alone of those 1879 towns survived, but the others helped to open the area to settlement and start its development. Therefore, their names are important historically and should be remembered.

PHOTO BY DAVID S. DIGERNESS

The towering Maroon Bells—southwest of Aspen—are flanked by golden-hued aspens at Maroon Lake in this autumn view. The page opposite reveals Conundrum Pass with freshly-fallen snow on White Rock Mountain in this late autumn scene. Back-packers probably wonder about the size of the beavers that live in this lodge beside the trail to Conundrum Hot Springs in the lofty mountains above Aspen.

22

Fred Iselin — an expert on the ski slopes at Aspen.

The Smuggler Mine at Aspen produced the largest nugget of native silver ever mined—weighing 1,840 pounds.

24

Chapter V

10. **Independence, 1880.** Independence got off to a good start when in the fall of 1879 the Farwell Consolidated Mining Company was incorporated by a group of Leadville men. They were W. P. Dickerman, president; W. H. Phillips, secretary-treasurer; Robert Borsen, general manager; and others.

In 1880 the company secured title to several claims: the Independence 1, 2 and 3, Last Dime, Last Dollar, Legal Tender, Mammoth, Mount Hope, Champion, Sheba, Friday and Dolly Varden, and began the construction of a stamp mill. It had fifteen stamps and it got underway in January, 1881.

During that year it was enlarged to thirty stamps. Each of these weighed 850 pounds and dropped ninety times per minute. The copper plates were twelve feet long and were supplemented by 400 feet of blankets. The mill was supplied with both steam and water power. Nearly $100,000 worth of gold ore was milled that year. However, the rich ore played out and the mill was shut down on January 21, 1882.

Several log houses were built; then a sawmill supplied lumber, and some frame houses and the large mill building were so constructed. The boiler at the mill required a lot of fuel and as coal was not available, timber was used. As a consequence, all of the easily available timber was cut and used.

During the summer of 1880 William B. Kinkead and Burton, town promoters, with the consent of a majority of the residents, surveyed the townsite for the purpose of securing a patent title to the land. They renamed the town Chipeta in honor of the then famous Ute woman and incorporated it on July 9, 1881. Kinkead applied for a post office and secured one called Sidney. He was its postmaster, having been appointed on January 4, 1881.

The Farwell Company officials resented Kinkead's actions and applied for a post office under their name. Their request was granted, and Farwell post office was established on July 14, 1881, with Theodore M. Van Eyck as postmaster.

Another group who didn't like either Sidney or Farwell secured still another post office, which they called Sparkill. It was established on February 1, 1882, with Hiram McHenry as postmaster.

Thus this small community of some 350 people now had three post offices at the same time. However, Sidney was discontinued on March 20, 1882, and Farwell, on July 3, 1882, leaving the field to Sparkill. Theodore Ackermann replaced McHenry as its postmaster on November 20, 1882.

The business directory for 1881 lists four grocery stores, three saloons and four boarding-houses at Independence. A newspaper, *The Independence Miner*, was started that year, its first issue appearing on October 8. George C. Hickey owned and edited the paper, which was published for only a short time.

11. **South Independence, 1880.** In the spring of 1880 some of the men at Independence went over Green Mountain and began to prospect on the South Fork of Roaring Fork River (Lincoln Creek). They found a few veins of good silver ore, and as soon as the news spread many other men joined them.

Two or three camps were set up near timberline in the head of the gulch, the main one being Hurst's Camp. Hurst, Kinney, Spencer, Smith, Fowler and Field were some of the prospector-settlers. Others were I. F. Young, John Larson, P. N. Balcomb, William Anderson and H. Berry.

Some of the claims staked were the Jennie Larson, by John Larson; the Lone Boy, by Balcomb; and the Scottish Chief, by Kinney. They were good producers and the ore from them was packed out by jack train over Red Mountain,

Castle Peak rises above the surrounding countryside in this view along the trail leading out of Castle Creek Valley south of the ghost town of Ashcroft.

thence down the Lake Creek-Taylor Park Trail to Everett. From that point it was hauled to Leadville.

Some of the other claims there were the Little Della, Osage, Windsor, Fortune, Tenderfoot and North Star, but each proved to be worthless.

In September, 1880, the men at Hurst's Camp decided that a mining district should be formed. Word of their intentions was circulated and two weeks later fifty-six miners assembled there and formed the Lincoln Mining District. At that time someone suggested that the South Fork of Roaring Fork be renamed, because (to quote his words) "the name was danged near as long as the crick." Dr. Ashbaugh, a new arrival, then suggested that they give it the same name as the mining district,

and after some discussion the name Lincoln Creek was accepted.

Three of those early immigrants left their names attached to geographical features there. They are Larson Peak, Anderson Lake and Youngs Creek, and the names originated because Larson, Anderson and Young lived at those places. In later years the name South Independence (generally applied to the locality) and the name Hurst's Camp (generally used by the local miners) gave way to the name Ruby, which was derived from nearby Red Mountain.

12. Aspen, 1880. In February, 1880, B. Clark Wheeler became anxious to see what he had bought from William Hopkins at Ute City; so,

The south side of Cathedral Peak is honeycombed with miners' prospect holes—high above timberline. One may hike along, and now and then hear tumbling rock as if the old prospectors are still searching for elusive Golcondas.

27

accompanied by Captain Isaac Cooper, Jack King and Dr. Richardson, he crossed the Divide on snowshoes, and eventually arrived at the Ute Spring camp, or Ute City, as it had been named by Gillespie in November, 1879.

Before he left Denver he obtained permission to survey a townsite there, and after he had examined the claims, he and his associates surveyed a townsite and marked its exterior boundaries on February 24, 25 and 26. Wheeler filed the plat with the Gunnison county clerk and recorder on March 25, 1880. In miner's phraseology, he deliberately "jumped Gillespie's claim." Many years later that act was taken into court, but the outcome of the legal action is not known.

Wheeler didn't like the name Ute City and conferred with other men. He told them that such a beautiful site should have a more appropriate title, so Walter Clark suggested that the name Aspen would be appropriately descriptive, because of the surrounding aspen-clad valley and mountains. Wheeler liked the name and though there was some objection, the name was bestowed. Therefore to Clark went the honor of naming the new town. He had located claims on the mountain south of the townsite and had already considered that name for it, so Aspen Mountain naturally followed. Clark lived in the town for the remainder of his life, and in 1916, when I first met him, he proudly told of having named the town.

Wheeler's investigations of the mines around Aspen proved to him that there was an abundance of rich ores in that locality. When he returned to Denver his glowing reports of what he had seen advertised the Roaring Fork mining field across the nation and interested unlimited capital for the development of the mines. David Hyman, his backer, soon paid off his bonded indebtedness and advanced money for development work.

Accordingly, in the spring of 1880 Wheeler sent three men to Aspen to set up a camp, and on May 8-11 he and Hallam with seven assistants crossed the Divide to Aspen on foot to begin work on the mines. The seven men were Josiah W. Deane, Byron E. Shear, Charles McBride, Mitchell Lorenz, George Constantine, Big Bill Watson and Jenks, a surveyor. Two newspaper reporters, W. W. Williams and W. H. Higgins, accompanied them.

Later, in the *Commonwealth Magazine* of September, 1889, Deane vividly described the trip in an article which he entitled: "Early Days in the Roaring Fork." The men had undoubtedly encountered a lot of snow, but he did not mention snowshoes. The following statements are from the article:

"Our party of nine men outfitted at Leadville, and with the assistance of a mule team made Twin Lakes in season for supper . . . Just out of Twin Lakes, we encountered snow enough to abandon the team and with our traps on our shoulders we tramped on to Seaton's ranch . . . Six hundred pounds of flour belonging to us had preceded us . . . Such of our party as could attempted each to carry one of the 50-pound sacks.

"We made it over the range the second day out just at sunset . . . At Langstaff's we breakfasted, and after a whole day's hard work, we came to the Roaring Fork but seventeen miles from Aspen. All day up and down on hogbacks, and on the night of May 11, 1880, we entered Aspen. The five or six men there were glad to see us with 300 pounds of flour and 20 pounds of bacon we had brought in."

Sam Lee, a cook, F. L. Johnson, a packer, and one other man, who had preceded Wheeler's party, had a camp set up for them. That was a blessing to those trail-weary, flour-laden travelers and their spirits soon revived. Two other assistants, John B. Brooks, a mineral surveyor, and Northrup, an assayer, arrived the next day. Work was started and as soon as snow conditions were favorable, Johnson began to pack in supplies and equipment.

Deane, who had studied law, established a charcoal pit and produced charcoal for use in sharpening tools as his first venture. Afterwards he acquired a tract of land south of the townsite and it became the Deane Addition. He later practiced law and was the first judge of Pitkin County. Hallam acquired land north of the townsite and it became the Hallam Addition. Shear later associated himself with H. B. Gillespie and made a stake in the fabulous Mollie Gibson Mine.

John B. Farrish, an experienced mining engineer, was employed by Hyman and he followed the Wheeler party to Aspen. He set Brooks to surveying the claims and Northrup to assaying the ores while he investigated Hyman's holdings. He recommended that development of the mines, especially the Durant, be pushed as fast as possible as a matter of precaution and protection.

The Durant, Spar and 1001 covered the apex of the great contact vein as it extended along the ridge of Aspen Mountain. The Emma, Aspen, Vallejo and other mines were along the side of the Durant, covering the vein on its dip or downward inclination. This phase of the situation caused several legal contests when those last-named mines reached the vein ahead of the first-named group. If Farrish's recommendation had been followed, it might have prevented the subsequent apex vs. side line litigation by giving the original locators safe title by right of possession.

Judge Josiah Deane was a good friend while I lived in Aspen. He was a staunch supporter of Forest Service policies and gave me strong support in carrying out those policies in that locality. He also gave me much of the material that is included in this account.

He was Governor Pitkin's choice for the new county's judicial post. Afterwards, he acted as county attorney for a few years. He took an active part in the apex-side-line case mentioned above, and worked long and faithfully to secure approval of the Independence Pass Highway project.

With reference to his article, partially quoted above: "Seaton's ranch" was up near the junction of the forks of Lake Creek and the town of Everett, which was later developed there. His statement "we came to the Roaring Fork" might be misleading, as he was following that stream. He referred to present Lincoln Creek which was then the South Fork of Roaring Fork. His "17 miles" were actually ten by the present highway mileage chart.

PHOTO BY THE LATE JOHN B. SCHUTTE

The fine arts were considered a part of life by people in the mining camps and towns, as illustrated by the Wheeler Opera House in Aspen.

Inside the Wheeler Opera House one could enjoy comedy, musical concerts and grand opera with the stars in full costume.

DENVER PUBLIC LIBRARY, WESTERN HISTORY DEPARTMENT

Chapter VI

13. Aspen, 1880. Before B. Clark Wheeler left Denver, he, Isaac Cooper and other men, on March 6, 1880, organized the Aspen Town & Land Company. That project had been proposed by Wheeler and directed by Cooper, and other known members were C. A. Hallam, W. L. Hopkins and D. M. Hyman. Their object, of course, was to promote the Aspen townsite.

Accordingly, as soon as possible after he arrived at Aspen, Wheeler hired A. Rittenhouse, a newly-arrived surveyor, to make a more perfect survey of it. Streets were laid out and lots were platted and numbered. And as may be seen, when the streets were named some of the land-company members were honored.

Thousands of men arrived that year and thousands of mining claims were staked. Many town lots were sold and about fifty log houses and over 100 tents were raised. A few interesting items concerning those early pioneers have been found, to wit:

Charles Jacobs and James and Angus McPherson went to Highland and opened a store, but returned to Aspen in the fall and opened a store there. James McLaughlin started to build the Clarendon Hotel. David David and a brother opened the Delmonico Restaurant, and J. E. Slagle, a drug store. George Crittenden tried to jump the Aspen townsite, but was restrained from doing so by Captain Thatcher, Deane, Hopkins, Shear and others. T. A. Marshall was appointed a deputy sheriff of Gunnison County and served the community until Pitkin County was organized.

When Julius Berg arrived he was leading a milk cow and he was immediately beseiged by the milk-hungry populace, all of whom wanted to buy milk. He had a good bass voice and was always willing to lead the singing at the various forms of entertainment. He later started and ran a confectionery store for many years.

Two of the men—William Reading and George Perry—met with fatal accidents soon after they arrived; Reading was drowned in Castle Creek and Perry was killed in a snowslide in Conundrum Gulch. Also, Walter Haustrauser was killed by John Ryder at Tourelotte Park. They had staked adjoining claims and had quarreled over some unimportant matter. Ryder went home, secured a gun, returned and shot Haustrauser. He was captured and jailed, but he escaped before the case came to trial.

At the confluence of Roaring Fork River and present Lincoln Creek, Joe Sendelbach built a log house and fed and lodged Aspen-bound way-farers. His place was known as Junction House. While there Joe sent a message to Deputy Sheriff Marshall, asking him to come up and help run off a big bear that was pestering him. Marshall sent back word that he (Joe) could do his own bear chasing as he hadn't lost any bears.

James W. Curtis and his wife, Lizzie, who were heading for Aspen, stopped at present Tagert Lake, built a log house, and likewise fed the people who passed by. Mrs. Curtis gained recognition as a baker of delicious pies—a rarity in those days. She mixed wild berries with dried fruits and sold her pies as fast as she could bake them at one dollar each. (Pies then were usually sold for twenty-five cents). The name is still preserved in Curtis Hill, the first leg of the Independence Pass Highway.

Eugene and Lloyd Grubb started a blacksmith shop which they ran for a few years. They then went down the valley and traded for a ranch a few miles south of present Carbondale. Gene specialized in the raising of potatoes and gained considerable recognition along that line.

Joshua Dustin, who was the host at Seaton's ranch in 1879, followed the crowd to Aspen and became the first constable. He was active in civic affairs for several years. Once he made the headlines in an issue of *The Aspen Times* when he publicly twisted the nose of his female companion. He was haled into court and fined. He learned the next day that he had been over-fined and went on the warpath until he secured a rebate.

William Blodgett, Frank Thompson and Walter Seaton organized a transportation company, and contracted to pack and haul the ore from the Spar Mine to the Leadville smelter. Until the road over Independence Pass was completed, it was a hard and unprofitable venture. But with tenacious persistence, they managed to keep going most of the time.

14. Roaring Fork, 1880. In the spring of 1880 a group of Leadville men, headed by Dr. A. A. Smith, the Leadville postmaster, and Judge J. W. Hanna, attempted to start a rival settlement just west of Aspen. They formed the Roaring Fork Townsite Company, and their surveyor, H. T. Buckley, laid out a townsite on an area between Castle and Maroon Creeks, which the company called Roaring Fork.

Buckley made a fine plat of the new town and displayed it in the Clarendon Hotel; as a result, many lots were sold. The company built one

house and several tents were raised.

About that time H. B. Gillespie, who was still Aspen's foremost booster, made a trip to Washington, D. C., to arrange for a post office, a postal route and a telegraph line. He had been successful, but by some political maneuver when the post office was established the promoters of Roaring Fork had it assigned to that place.

Their attempt was unsuccessful, for Gillespie and W. C. Koch, who had been appointed as postmaster on June 7, soon persuaded the postal authorities to move the office to Aspen.

As a result of the questionable methods in promoting Roaring Fork, the project failed early in the year.

15. Aspen, 1880. During his trip, H. B. Gillespie secured a license to construct a toll road from Aspen to Taylor Park. During the summer of 1880 he promoted and financed the project, and it was constructed by Stevens & Company. It extended up Castle Creek to Castle Forks City (Ashcroft), across Taylor Pass to Grandville (Bowman) and paralleled the Taylor River to Old Man's Cabin (Denny's). At that

COLLECTION OF THE LATE JOHN B. SCHUTTE

John Schutte was but a baby when his parents ran this bakery in Aspen. John later became famous in the Glenwood Springs area as a photographer.

31

point it joined the toll road which ran from Buena Vista across Cottonwood Pass to Hillerton and Tin Cup, both lively towns within the Park at that time.

B. Clark Wheeler, at about that time, began to promote a toll road across the Continental Divide at Independence Pass to Twin Lakes. He was not so successful as Gillespie and the road wasn't built until the next summer. In the meantime, Wheeler and other business men had a trail constructed from Aspen to Seaton's ranch.

Wheeler then organized an express and jack-train service to Granite, the nearest railroad station. Others started jack-trains and many long lines of burros and mules plied back and forth over "the hump," as the Divide was usually called, packing ores out and supplies into Aspen. Some of the ore was packed directly to the Leadville smelter for four cents per pound. Each round trip was a difficult task which required much time and much hard work for the animals and the whackers.

All kinds of things were packed into Aspen, and one of the most difficult objects to transport was a wagon. J. B. Girard brought it in from Twin Lakes in June. A month's time and about 3,000 man-hours of strenuous effort were required to accomplish the job.

16. **Highland, 1889.** The influx of prospector-settlers into the valley in 1880 was not limited to Aspen, for Highland developed faster than that town. Most of the lots were sold; about forty cabins were built and about 150 tents were raised on other lots. The remainder were marked with a set of foundation logs or by a notice of ownership on a stake or a post.

Several tent-stores, besides Woods Brothers (previously mentioned), were opened. Known operators were Jacobs & Company, Boulter & Company, and Kingsbury & Irions. Prices charged were extremely high for those days because of the time and effort required to pack in the merchandise.

However, despite its propitious outlook, the town faded out when none of the claims produced paydirt. Its residents moved to Aspen or Ashcroft and by fall the town was almost deserted, thus becoming the first ghost town in the valley.

A few years later one of B. Clark Wheeler's ventures, on Carbonate (Richmond) Hill, paid off when rich ore was found in the Little Annie Mine. It was a good producer for a while, and had the strike occurred in 1880, the town of Highland might have existed for several years longer. A large mill and several houses were erected about 1890 and were used until the ores played out.

About 1910 an attempt was made to reach the Little Annie vein by boring a tunnel to it from the Castle Creek level. A group of local men organized the Hope Mining Milling & Leasing Company, and beginning about one mile above Highland, bored a three-mile tunnel eastward. However, to the sad regret of the officers and the thousands of shareholders who had invested in the project, very little valuable ore was found.

In the early 1920's, after a long and desperate struggle, the famous Hope Tunnel was abandoned and with its passing went many hopes of the local people for the revival of the old "boom" days. At the time, Ben Kobey was the president of the company and James Hetherly was superintendent of the mine, and their long, hard fight for the success of the project is commendable.

At the present time Highland and its environs are the scene of some skiing activity, and the locality may see further development along that line. The Highland-Bavarian Lodge, erected in the 1940's, may eventually become the forerunner of a large winter-sports project.

The Henry Gillespie house—later called a "ghost house,"—in Aspen was typical of the fine architecture of that day.

The Forest Service built this cabin along the trail near Conundrum Hot Springs as a shelter for rangers and others making long trail rides to patrol the area.

Conundrum Hot Springs pool was built by the Forest Service in 1912 and was once covered with a roof so that one could soak in the warm water without being burned by the intense high altitude sun rays.

Chapter VII

17. Tourtelotte Park, 1880. The name, Tourtelotte Park, came into existence when Hank Tourtelotte climbed up Spar Gulch in the spring of 1880, looking for ore veins. When he camped at a spring in the beautiful mountain park, he did not know that his name would be linked with the spot for all time thereafter.

Unknowingly, he had crossed some of the richest veins in the region, but in his case ignorance was bliss, for there he found the place that exactly suited him. He built a cabin and staked several claims, one of which—the Buckhorn—eventually paid off.

Other prospectors came by, stopped to visit, and bewitched by the natural charm of the place, stayed. They located claims, built cabins and formed a small settlement which for several years had no outlet but a steep mountain trail.

And, oddly it seems, the camp had no town promoters and was never surveyed or laid out as other towns were. Also, all of the names of the early settlers (except Hank's) seemed to have vanished into thin air.

During late July and early August, ex-President U. S. Grant and ex-Governor J. L. Routt made a wagon-trip into the Crested Butte area, and eventually they reached Gothic. Pete Barthel, a long-time resident of present Carbondale (then a boy), saw Grant sitting on the porch of the Gothic Hotel, smoking a cigar.

Hearing of the then much-advertised town of Schofield, those illustrous visitors decided to go up and look it over. As there was no road between Gothic and the new town at that time, they rode mules. At Schofield they visited many of the prospects, duly escorted by some of the town's officials who hoped to sell them claims. One day they were taken to the brink of a deep, dark

canyon north of town to view the fearful chasm. Locally it was known as Sonofa B — Basin, and when Grant learned its name, he laughed and said: "You Westerners certainly name things appropriately!"

Their arrival at Schofield had been a matter of great moment to the townspeople, who went all out to celebrate the occasion. They were royally welcomed and responded pleasantly to the greetings.

18. Schofield, 1880. Schofield continued to grow during the summer of 1880, although not much paydirt had been found. Several houses and a large mill were built, and much development of claims was done by prospectors who flocked in from Gothic and Crested Butte.

During the jubilee which followed, a barrel of whiskey was sent out for free consumption. According to rumor it had been made hastily from ingredients at hand and was only a little less deadly than poison. But even rumor does not tell whether the guests partook of the refreshment. Grant and Routt stated later that the trip, especially the jaunt to Schofield, was the most enjoyable one they had ever taken.

19. Crystal City, 1880. Some of the Schofield prospectors drifted on down Rock Creek during the summer of 1880 and found rich silver ore at a point on the north fork of the stream. Among the many claims located was the Lead King. It was a good producer and the ore was packed to Schofield and milled there or at Gothic.

A small settlement grew up around the mine and after a road reached the place a few years later a large mill was erected there. The area around the mine and mill became known as Lead King Basin, a name which still persists.

Other prospectors gathered at the confluence of the North and South Forks of the stream where more good ore was found. A small settlement called Crystal City was started in the fall of 1880, and some of the early arrivals there were William D. Parry, G. D. Griffiths, William Wood, Frank and Charles Avery, Tom Boughton, and Mead.

The prospectors found a crystalline, or crystal-like quartz, in their diggings, and from this discovery originated the name Crystal City. According to stories told by some of the old-timers, many of the crystals were very beautiful. In the 1890's a prevalent rumor gave W. D. Parry the honor of naming the town.

Other early residents were John Sugar, James Riland, Frank Williams, John Mobley, William, Pete and Ed Barthel, A. A. and F. C. Johnson. The Johnson Brothers started a store and Mrs. G. W. Melton, a boarding-house.

20. Clarence - Marble, 1880.   John Mobley and William Wood moved on downstream from Crystal City in 1880, and each located homestead claims at the confluence of Rock and Carbonate Creeks. Each laid out a townsite on his land; Mobley called his Clarence, Wood called his Marble. Over the years small settlements developed and seemingly there was considerable rivalry. According to rumor Clarence predominated at first, or at least it was more widely known than Marble. However, Wood's group won out; it secured a post office with James Riland as postmaster, and shortly thereafter the two settlements were united as Marble. The town was incorporated on August 5, 1899.

Mobley had brought his wife Julia, three children and their worldly possessions from Gothic on burros. He was twenty-nine and she twenty-eight years of age at the time. Again they moved on downstream and camped at the confluence of Rock and Avalanche Creeks.

Some prospecting and mining was done in the vicinity of Marble and a smelter was constructed and operated for several years. The chief interest, however, was in the marble beds which William Wood and W. D. Parry had discovered on Yule Creek in 1882. A few attempts to quarry some of the marble were made in the late 1880's.

In October, 1890, A. J. Mitchell and Dr. Klein of Philadelphia, who had become interested in the marble beds, came in to look them over. They were well pleased with what they saw and soon afterward started a movement which ran into a development of the marble deposits, later.

In 1892 John C. Osgood, who was interested in the Rock Creek coal fields, quarried a large block of marble to send to the World's Columbian Exposition at Chicago. It cost him $1,700 to show the block, but it attracted much attention to that part of the valley. In 1895 and 1896 he and others quarried more of the marble, and it was hauled to Carbondale and shipped to finishing mills in the East.

21. Castle Forks City, 1880.   In the spring of 1880 William F. Coxhead of Leadville began to prospect on Castle Creek about twelve miles south of Aspen. He filed on a placer claim which he called Castle Forks and laid out a townsite which he called Castle Forks City. A few prospectors bought lots and a small settlement was started. Some of the early arrivals there were John M. Leahy, Calvin Miller, Milo Dawson, and William Lipps.

Coxhead struck good ore in the Highland Mary claim soon afterward and lost interest in the town he had started. He sold out what rights he had to T. E. Ashcraft, when his venture at Highland failed. Ashcraft and his associates took over in the spring of 1881 and began to promote the town. They didn't like the name Castle Forks City, so changed it to Ashcraft, over the protest of T. E., 'tis said.

Daniel McArthur, a long-time resident of the town, arrived in 1881 but went down the valley to the site of present Glenwood Springs. There he almost ran into a small band of Utes, but saw them first and hid in the timber until they left that locality. He soon turned back and immediately found more trouble; the rivers were at flood tide and his two jacks wouldn't cross them. He did some prospecting and finally got back to Ashcroft in the spring of 1882. There he remained for over forty years.

About 200 people came into the camp in 1881, but only half of them spent the winter there. However, they and hundreds of others returned when the boom started in 1882, the account of which followed shortly.

Ashcraft, like Coxhead, soon lost interest in the town; he started prospecting and discovered or otherwise gained an interest in the North American Mine up near present American Lake. According to Jack Leahy, Ashcraft made a small stake there, then sold out and went back East. Although he lost interest in the town and deserted it, it still bears his name and probably always will. It has become a well-known landmark in the valley.
In the 1940's Stuart Mace opened a lodge there and operates some kind of a dog-sledding business.

22. Aspen, 1880.   Although settlement of the valley in 1880 began to spread to outlying districts, Aspen was still the center of activity. And though sadly handicapped by its isolation from the marts of trade, its development slowly advanced.

The completion of the Taylor Pass toll road, late in September, brought considerable relief. The section between Castle Forks City and Taylor Pass was the last constructed, and before it was finished, wagons began to arrive, the first about July 1. The wagoners had to by-pass that section and to do so, followed timberline from the Pass to a point directly above Castle Forks City. They then lowered their wagons to Castle Creek Valley and the finished section of the road with winches and ropes around trees.

Immediately after the road was completed, Stevens & Company started a stage line between Aspen and Buena Vista. They charged other users of the road a toll, to wit: single animals, $1; team and wagon, $2.50; and 4-horse outfits, $5. George F. Elrod drove the first wagon over the completed road. Amos Bourquin was one of the first tollgate-keepers on Taylor Pass.

Later, Rockwell & Bicknell and Wahl & Witter ran stages over the route, and other men did likewise. Atkinson & Holbrook had one (the first) of the many large freight wagon-trains that hauled ore and supplies over the road.

One of the first wagon-outfits to reach Taylor Pass was owned by Andy McFarlane, who at that time, or later, brought in the first sawmill. H. P. Cowenhoven and D. R. C. Brown and two assistants followed him with two wagonloads of merchandise, which Cowenhoven had purchased in Buena Vista. They had to follow the route described above and their descent from timberline, according to Brown, was hazardous and difficult. William Blodgett, a horseback traveler, who had seen and talked to the Cowenhoven party at Twin Lakes, put out, later, a good description of the trip. It is shown in part as follows:

"From Buena Vista we managed shortly after nightfall of the second day to reach the Taylor River—Proceeded up Taylor River next morning—Reached the foot of the range at nightfall—Reached Taylor Pass a day and a half later.

"Followed McFarlane's track to the head of the South Fork of Castle Creek (Express Creek) . . . At timberline Cowenhoven's wagon plunged into a bog. It took a day with windlass to get it out. The second wagon was unloaded and the goods packed around the bog and reloaded.

"Next morning came to a sheer bluff, 40 feet, unloaded wagons, took them apart, lowered and reassembled them. It required two weeks to go ten miles. Finally, we reached a place 1,000 feet above Ashcroft. Brown went down and hired two more men—Cut down trees for brakes, used guy ropes.

"Got to Ashcroft at 3:00 p.m., made eight miles that night. Arrived at Aspen at 2:30 o'clock on July 21, 1880."

However, the risk and the trouble encountered were well worth while as the group reached Aspen well in advance of other merchants. Cowenhoven erected a building at the corner of Cooper and Galena and started the first store. Brown clerked for him for awhile and then became a partner.

SUNDANCE BOOKS: RUSS COLLMAN

A spectacular vista may be enjoyed at Cathedral Lake—locked in a cleft of Cathedral Peak at timberline. Trails originally used by Indians and prospectors wind in and about the area. Sourdough miners packed their ore down into Ashcroft from here.

Those early wagons followed the Cottonwood Pass road from Buena Vista to Taylor Park. But in 1882 another road was built from the Arkansas River Valley to the park, via Chalk Creek, St. Elmo, Tin Cup Pass and Tin Cup. Thereafter, it was used as much as, or more than, the Cottonwood Pass road by immigrants bound for Aspen.

The Taylor Pass road was used for about forty years by wagons, then it was abondoned by all but foot and horse travelers. According to current reports, travel from Aspen and Ashcroft can now be made by truck across the pass to Taylor Lake, and although difficult, by jeep to the park.

In the fall of 1880 much interest in the first election was evident. More than 300 names were registered but only 209 men voted. The Republican presidential electors received a majority of eight votes; Governor Pitkin, a majority of twenty-one. Warner A. Root, who had been appointed justice of the peace in April, was elected as such, and Joshua Dustin was elected constable.

Several women came to Aspen that summer and fourteen of them wintered there. They were Mrs. H. B. (Sarah) Gillespie, Mrs. H. P. Cowenhoven, Miss Kate Cowenhoven (later Mrs. D. R. C. Brown), Mrs. James McLaughlin, Mrs. Charles H. (Minnie) Jacobs, Mrs. Henry (Julia) Webber, Mrs. James W. (Jennie) Adair, Miss Phoebe Phillips, Mrs. W. C. Corkhill, Mrs. P. M. Williams, Mrs. Peter O'Reilly, Mrs. J. W. Currie, Mrs. L. C. Wellman and Mrs. White.

Those women, according to Judge Deane, "were a blessing" to that snowbound group of men that winter. Mrs. Gillespie started a Sabbath school and helped to start a singing circle. The latter became so popular that H. B. had to pitch a large tent to accommodate those who wished to attend (which was usually everyone in the camp).

And undoubtedly another blessing was the organ which Gillespie had brought in shortly after the road was opened. Night after night its melodious tones resounded from the tent as the women and some of the men joyously sang the hymns and the songs of the day.

At Christmas-time the women prepared a delicious dinner to which all of the people were invited. The dinner was a real treat to that group of about 300 men who hadn't had a "woman-cooked" meal since they left Leadville or Denver. They praised it highly and thanked the ladies profusely before they turned their well-filled tummies homeward.

On New Year's Eve the men reciprocated by preparing a dinner for the women. The best

The Cathedral Lake trail led out of Ashcroft to the mines surrounding the lake.

cooks among them prepared the food and the others served it. The women enjoyed it as fully as the men had enjoyed their dinner, and were as generous in their praise and thanks as the men had been. So in that and many other friendly ways, those early Aspen settlers learned to mould those hard frontier conditions to meet their needs.

Chapter VIII

23. Newspaper Comments, 1880. Before the story of 1881 and future years is recounted another picture of Aspen and the surrounding country should be presented. It is the one that was shown by the newspapers of the day. I believe that the items shown here are far more accurate than any record that can be produced seventy-eight years later, even though they may be slightly biased by the writer.

The following excerpts are taken from *The Daily News*, a Denver newspaper:

October 1, 1879. "Highland townsite was surveyed September 21, 1879, and the town company filed letters of incorporation with the Secretary of State."

February 21, 1880. "Ute City. The leading mining claims are the Monarch, owned by Haskins, Fellows & Company; Pioneer, by Hopkins Brothers of Denver; Galena and Spar, by Steele and Pratt; Little Pittsburg and Addie, by D. McPherson of Leadville; Hope, by Evans, a prospector; Iron and Haskins, by Haskins, a conductor on the K. P. Railroad."

"On Hunter's Creek, Blodgett, Staats, and Root. Nearly all of the stock are dead from starvation, and most of the miners have gone to Leadville to remain till about April 1, when the snow will be nearly gone."

As shown by J. W. Deane's article, hereinbefore quoted, the reporter's estimate of the miner's return to Aspen, April 1, was far too early. They hadn't yet returned when he got there on May 11.

May 6, 1880. "Roaring Forks, Colo. Postmaster, post office established."

July 1, 1880. "Aspen had mail service beginning July 1. The first post office was in the Roaring Forks townsite. It was moved to Aspen July 10."

August 4, 1880. "Roaring Forks. Building sold and moved Aspen."

July 6, 1880. "Highland. The Three Hills, Richmond, Copper and Fisher. The route from Buena Vista to Roaring Forks. Highland, July 1, 1880. Owing to the liberal policy of the town company of which T. E. Ashcraft is president, granting four lots 25 x 100 feet to those who would build improvements on two of them, the town with its motley collection of log huts sprang rapidly into existence. The principal merchants are Boulter & Company, McPherson, Jacobs, and M. L. Woods of Woods Brothers of Buena Vista, who was first to display goods in Highland, having accomplished the journey from Buena Vista via Twin Lakes and Independence, through a series of obstacles which would appal a less determined and energetic person.

"Richmond Hill, where the claims of Stevens & Leiter are located, and Cooper Hill where the Cree Brothers and Col. Gray have sunk several shafts, are producing large quantities of pay mineral. On the same range and about midway between Taylor Forks and Aspen is Fisher Hill, so named in complement to C. W. Fisher, general superintendent of the Denver, South Park, and Pacific railroad, where, if surface indications may fortell results, the choicest prospects of the district are found.

"Associated with him are Frank P. Morgan of Buena Vista and D. Brainard of Denver, who brought with them a large outfit of men, provisions, and pack animals, and have located a large number of claims which they are developing with the dispatch and enthusiasm which foreshadows success. The best known of these are the Florence lodes, the Sheridan lode, the Pittsburg, Amy Powell, Lena, and Silver King."

July 15, 1880. "Two thirds of the Eva Bella lode, located in the Highland mining district, Gunnison County, near the town of Highland, on what is known as Copper Hill, owned by A. W. Zern, C. C. Harris, and N. C. McAlpine, was recently bonded for $30,000. At a depth of ten feet ore was reached that assays 350, 340, and 331 ounces silver per ton. An assay on croppings on the Little Russell lode, located on the same hill, runs 90 ounces silver per ton."

July 21, 1880. "S. W. Sladen has purchased a smelter, which is already completed at Chicago, and will soon be in operation. The cost will be $15,000, and it is expected to handle about 10 to 15 tons a day. The road from Grandville to Aspen will soon be in complete order to travel."

August 14, 1880. "From W. F. Coxhead who has just come in from Castle Forks (or Ashcraft, as it is now called) we learn the following interesting items: The Bennett lode, owned by the Girard Company, is actively pushing developments. Not far from the Bennett Mr. Coxhead is working the Highland Mary, where he struck mineral at the surface. A toll road from Buena Vista, through Cottonwood Pass and Taylor Park, passes within three miles of the place, and has lately been traveled over by a number of wagons."

September 23, 1880. "Ashcraft better known by its former name Castle Forks, is the center of a rich mining district and is fast building up.

"Highland at one time during the spring saw a population of 500 but is now depopulated."

September 16, 1880. "Aspen's population is about 900. D. H. Bradley is president of a saw-mill company which has a capacity of 12 M feet per day. The Spar-Gillespie Company tunnel is in 50 feet."

The Bureau of Mines report for 1880 states: "The Smuggler shaft is down 75 feet; the Traynon Tunnel is in 150 feet. About 250 men are working."

In this 1905 scene the Aspen Fire Department was located on Durant Street. Fire Chief William Wack stands at the left.

The Loges Peak Chair Lift rises to 11,800-feet and overlooks the Maroon Bells. Some of Colorado's finest skiing may be found around Aspen—with more than 50 miles of ski runs.

Chapter IX

24. A Reporter's Report, 1880. Two articles from the same newspaper which show opposing opinions about existing conditions are here presented.

July 11, 1880. Roaring Forks. How to get there and what is to be seen. What it costs to live and other interesting facts. From the Leadville Chronicle.

"Of the many letters which have been written to the press of this city about the Roaring Fork country, very few were entirely free from self-interest. To supply its readers with the truth, as it did in regard to the Gunnison district, the Chronicle has been to the expense of sending a commissioner to explore the entire section.

THE TWIN LAKES ROUTE

is the shortest, probably 72 miles, the points along the route being distanced as follows: Twin Lakes, 16 miles; Seiden's ranch, 28 miles; Independence, 38 miles; forks of Difficulty and Roaring Forks, 50 miles; the Lakes, 56 miles; Cotton's ranch, 60 miles; Aspen or Ute City, 64 miles; Highland, 75 miles. As far as Sieden's ranch a wagon road has been constructed, that portion from Twin Lakes being a toll road. Rates, saddle horses, 25c; two horses and vehicle, 50c. But at Seiden's it is lost in a trail which is well marked, but very rough and marshy to the foot of the range, where a zigzag ascent far above timberline is commenced.

"So rapid is the rise and so uncertain the trail is a matter to be conjectured from the score or more of dead animals which have missed their footing and rolled back into the valley. The Mountain Boy trail is a trifle longer and less steep. Almost any settler can point it out. The descent into Independence Gulch surpasses anything the wildest imagination can conjure. The narrow path seems to be perpendicular, if it does not lean a little toward the gulch. Many a burro has ceased from troubling before he reached the bottom.

"At Independence accommodations can be obtained. Meals, 75 cents; oats, 10 cents per pound. The grass, naturally luxuriant, is fed down by stock. Leaving Independence, for twenty miles the trail leads across more rocks and swamps than any other hundred miles of trail in the world. It is plain enough, there is no danger of getting lost, as where the biggest rocks and deepest sloughs are, there is the trail. A prominent feature is the toll bridges wide enough only for animal or for man. They occur every three or four miles and cost the traveler 25 cents each. Riding that twenty miles is out of the question. It must be walked and the horse led with great care, or more legs will be damaged. It is stated that the difficulties to be encountered in crossing in the spring are greater, the sensation experienced while sitting upon the snow with the feet dangling through the ice water, is something not to be forgotten.

"Cotton's ranch is under the bluffs that separate Hunter's Creek from the Roaring Fork. Good prospects are found, some of which are worked vigorously. Four miles to Aspen is over a good path, and more toll bridges. Of Aspen a description is necessary. Any and all of the people who bought lots last winter and paid their hard cash need not fear jumpers at present. Main and Central streets are occupied as a pasture by the more aristocratic horses and mules, while the suburbs and plaza are given over to the meek and lowly jackass.

"Upon the Aspen townsite are three or four cabins, but in Ute City and Deane's addition more enterprise has centered. The Lee House is

Looking west across Aspen, the productive Mollie Gibson Mine is seen in the foreground, served by both the Denver & Rio Grande and the Colorado Midland railways. The depot grounds of the D&RG are at center right—with the right-of-way entering town from the right. The Colorado Midland entered town in the far right distance and circled around the base of the mountain to the far left.

the only hotel, and board costs ten dollars and a half per week. It will be useless to ask for meals to be sent to your room, as the hotel contains but one. The kitchen is in the street in front. A second-hand store and three or four saloons is the business of the city.

"The Smuggler and Monarch mines are located on the opposite side of the Roaring Fork. Wm. A. Farrish, of Black Hills mining fame, is the superintendent. Various stories are told of these claims and the truth seems to be known only to the managers, who take great pains to show people certain portions of the mine. Castle Creek joins the Roaring Fork on the south side and has its source in the Taylor river range. At the point of confluence, a bar of a thousand or more acres has been formed. Aspen uses the eastern half, while the town of Roaring Fork is located on the western. One tent and one log house in course of construction is the present appearance.

"The only wagon in the Roaring Fork country is employed, at $20 per day on that block house.

"At Aspen the

TOLL ROAD TO HILLERTON

takes its start. It is completed to a few miles above Highland on the Fork side of the range. The eight miles to Highland are easy ones with a constant ascent. The place is located at the junction of East and West Castle creeks—both good sized streams. The site is a mile in length along a bench on the east side of the creek; contains three streets and about 30 finished and occupied cabins. Two hundred or more foundations have been put up to hold the lots. Timber is not scarce and is mostly cottonwood.

"Three stores, all of which depend on pack trains for their supplies, furnish the masses of provisions at the following prices: Butter, 90 cents per pound; salt, 65 cents per sack; bacon, 40 cents per pound; flour, 20 cents per pound; nails, 40 cents per pound; crackers, 37½ cents per pound; whiskey, 25 cents per drink. The stores are all in tents and run upon a very cheap scale; no clerk hire, no delivery wagons, no license, no subscription papers and no city scavenger.

"ERRORS HAVE GONE ABROAD

regarding the Roaring Fork country. There is no boom in any of the towns, any writer to the contrary notwithstanding. There are no smelters or sawmills yet, although the timbers for one have been whipsawed at Aspen. The first mail accommodations were had on July first, three times a week from Buena Vista. Wheeler, so far as the writer could find, has not charged stumpage for trees cut on the Aspen townsite. Certain it is that no signs of a tree are to be seen upon the ground.

"Time will, without a reasonable doubt, make good camps at Aspen and Highland. The ore is somewhat low grade on the surface, and only the croppings are thus far prospected, but every evidence exists that better will be found. The road will remove the onerous burden upon prospectors by high prices. This class seem more than usually indolent, and are well described by one of their number as 'sleeping a great deal, working very little and eating all they can.' No mines have been found, only prospects. Over 10,000 claims have been located. A foot passenger can go by Twin Lakes, but it is folly to take animals that way. From Aspen down the Roaring Fork to Grand River the distance is forty-five miles, over a hard trail.

"Leadville has two routes open to secure a rich trade, via Red Mountain, and via Red Cliff and Eagle River. Either way is practicable, and the trade is worth the outlay of a good deal of money. At present Buena Vista must be and is the supply point. The route via Independence does not seem (although it may be) practicable."

The reporter did some very good estimating of distances over a route such as that. The

In this view the Mollie Gibson Mine is in the foreground and the Smuggler Mine is located on the hillside behind. The tram track in the foreground is running along a sluiceway.

43

A Colorado Midland three-car passenger train was recorded in this photograph while crossing the Maroon Creek viaduct. The train is just about to enter Aspen. Below the viaduct a homesteader's field is in view.

distance from Twin Lakes to Aspen on the present highway is 38.5 miles. Seiden's (Seaton's) ranch was near one-time Everett. His "Difficulty" was probably present Lincoln Creek. The Lakes were first called Curtis', later Callicotte's, and still later, Tagert's. Cotton's was later called Cosseboom's and still later, Aspen Park.

A contradictory statement, refuting some of the *Chronicle* reporter's charges, was sent to the same Denver daily. It is given here:

"Aspen, July 8, 1880. Aspen is recovering from the bitter and insiduous attacks made upon her as a camp. The Roaring Fork townsite business has undoubtedly set our camp back more than a month in development, and driven away at least a thousand people. The toll road is finished from this place to Cattle Forks City, and only a short piece remains to be constructed between that place and the top of the range. A sawmill will be running in about ten days, and as soon as possible after the toll road is open smelters will be here. There is plenty of ore in sight on the Smuggler to keep a smelter running. The great group of mines that were bonded in 1879 have been paid for, and are now being developed. There is a great demand for practical miners.

"The Smuggler, Mollie Gibson, Chamberlain, Venus, Claremont, and Crittendon and several others are working three shifts per day. New strikes are being made daily. Since the discovery of mineral in the Smuggler No. 2, Johnson's Hill has been covered with busy diggers, some looking for carbonates and others for the continuation of the vein. The vein will soon be known as one of the wonders of the world. It is known as the Spar vein and is about 28 feet wide. It has been traced and located for more than nine miles, holding to its course through the mountains as steadily as a mariner's compass points to the north. Assays of mineral run as high as 8,000 ounces.

"Aspen has now more than a hundred cabins and tents erected, and twenty or more in process of erection. Town lots are selling rapidly, and a cabin is being put up, on every lot that is sold.

"Our post office has at last reached us (no thanks, however, to the postmaster at Leadville) and we receive mail three times per week via Buena Vista and Hillerton. All mail should be directed via Hillerton.

(Signed) Byron E. Shear."

44

Chapter X

25. **Aspen, 1881.** During the winter of 1880 the men at Aspen held several meetings in Henry Webber's cabin to arrange for the incorporation of the town and the organization of a new county. Warner A. Root, the justice of the peace, prepared the papers that were necessary and sent them to the County Commissioners. Their petition for incorporation was granted on April 11, 1881.

An election was held and the following officials were selected: George Trippett, mayor; James W. Adair, Angus McPherson, George F. Elrod and Rheumanalor C. Wilson, trustees; N. J. Thatcher, clerk. Warner A. Root was appointed police magistrate and Joseph H. King city attorney.

The organization of the county met with considerable outside opposition. However, the Aspen forces, led by Captain Thatcher, B. C. Wheeler, Jason Freeman, William B. Root, Byron Shear and others came off victorious. On February 23, 1881, the State Assembly organized Pitkin County from a part of Gunnison.

Governor F. W. Pitkin, for whom it was named, immediately appointed as County officials: Andy McFarlane, sheriff; W. B. Root, clerk and recorder; H. P. Cowenhoven, treasurer; J. W. Deane, Judge; Frank Rice, Assessor; Dr. J. B. Perry, coroner; W. L. Hopkins, G. F. Elrod and Charles L. Moore of Independence, commissioners. Aspen was named the county seat, so the new officials rented a building and used it until a court house could be erected.

More men came to Aspen in 1881 than in the previous year, but only eight names of the many arrivals have been found. They were Davis H. Waite, Thomas A. Rucker, Fred H. Stockman, Amos Bourquin, C. W. Brooks, W. E. Turley, William M. Dinkel and Robert Zimmerman.

Waite was an attorney and a journalist, and practiced both professions. He went to Ashcroft when it boomed and established a newspaper, the *Ashcroft Herald.* Later he returned to Aspen and worked on the *Aspen Times* with B. Clark Wheeler, who incidentally was his son-in-law. He affiliated with Aspen Lodge No. 21, A. O. U. W. (which was organized on November 27, 1881) and was secretary of that assembly. During that time he published a labor journal, *The Union Era,* and through it gained the public recognition which led to his election as governor in 1892. Rucker practiced law, was judge for five years, city attorney for two years and then became judge of the ninth judicial district. Three of the other men started local businesses. Dinkel and Zimmerman went down to the vicinity of present Carbondale and started the first store in that

Three other arrivals in 1881 were Sonny Russell, Dale Osman Jacobs and Eula Webber. Sonny, the son of Mr. and Mrs. H. Russell, was the first child born in Pitkin County while it was still Gunnison. He possibly and probably was born at Independence. Dale, the son of Mr. and Mrs. C. H. Jacobs, arrived on April 12, thus making him the first child to be born in Aspen. Eula, the daughter of Mr. and Mrs. Henry Webber, was the first girl.

Aspen began to expand immediately after it was incorporated in 1881. A school district was formed, a school board selected, a small building was rented for use as a schoolhouse and a teacher—Miss Hattie Whitman—was hired. She had about twenty pupils at first, but the number was soon increased to fifty; and the school board had to start plans for a city-owned building.

In February, 1882, the town board issued bonds in the amount of $5,400 and built a 2-story, 4-room schoolhouse which would seat about 200 pupils. School was opened there in the fall with Miss Whitman as principal, and Miss Nellie Muir and Mrs. Eugene (Isadore) Grubb as teachers.

A fire department was organized in the spring

In 1961 the Denver & Rio Grande Western's depot at Aspen sported a gayly painted baggage door, perhaps the work of the station agent. This view looks toward town with the Independence Pass area in the background.

PHOTO BY JOHN W. MAXWELL

Engine Number 1153 of the D&RGW chuffed into Aspen with a freight train near the end of steam operations on the railroad. Aspen's city fathers have since gotten rid of the tracks and the depot has been removed to a site near the edge of town. The railroad now terminates at Woody Creek.

PHOTO BY DEL GERBAZ

PHOTO BY ROBERT A. NORRIS

The D&RGW's Number 956, a 2-8-0, was photographed at Aspen in 1946 with the local freight. Here she would be turned on the turntable prior to the return trip downgrade to Glenwood Springs.

A fire department was organized in the spring of 1881. The town board appropriated $200 for equipment and the citizens volunteered as firemen. A bucket brigade was formed first, then when water hydrants were installed, hoses and hose carts were obtained. Later, the town had several kinds of carts and an engine drawn by horses. Many fires have burned parts of the city and on several occasions the volunteer firemen have saved it from almost complete disaster.

The first post office was located on Hopkins Avenue and it was operated there for about four years. When the wagon road across Taylor Pass was opened, mail was brought in intermittently from Buena Vista. After the Independence Pass road was opened there was a daily mail stage from and to Buena Vista (later from and to Granite) via the new route.

Two stages also plied daily between Aspen and Leadville and those daily communications with, and outlet to, the outside world were a great boon to the citizens of this frontier settlement.

Two weekly newspapers, *The Aspen Times* and the *Rocky Mountain Sun*, were started that year. The first issue of the *Times* appeared on April 23, 1881, and the first issue of the *Sun*, on July 9. The former paper was published by the Aspen Printing & Publishing Company which had been organized by Ed O'Connell, Geoff Levelle, George F. Crosby and James C. Connor. The latter paper was published by Mason, Mackey & Giffney.

Connor was the second postmaster; he replaced Koch on December 27, 1881, and was reappointed on February 2, 1885.

The first church services were conducted by the Rev. E. A. Paddock, a Congregational minister, and the Rev. M. M. McCarthy, a Catholic priest. According to Judge Deane those clergymen preached on the street corners, in tents and in cabins, and occasionally in a tent-saloon which the owners had donated for their use. Both men were well liked and their meetings were usually well attended.

Many business buildings were started in 1881 and a few were completed. *The Aspen Times* erected a new building on the corner of Mill and Hyman, which was opened on July 1. On July 4, the owners raised a large U. S. flag over it, and this, according to its current issue, was the first public display of the flag in Aspen.

James McLaughlin completed the famous Clarendon Hotel that year. It was 100 x 100 feet and had 75 rooms. McLaughlin and his wife operated it successfully for many years. In it many mining plans were formulated and many conflicts were settled. Many stupenduous games of poker also occurred in it—and when mining magnates foregathered there, the stakes sometimes ran into thousands of dollars. It was also a social center and was used extensively for dances and parties.

The Tudor Theatre Comique, the first theatre, was built that year by John Tudor, who opened it on July 30, 1881. It featured burlesque shows which were staged by the Tudor family. The glamorous Mamie ('tis said) was really worth seeing.

Several boarding-houses and two more hotels were opened during 1881 and 1882. The Aspen Smelter was built in 1882-1883 for Jerome B. Wheeler by his mining engineer, Walter B. Devereux, who then managed the operation. It was blown in during August, 1884. A lead mill and other mine structures were built during 1882 and 1883.

Phil Carbary started the first newstand and he kept it well-stocked with current periodicals. Mitchell started the first brickyard, somewhere in the north end of town. He employed several men and moulded some 100,000 bricks to be used in the construction of the Aspen Smelter. J. W. Atkinson and a brother owned and operated that or another yard later. Many of the buildings in Aspen were constructed from bricks made at the Atkinson yards.

One of the festive occasions of 1881 was the marriage of Miss Kate Cowenhoven to David R. C. Brown in October. Their romance had begun on the trip from Buena Vista to Aspen and subsequently developed while Brown worked in Cowenhoven's store.

In the spring of 1881 B. Clark Wheeler started the construction of the toll road that he had been promoting. A survey was made from Twin Lakes to Aspen by C. L. Moore and others, and work closely followed the survey. Dr. J. E. (Doc) Rice, a long-time resident of Twin Lakes, built the road, and received a lump sum of $10,000 upon its completion from Wheeler and his associates. The road was nearly forty-three miles in length and followed almost the same route as present State Highway No. 82. In fact, parts of the old road can be seen all along that route. The greatest divergence from the old route was at the lower end of Mountain Boy Park on the east side of the Divide. The present highway cost nearly fifty times as much as the original road.

Construction of the road was completed in November and travel over it commenced as soon as snow conditions would permit in 1882. J. C. Carson (usually called Kit) and a brother put on a line of fine coaches and teams and made daily trips to and from Leadville. Two of their stage drivers were Walter Goff and James Davidson. Wahl & Witter and Rockwell & Bicknell later moved their stage lines from the Taylor Pass route to this one.

There were other stages, and scores of freighters started wagon trains to bring in the large stock of supplies and machinery that had accumulated at Granite on the Denver & Rio Grande Railroad. For the most of the summer they ran day and night, and according to Jack Williams, they were often a continuous line which varied from one mile to one-and-a-half miles in length. Atkinson & Holbrook moved to this route, as did most of the freighters who had "skinned" mules over Taylor Pass. Jackson, Thompson, McGee, Moore, Hill and Davis were other freighters.

Toll gates were set up at Weller, Bromley and Twin Lakes. Weller and Bromley ran the stage stations and boarding-houses at those points. Weller Station was about one-quarter mile below the confluence of Lincoln Creek and Roaring Fork. Sometime in the 1890's all of the buildings were destroyed by fire. Bromley Station was about three-and-one-half miles east of the Pass in Lackawana Gulch. A few tumbled-down cabins still exist.

Toll charges on the road were the same as those on the Taylor Pass route. One of the early gate keepers at Bromley was named Stevens and he was succeeded by George Finnegan. Weller had three sons and their family name is still preserved in Weller Lake, a beautiful mountain mirror which lies about two miles west of the old stage station site.

Also during 1881 Henry Gillespie arranged with the Western Union Company for telegraphic service and the company constructed a telegraph line from Granite to Aspen in 1882 and 1883. As postal service was slow at that time this faster means of communication with other parts of the state and nation was greatly appreciated by the businessmen of Aspen.

Chapter XI

26. Ashcroft, 1881. During the summer of 1881 Ashcroft had a population of 500 people, and it had a daily mail-stage service to Aspen, Independence and Leadville. The town was incorporated and an election was held; Peter Lonergan was chosen mayor; A. L. Teuscher, C. E. Roach, T. C. Monaghan and Peter Kearney trustees; W. S. Boyd town clerk.

Late in May a group of citizens met and planned a Fourth-of-July celebration. Mayor Lonergan presided and T. J. Flynn was chosen president of the forthcoming affair. Mayor Tannifield of Aspen and Mayor Shum of Independence were named vice-presidents. Some of the committee chairmen were Peter Kearney, T. C. Monaghan, A. A. McFarlane, Fred Maxwell, James Hawkins, Peter O'Hare, Judge J. H. King and Judge Davis H. Waite.

From newspaper accounts later, the celebration was a real jubilee with plenty of patriotic speeches, sports and fireworks on tap.

The town acquired a post office during the summer; it was called Chloride. Lewis T. Teuscher was appointed postmaster on August 5. However, the name Chloride wasn't liked and it was changed to Ashcroft (spelled with an *o*) on January 3, 1882. Thus, officially, Ashcr*a*ft became Ashcroft and has continued as such.

An item in the June 5, 1882, issue of the *Rocky Mountain News* stated: "Ashcroft. Fifteen men at work clearing and grading streets. Hotels fast nearing completion. Boom has arrived. Snow fast disappearing, roads improved."

During 1881 and 1882 some rich silver ore was found in the Pine and Express Creek areas and pockets of rich gold ore were discovered on Michigan Ridge above Blue (Cathedral) Lake. These discoveries boosted the camp's development. A trail was built from the town to the ridge and a long pack-train plied daily between the two to bring out the ore. When I built the Panorama Trail from Ashcroft to Conundrum Creek across Electric Pass in the 1920's, I used parts of that old trail. At that time Jack Leahy pointed out the old diggings and trail above the lake, and told me of the early activity there.

The fabulous strike which boomed the camp was made in the spring of 1882, when Fitzgerald Brothers and Jake Sands found rich ore in the Montezuma/Tam O'Shanter mines southwest of the town. They were leasing the claims which had been located in 1880 by Nick Atkinson and Jim Chaney. At that time the Tam O'Shanter had been called the Elkhorn, but for some unknown reason the name had been changed. After they struck paydirt the leaseholders tried to have the lease renewed but failed to do so. They therefore worked all the men they could hire and took out ores worth $196,000 before the lease expired. The ore was packed out by burros to a point about two-and-one-half miles above Ashcroft, from which point it was hauled to Ashcroft or elsewhere.

According to Jack Leahy the lower end of the pack-train route was called Jacktown, because so many jacks—200 to 300—were kept there. Their braying could oftentimes be heard as far away as Ashcroft. The place later became the settlement called Kellogg, because a man named Kellogg built a mill there to treat the ores, and his workmen resided near the mill.

Atkinson and Chaney had been grubstaked by S. E. Bruckman of Leadville, and his name had been put on the location notices of the Montezuma and Elkhorn claims. After the rich ore was found by Fitzgerald and Sands, Atkinson, Chaney, and Bruckman disagreed over rights. Atkinson and Chaney sold out to William Parker and Jake Sands, and they bonded the mines to Horace Tabor and Joel Smith of Leadville.

The author and son are shown here removing Forest Service file cases on Hyman Avenue in Aspen the day after the big fire on November 16, 1919. Fires destroyed many fine old buildings in the mining towns due to the carelessness of adults or children "at play."

Bruckman immediately filed suit against them and there was a long legal contest. The courts eventually decided the case in favor of the Tabor group and they went ahead with the development of the mines. The output from them was enormous, but mismanagement of the work at the mines and the failure of a Leadville bank, where Tabor had deposited $95,000 as payment on the purchase price of the mines, took away much of the profit.

The mines produced heavily in 1882, and Kellogg built the mill mentioned above and Brooks & Bethusen built the Castle Peak Smelter at Ashcroft. However, those facilities couldn't handle the ore and a wagon road was promoted and constructed across Pearl Pass and onward to the railroad at Crested Butte. The railhead of the Denver & Rio Grande Railroad had reached The Butte on October 21, 1881, and as soon as the toll road was opened, on September 7, 1882, much of the ore was hauled there and shipped to smelters at Canon City and Leadville.

Tabor first rented then bought the smelter at Ashcroft from Brooks and Bethusen. He made frequent trips to Ashcroft in those days and according to Leahy, there was some jubilation each time he came to town. But on the day in 1883 when he arrived with his new wife, Baby Doe, a stupenduous celebration was staged. Among other things, there was a banquet and a ball, and no one slept for twenty-four hours, while at the thirteen saloons then existent all of the drinks were on Tabor.

Some of the businessmen and firms at Ashcroft in 1882 were Charles E. Boesch, meat market proprietor; John B. Brooks, U. S. Deputy mineral surveyor; Castle Peak Smelter; Covert House, W. H. Covert, proprietor; Edward A. Hughes, saloon keeper; Issley & Lloyd, civil engineers; Peter Kearney, saloon-keeper; G. D. Kilborn, assayer; Conrad Kruse, lime kiln operator; Henry Kunz, justice of the peace; Rev. M. M. McCarthy;

McCarthy & Flynn, general merchandise; O'Connell & Overman, contractors and builders; P. O'Hare, notary public, Miss Emma Perry, teacher; Richard Perry, boot and shoe-maker; Perry & Carbary, newspaper and stationery; Riverside Hotel, Boulton Brothers, proprietors; C. H. Smith, groceries and clothing; B. L. Sowle, assayer; Sowle Brothers, livery and feed; Teuscher Brothers, livery and feed; L. T. Teuscher, postmaster; S. R. Walters, constable; P. J. Watkins, blacksmith.

27. Schofield, 1881.   Schofield thrived during 1881. Considerable development work was done in the town and in the prospect holes around it. A mill for treating ores was erected. By 1882 it had become a lively town of some 200 people.

Some of the business firms and men of 1882 were William Bridges, carpenter; C. Buddee, general merchandise; Cannon Brothers, saloon-keepers; Consolidated Vanderbilt Mining Company, S. H. Butler, superintendent; Cay, Darland & Company, groceries; John Engstrom, boot and shoe-maker; F. M. Gregory, saloon-keeper; A. H. Hale, carpenter; J. C. Harrod & Company, saloon; C. J. S. Hoover, attorney; Holman & Morrison, meat market, lumber mill; William Miller & Company, restaurant; New York Concentrating Works, J. H. McCoy, superintendent; Schofield House, hotel; Schofield Mining & Smelting Company; West Virginia Mining Company, C. H. Scheue, president; Wichita Mining Company, J. W. Phillips, superintendent.

The town had daily mail-stage service to Gothic and Crested Butte, and flourished until about 1885. At that time some of the residents were William Bright, restaurant; P. Brown, general merchandise; William D. Parry, carpenter; R. R. Ross, blacksmith; John Sugar, barber; Mrs. Louise Scheue, deputy postmaster.

However, no rich ores were found in that locality and the town declined. In 1885 the post office was discontinued and the residents began to move to other places. Today it is a ghost town that is known to only a few persons, because it is so far away from human habitation or passable roads.

28. Elko, 1881.   A townsite called Elko was laid out a few miles west of Schofield on October 1, 1881, by a group of men from Crested Butte. They were D. E. and W. A. McGloughlin, Samuel Blachtell, R. J. Walter and John Engstrom. A small settlement developed and flourished into the 1890's, but nothing is known about its residents or its business activities.

The September 25, 1889, issue of the *Carbondale Avalanche* stated: "The mining camp of Elko is quite busy these days."

29. Jerome Park, 1881.   The "coal banks" in western Pitkin County were discovered by John Murray in the summer of 1880. They lay on Coal Mountain, west of Jerome Park. In later years they were generally referred to as the Jerome Park coal banks and still later as the C F & I coal mines.

Over the years several men found exposed seams along the deposit from Sunshine on the north to Coal Basin on the south. William Dinkel found the seam at Marion in 1881 and William Gay found the one at Spring Gulch in 1882. The deposits at Sunshine on Fourmile Creek and at Coal Basin on Coal Creek were found at about that time. Numerous other discoveries were made a few years later.

However, it seems that Murray was the first person to try to exploit a mine. Just what he did is uncertain but it was enough to establish a right to his findings. For when Jerome B. Wheeler of Aspen began to look for coal to use in his smelter, Murray sold out to him. In 1883 Wheeler promoted and had a wagon road built from the Rock Creek valley to Coal Mountain, and J. C. Eames opened one of the seams and hauled coal to the smelter at Aspen. Other mines were opened and coal was supplied to most of the towns in the valley.

From this small beginning arose the great coal industry of that region which was promoted and developed by the Grand River Coal & Coke Company, the Colorado Coal & Iron Company, the Colorado Fuel & Iron Company, and the Rocky Mountain Fuel Company. It also led to the construction of the Colorado Midland Railway, for the original intent of that company was to provide transportation for the coal which those companies produced.

The source of the name Jerome has never been definitely decided. Some say it was named for Jerome B. Wheeler, previously mentioned, while others claim that it was named for J. L. Jerome, one of John C. Osgood's associates in those days, who handled much of the business there. After careful study it is my opinion that it was named for J. L. Jerome.

30. Frying Pan, 1881.   The Frying Pan country has always been divided by an east-west county line which was fixed when Summit and Gunnison counties were established in 1861. The same line still exists between Eagle and Pitkin Counties since they were organized in 1881 and 1883. Until the land was opened to settlement the lower end (wherein lies present Basalt) was in the Ute Indian Reservation.

During 1881 and 1882 the area was thoroughly prospected and many lode claims were staked. Some fairly valuable ore was found in the Bessie Mine, south of present Thomasville on Porphyry Mountain, south of present Meredith, and in the mountains northwest of present Wood's Lake. The ores at those places, however, soon played out.

The Aspen Sampler was in the process of expanding its facilities when this photograph was taken in 1889. The Sampler was located on the south side of Aspen and was served by both railway lines.

PHOTO BY DAVID S. DIGERNESS

One may tour by dog sled for much of the year in the Ashcroft area. Because of the sheltered condition in the valley, snow often covers the ground from late fall until early spring.

Homesteaders also located many agricultural claims. Among the first of these were Gabriel and Otmar Lucksinger who settled at the present site of Basalt. Otmar soon sold his claim to his brother Jacob, and he and John Ruedi moved upstream and settled at present Sloss and present Ruedi.

In the early 1880's the Aspen Smelter and other industries at Aspen needed charcoal, so in 1882 a group of men constructed some kilns near the confluence of the Roaring Fork and Frying Pan Rivers and began to produce it.

Pinon trees were plentiful in that locality and they made good charcoal, so the business thrived.

A small settlement of tents and shacks grew up around the kilns. It was first referred to as "the Frying Pan Kilns," then a few businesses were started and it became known as Frying Pan. Dennis Barry opened a tent-store and Red Duggan had one of several tent-saloons.

When the Colorado Midland Railway Company established the town of Aspen Junction across the river in 1887, Frying Pan soon disappeared. Only a few old kilns now mark the spot.

53

Chapter XII

31. Natural Resources. Readers who have followed the trails into and through the Valley have undoubtedly seen how its settlement and development progressed with each new discovery of some rich mineral. When someone found gold, silver, lead, zinc, coal or marble, other men rushed to that spot and a camp or a town was started. Only the abundance of other natural resources made this continuous advancement possible. Game, timber, grass and water were easily available, and on these resources the prospectors and their animals could subsist while they overcame the harsh wilderness conditions. Later, the land itself provided food for their sustenance.

Game was the most important of those resources to the early settlers. Deer and elk were so numerous that a prospector could kill one at any time. Without that meat the great immigration would have been impossible. Besides the deer and elk there were mountain sheep and antelope. Jack Williams saw one moose killed in Lost Man Gulch in 1880. No record of the killing of buffalo has been found; but they existed, for skulls and horns were found even in the higher valleys. Bear were plentiful and added zest and sometimes trouble to the settler's early occupation of the region. Mountain lions, wolves, coyotes, foxes, lynxes and all the lesser predatory and furbearing animals were abundant. Grouse, prairie chickens and rabbits were found all over the area.

In 1882 some prospectors encountered a grizzly bear in Conundrum Gulch, south of Aspen, and one of their number was severely injured. Some of the old-timers claim that he died and was buried nearby. There is a grave beside the trail about one mile below Conundrum Hot Springs, and a board nailed to a tree bears the incription: "Here lies Dick Reynolds. Died only God knows how." Diligent search failed to reveal whether the two incidents were related.

Not content with taking from the wildlife of the country that which was necessary for their subsistence, some of the early settlers began to commercialize that resource and game was slaughtered indiscriminately. With the growth of the towns, the construction of the railroads, and the development of the coal camps, game was killed and sold by many not engaged in those pursuits until the once plentiful supply dwindled to almost nothing.

Frank Dickens of Satank—later a trapper for the State Game & Fish Department—once stated that he killed eighteen elk on North Thompson Creek to supply the Spring Gulch camp. Solon Osgood, a resident of the Captiol Creek valley, once pointed out a place where he had killed twelve elk to sell in Aspen. Such depredations continued even after game laws were effected, and the elk herds were almost exterminated. Deer herds were greatly but not wholly depleted.

In 1912 the Elk's Lodge of Aspen, and residents of Pitkin County generally, fostered a movement to bring in a few elk to restock the country. Three shipments were obtained from herds in Wyoming. On April 17, 1913, sixteen head were released on Smuggler Mountain, and another herd of twenty-two head, on March 14, 1914. The third herd of twenty-four head was released at Meredith, in the Frying Pan valley, on March 7, 1915. Those herds were carefully protected and elk are now plentiful again. Deer, under better law enforcement, naturally increased and are now found in most of the mountainous parts of that region. A few bands of mountain sheep have held even in numbers. Grizzly bears and wolves have been completely destroyed. I saw three wolves in 1913, which were the last encountered. Considering the wasted state of the game resources in 1910, the officials and residents of the valley may well be proud of the greatly improved conditions.

Timber was next in importance to the early settlers. There were fair to dense stands of lodge-pole pine, Engelmann spruce, Douglas fir and a few minor species in most of the mountainous

54

areas. At first settlers built log cabins and houses, but as soon as lumber was available, frame houses supplanted most of them in the settled communities.

Andy McFarlane and D. H. Bradley were early sawmill operators at Aspen in 1880. They received $70 per thousand board feet, which was a very big price in those days. George Bennett ran a mill in the vicinity of Glenwood Springs in the 1880's. Some of the other early operators were Wilder & Roberts and Tom Owen on Brush Creek; Clarence Reed on Difficult Creek; Scott Brothers, Tom Owen and Frank Gowen on Woody Creek. On the Frying Pan, some of them were Robert & Anderson, H. B. Biglow, A. J. Dearhamer and Lige Thompson. Anderson & Davis operated on Cattle Creek and John Thomas on Mount Sopris. On Hunter, Castle, and Fourmile Creeks and Crystal River many old settings may be seen and their large slab-piles testify to the settler's enormous use of the timber resources.

H. G. Koch began operating about 1890 and at one time had four sawmills, the largest being at Aspen. He had a contract for awhile to furnish the Smuggler Leasing Company with 600,000 feet of mine timbers per month. Most of that timber was supplied from his operation at Norrie. According to an October, 1890, issue of *The Aspen Times,* the eight sawmills on the Frying Pan were turning out about 100,000 feet of lumber daily.

One of them was probably operated by Robert Reed, who ran a mill at different places in the Frying Pan valley. In 1913 he was operating on the North Fork of the Pan and continued to do so until the Colorado Midland Railroad was shut down in 1918. The Koch mill was also shut down at that time.

The need for charcoal before coal was available made it necessary to construct charcoal kilns here and there in the valley. Besides the ones at Frying Pan, there was another group about four miles south of Aspen on Castle Creek. Much of the timber on that watershed was cut to supply them. A. G. Sheridan, usually called "Phil," had charge of the timber operation, possibly of the kilns. The area around Independence was completely denuded to provide fuel to the stamp mill there. The barren area was planted with seedlings during the 1930's by one of the government work agencies. Many cut-over areas show the waste of timber in early-day cuttings by the 3-to-4-foot stumps which still bear silent testimony.

Forest fires destroyed a large amount of the timber. In 1879 one fire burned out the upper end of the Roaring Fork valley; it was caused by careless prospectors. Another fire swept the Hunter Creek area in 1889; it originated when one sawmiller burned the set of a rival operator. In the Owl, Willow and Maroon Creek watersheds

Colorado Midland locomotive Number 32, built by Schenectady Locomotive Works in 1888, posed smartly with a special passenger train between Rathbone and Cosy Point about 1910.

Tourists and local residents are afforded many excellent views along the Roaring Fork River between Glenwood Springs and Aspen. Many Coloradans feel that autumn is the most beautiful time of the year in the Rocky Mountains.

a fire burned over a large area when ditch builders burned the debris along their right-of-way. Most of the old sawmill settings have their adjacent burned areas, showing that the sawmillers had been negligent or had purposely burned their slash.

In 1889 two fires destroyed much of the timber around Crystal and Marble, according to Tom Boughton, a long-time resident of that region. In 1895, a fire at the east base of Mount Sopris destroyed a large block of timber. It burned for several weeks and was at night a spectacular sight from Carbondale and the surrounding country. In 1910 I worked for Frank Childs, who harvested a large quantity of the dead poles for mine props.

Grass was almost as essential to the early.

In 1960 the Colorado Midland depot in Basalt looked like this—brightly painted in red, white and blue. The depot now rests up-river about fifteen feet from its original site. Since this picture was taken the appearance of this building has been changed again.

PHOTO BY ROBERT A. LEMASSENA

D&RGW 2-8-0, Number 1137, backed downgrade through Snowmass on the Aspen Branch, shown here in 1955 with the mixed freight. Backing was necessary because the train had not gone into Aspen where the engine could be turned.

settlers as game and timber, for their animals also had to have food. There was an abundance of grass almost everywhere and in many places large meadows existed where wild hay could be mowed. In 1887 my father made several trips to a meadow near Wheeler where he cut with a scythe and brought home wagonloads of hay to feed his milk cows during that winter. Fred Light of Sopris Creek once told that in 1880 he cut six sacks of wild hay from his homestead, took them to Aspen, and sold them for $60.

However, transient herds of cattle soon overran the open ranges. In 1880 John Eames brought in 400 cattle from the Eagle River valley. Soon afterward Yule Brothers and John Murray brought in 700 cattle and 100 horses. Other stockmen did likewise and the grass crop was soon sadly depleted. But this type of grazing soon vanished as the winters were too severe for the stock to survive without hay.

Many of the settlers brought in a few milk cows or small herds of range stock and after hayfields had been established and winter feed became more available some of the small herds were increased. Some of the ranchers who ran the earlier herds in the Roaring Fork valley were Borum & White, Nuckolls, George Banning, Fred Light, Jack Williams, Milo Carroll, Price Sloss, Timothy Stapleton, Benedict Bourg and Bob Roberts. Some of them in the Crystal River valley were Jim Zimmerman, Jim Dalton, Eugene Grubb, John Thomas, Fate Girdner, George Swigart, Oscar Holland, Dan Flynn and Wald Brothers.

Nowadays, grass is almost as valuable as gold was in the early days. Under the regulated grazing system of the U. S. Forest Service the ranges of the valley furnish summer pasturage for thousands of cattle and sheep annually.

Water was so abundant that it scarcely needs mentioning. Its availability for irrigation is, of course, responsible for the enormous crops that are produced on the lands within the valley.

Another trainload of goods heads upgrade for Aspen behind the D&RGW's locomotive Number 1159, a husky Class C-48 2-8-0.
PHOTO BY DEL GERBAZ

Chapter XIII

32. **Independence, 1882.** Sparkill post office existed at Independence from 1882 to October 18, 1887, when it was discontinued. During that time the camp was known by either of those names: business directories sometimes used both names. A list of 40-odd business names, which are shown at the end of this section, was carried under the name Independence in 1882, and some of them under the name Sparkill later. Langstaff's flophouse was now shown as the Grand Hotel. Jack Williams, his partner, had moved to Aspen.

While at Independence, Jack had intermittently run a jack-train or prospected in the hills around the camp. As he once expressed it, he earned money with his jacks to plant-in his prospect holes. On one of his pack-trips he bought a large jack in Leadville for $30. He loaded it with supplies and packed them to Aspen where he received $30 just for the packing job. At another time he was paid $100 for packing two children from Leadville to Aspen. He made box panniers, placed a child in each, and packed them safely across the Divide to their new home, while their parents trudged along with Jack the full 65 miles. This incident shows the courage and resourcefulness of those old pioneers and is to me the highlight of this story.

On one of his prospecting trips, while digging in the mountains north of town, a government surveying party came by. Their leader conversed with Jack and asked him his name. After Jack had answered, he asked for the name of the mountains. Jack told him they had no name, whereupon he grinned and said, "Well we'll have to fix that Mr. Williams." He then wrote on his map and showed it to Jack; across it were the neatly-lettered words—Williams Mountains—. And today as such they stand, a lasting monument to a fine old pioneer who did his bit in the development of that fair valley.

Jack remembered the only shooting affray at Independence, but had forgotten the names of the men concerned. One of the men, the town marshal, attempted to arrest two half-drunken men who were shooting up one of the saloons. They resisted and started to draw guns, so the marshal shot and killed both of them. They were buried in the small cemetery on the hillside and in 1920 their graves were still visible, although no names could be distinguished.

The businessmen and concerns at Independence in 1882 were Theodore Ackermann, grocery and restaurant owner; H. C. Albertson, saloon-keeper; Bank of Pitkin County, R. Bailey, cashier; Briner, Lavender & Company, dry goods and clothing; Carson Brothers, daily stages to Aspen and Leadville; Conners Hotel, J. R. Conner, proprietor; T. Craig, constable; Cunningham & Small, bakery; Delmonica House, T. Bradford, proprietor; C. H. Demarest, surveyor; Farwell Consolidated Mining Company, Thomas M. Swain, general manager; Grand Hotel, Langstaff & Meeney, proprietors; Conrad Hanson, sawmill operator; C. L. Harding, druggist and stationer; Frank Harper, board and lodging; W. P. Harris, blacksmith; Wilmot Heard, attorney; Mrs. W. Hodges, restaurateur; Independence Hotel, T. Ackermann, proprietor; Independence Miner, George C. Hickey, proprietor; Lee Jones, saloon-keeper; G. Kirkbride & Company, drugs; King & Company, livery and feed; H. T. Kneeland, grocery and hardware, store owner and justice of the peace; Mrs. Maggie McCalley, laundry; New England House, J. B. Cunningham, proprietor; F. W. Neubauer, saloon keeper; Joseph B. Nine, liquor store entrepreneur; Phoenix Hotel, C. H. Demarest, proprietor; Quinn & Kelly, saloon-keeper; Charles Reagan, saloon-keeper; Joe Reynolds, postmaster (probably acting or deputy); Rockwell & Bicknell, livery and feed, daily stages to Leadville; Joe Ruddy, barber; Shinn & Cain, livery; Shinn & Hasley, meat market; Shinn & Reynolds, groceries; Simon & Rupp, saloon-keeper; A. Taft, saloon and billiard hall owner; G. L. Thomas & Sons, groceries; Peter Toohey, saloon-keeper; Joseph Vanines, liquor and cigar store proprietor; William Vining, saloon-keeper;

Wellington & Burnett, wood peddler.

33. Carey's Camp, 1882. Conundrum Gulch was the scene of much activity in the early 1880's. The earliest settler was Abe Lee who built a cabin about eight miles above Highalnd and ran a small flock of sheep up around the hot springs.

Several placers and lode claims were staked. Prospectors found gold float in the sandbars and hunted high and low for the Mother Lode but never found it. It was a puzzle which they couldn't solve. And that fact accounted for the change of the name, West Castle, to Conundrum Creek, when one of them said, "It sure is a Conundrum."

In 1882 Captain Carey located claims and started a camp about seven miles above Highland. He worked several men and about a dozen cabins were built. A commissary of some sort (maybe a small store) was set up and on August 21, 1882, William Schwartz opened a post office there and was the postmaster. He held the post until the office was closed on January 1, 1884.

At about that time disaster in the form of a large avalanche struck the camp. It buried the cabins and suffocated five men—the only ones in camp at that time—as they sat around a table in Jim Thorn's cabin. A rescue party, one of whom was Joe Sparger, reached the camp about twenty

Basalt was first known as Aspen Junction in 1887 when this photograph was taken. This view looks southwest across the depot grounds. A freight train may be seen pulling into town, heading toward Leadville. This depot probably burned prior to 1890.

In this view of Basalt — C. 1904 — Mount Sopris dominates the horizon. On this warm summer day all activity centered around the railroad yards as a train was being switched on the Aspen leg of the wye. Six locomotives are in view, possibly indicating that trains could be expected that would require helpers for the climb up to the tunnel at the Continental Divide.

days later and found the corpses. They also found Thorn's dog alive, took it to Aspen and it survived. Carey visited the camp during the following May, but how long he continued his operations is not known.

The largest mine operation in the gulch was at the Cummings claim about one-half mile below Carey's Camp. The miners and the laborers who cut fuel-wood for the mine's boiler lived at the camp. The claim was owned by Major R. J. Pickeral, Tom Ozburn and F. X. O'Brien, and Pickeral and Ozburn had charge of the mine. It was located at the base of the steep mountainside and all of the mine machinery was housed in a large underground room which had been excavated for that purpose at the entrance of the mine. That work had been done as a precautionary measure because of snowslide conditions.

I went into the room once in 1921. Everything there was apparently just as it had been left when the mine was closed. The large engines were covered with a stiff white grease.

A wagon road was built as far as Carey's in 1883 and it was extended later to Lee's cabin. At that time Pitkin and Gunnison Counties planned to construct a road connection between Aspen and Gothic over the Conundrum-Copper Creek divide.

Gunnison County built its part to the top of present Triangle Pass, but Pitkin County reneged and did not make the connection.

In 1912 a group of Aspen's citizens with some help from the U. S. Forest Service excavated a small pool near the hot springs and built a bathhouse over it. The Service constructed a small station cabin which was available to all visitors. The cabins were about sixteen miles southwest of Aspen and they were erected by or under the direction of John Parsons, who will be remembered as Aspen's most able stone mason and a builder of excellent fireplaces.

In 1929 I had to replace the sixty-four feet of 2-inch pipe which Parsons had installed to carry the hot water from the spring to the pool, and I remember it as the most difficult packing job I had ever tackled. I had the pipe cut into eight-foot lengths and after four hours of trial and error I found a hitch that would hold it in the proper position on my two pack-horses. I arrived at the hot springs at 8:30 p.m. after thirteen hours of strenuous labor, tired but happy.

In 1938, when I traveled that way with a trail-rider group, the bathhouse had been removed because of the rotted condition of the logs. However, a tent was set up over the pool and every

In 1894 the Peach Blow quarry was active furnishing sandstone for
sidewalks and building materials for Denver and Colorado Springs.
The quarry operations folded with the use of concrete in the place
of this beautiful stone. A Colorado Midland spur served this quarry
where the sandstone was loaded onto flatcars with a hoisting boom
powered by an upright steam boiler located in the shed. The stone
was transported by rail across the river where the quarry was located.
Looking up-river the valley opens up at Ruedi.

PEACH BLOW QUARRY
C. M. RR. No. 1062

rider enjoyed a bath in the naturally hot water.

34. Defiance, 1882. The land at the confluence of the Roaring Fork and Grand (Colorado) Rivers was first acquired by James M. Landis; he "squatted" on it in 1880. It was then in the Ute Reservation but in some way he managed to hold on to it, and from that small beginning arose the now thriving city of Glenwood Springs.

In 1882 Captain Isaac Cooper, who had first visited the valley at Aspen in 1879, and some of his associates—John C. Blake, William Gelder, Frank Anzensperger and Hy P. Bennett of Denver—bought his rights for $1,500. They organized the Defiance Town & Land Company and laid out a townsite which they called Defiance.

The name Defiance had first been applied to a small settlement that had survived for a while at a point several miles eastward. Cooper had been interested there and wished to preserve the name. However, his wife, Mrs. Sarah F. (Hall) Cooper, persuaded him to rename the town Glenwood Springs to honor their home town, Glenwood, Iowa. It was a very appropriate designation for such a beautiful spot.

Below a Leadville-bound train, Number 4 may be seen backing down to couple onto a Pullman observation car during 1908. The larger 2-8-0's were generally used as helper locomotives.

This unusual view shows all four of the Colorado Midland's largest 2-8-0 helper engines in Basalt on a summer day in 1908. These locomotives were purchased in 1907 and were the most powerful steamers the Midland owned.

The town, like most of the early settlements, was largely housed in tents. F. A. Barlow had a restaurant-hotel in one; M. V. B. Blood taught the first school in another. Barlow secured a post office in his name, and Mrs. Garretson became the first postmaster. A toll road, which is described later, was built from Aspen to the new town in 1883, and Barlow & Sanderson ran a semi-weekly stage between the towns. Charles Fravert and John Goff were early stage-drivers.

Also, during that summer the Grand River Bridge Company built a toll bridge across the Grand River. It was known locally as the Cooper Avenue bridge and was used until 1891 when the State Highway Department built a new bridge on Grand Avenue. It was then moved to a location on the Roaring Fork River near present Cardiff. Mrs. Perry (Eleanora) Malaby of Glenwood Springs (who has lived there in the same house for seventy-two years) recalls that the Cooper Avenue bridge replaced a suspension footbridge which had been previously constructed. She was the last person to cross the footbridge.

According to Carroll Clark of Glenwood Springs, toll charges were established by the county commissioners at a meeting held at Carbonate, August 1, 1883. They were team and wagon, $1; extra team, 50c; saddle and pack animals, 25c; cattle and sheep, 15c; footman, 10c.

High Street was the county road in Basalt before the 1900 fire. The D&RGW ran through the trees beyond the river to Aspen.

The Frying Pan River is strikingly beautiful just east of Basalt—along the old grade of the Colorado Midland.

Incidentally, Jim Landis went east after he sold his land rights to the town company, married Dolly Barlow, returned to the town, and established a home and a business. And fittingly, it seems, their son Harry was the first child born in Garfield County.

35. Glenwood Springs, 1883. Just when the name Defiance gave way to Glenwood Springs hasn't been determined. It probably was about the time that Garfield County was organized, February 10, 1883. However, the town didn't become the county seat until sometime later, for a town called Carbonate, which lay about fifteen miles north of Glenwood Springs, had been previously so designated.

Carbonate soon declined and the appointive county commissioners adopted a resolution on August 21, 1883, whereby the county records were to be moved to Glenwood Springs for safe keeping. Accordingly, the records were transferred soon thereafter from one town to the other by Frederick C. Childs, John Noonan, Perry Malaby, and Henry Brown. They had been duly appointed to do the job by the commissioners.

Glenwood Springs was soon designated the county seat, and Governor James B. Grant appointed the following county officials: John Blake, sheriff; C. A. McBriarty, clerk and recorder; George C. Banning, treasurer; William Gelder, judge; J. F. Clements, surveyor; C. S. Cooper, assessor; F. C. Childs, Frank Anzensperger and George P. Ryan, commissioners; G. G. Minor, attorney; and Forbes Parker, clerk of the district court.

John Blake built the first house in 1883 and F. A. Barlow the first hotel—the St. James. He replaced it several years later with the Barlow Hotel. Dr. Baldwin opened the first drug store, and William Ragland, the first blacksmith shop. Dick Donovan opened one of the first stores; George Schram bought it and ran it, then passed it on to his son, Fred C. Schram. H. R. Kamm built a brick building (probably the first) in 1884 and opened a store in it.

36. Aspen, 1883.   Aspen's population in 1883 was about 1,000 people and not much greater in 1884. Many mines were opened and much ore was taken out, but its transportation to the railroad at Buena Vista or Granite by wagon-train was a slow and expensive operation which retarded the city's growth. Its development, however, kept advancing as more business firms were started and more houses built.

The names of four men who arrived in 1883 were Jerome B. Wheeler, William C. Tagert, C. F. Smith and George A. Richards. Wheeler, a New York capitalist, became another enthusiastic town booster, and promoted many projects. He bought the Aspen smelter and opened it in August; also he bought several mines. Then, needing coal and

The Aspen Branch of the Colorado Midland was hit by a tremendous snow slide in 1912 which called for the use of the rotary snowplow. The size of this slide may be measured by the eleven-foot diameter rotor wheel on the plow.

coke for the smelter, he promoted the toll road to Coal Mountain and the mine development there which have been previously mentioned. He started other projects some of which will be named later.

Tagert was a boy, nine years of age, and alone in the world when he arrived. He first earned a living by selling newspapers, then went down the valley and worked on ranches. In his early manhood he opened a hay and grain store in Aspen, and later he ran a livery, bus and stage business. Smith became Aspen's efficient fire chief and served as such for many years. Richards became a real estate dealer.

Seven men who arrived in 1884 were James McMurray, county assessor; Henry C. Rogers, school teacher and county judge; James S. Harrigan, blacksmith; J. D. Bransford, insurance agent; A. W. Hare, assayer; J. E. Rockwell, attorney, and Dr. A. J. Robinson, who became mayor in 1890. Jim Harrigan still plied his trade in 1916 and shod my horses occasionally. He then became master mechanic at the Hope Tunnel project on Castle Creek.

Along with his other activities, Wheeler organized the J. B. Wheeler Banking Company in 1884, with himself as president, Henry W. Woodward as vice-president, H. T. Tissington as cashier and Fred W. Adams as assistant cashier. A few other businesses listed that year in the directory, besides the Wheeler bank, were: Clarendon Hotel, James McLaughlin, proprietor: Garrison House, L. J. W. Vary, proprietor: C. S. Chatfield, grocery store operator; Koch & McFarlane, sawmill; C. A. Marshall, meat market owner; O. D. Sebree, livery stable proprietor.

Two bad fires occurred in 1884. One of them burned the Clarendon Hotel, but a new building,—larger and better than the first one—was erected within a short time.

The movement to construct church buildings started in 1883 and 1884. The first one built was the Congregational Church on Cooper Avenue. The Rev. E. A. Paddock led the movement and as its pastor preached the first sermon in it. It was later taken over by the Presbyterians. The Catholics and Episcopalians were the next to build, but the time is uncertain.

The Methodists began to plan for a building in 1884, but didn't get to it until 1885 and 1886. Mrs Ella Gilbert Beck of Denver, who was the organist of their church at a later date, has a brochure which shows much of their early activities. Baptists, Christians and Lutherans were also active at that time and built churches soon thereafter.

Chapter XIV

37. Aspen-Glenwood Road, 1883. The road which linked Glenwood Springs to Aspen and the outer world was constructed during 1881, 1882 and 1883. It was finished as far as Emma in 1883 with the exception of one bridge. It was forty-six miles in length and its route followed the line of least resistance. It went into the hollows and over the humps encountered with little thought of grade, curves, or tread.

The road began at the northwest corner of Aspen, dropped into the Castle Creek valley and crossed the stream near the point long known as the Henry Wurtz place. Barlow and Sanderson, the first stage operators, had a station there which (according to Jake Wurtz of Denver) was called Riverdale.

From that point the road crossed Castle Creek on a bridge that disappeared many years ago. It then traversed the bottom land south of the Roaring Fork which it crossed at Slaughterhouse bridge (so named because Joe Hunn had a slaughterhouse near by). The present bridge is a replacement of the earlier one. It then extended northwestward to and across McLean Flats to Woody Creek over nearly the same route as the present road.

From the Woody Creek bridge the road followed the flat about where the Denver & Rio Grande Railroad track lies for a mile, then followed nearly the same route as the present road to the junction of Snowmass Creek with the Roaring Fork. From there it followed the higher edges of the cultivated land east of the river to within two miles of present Basalt, then cut through the fields and crossed to the west side of the river over the County bridge (about ¾ mile above the present bridge near Basalt).

The route from there to the Hook bridge varied considerably from the present road, but passed Emma at the same point and took a more direct route to the bridge. From that bridge to Carbondale the road followed close to the route of the present Denver & Rio Grande Railroad track. Built in 1887, the track used a part of the wagon road and in places completely obliterated it.

About one-and-one-half miles east of present Carbondale, Bill Dinkel and Bob Zimmerman had a store and a stage station which was called "Dinkel's." The route then ran through present Carbondale and when that townsite was surveyed the surveyors used a part of the road for their Main Street. Mrs. Tanney built and operated an eating-house for the stage company near the east end of that street shortly before the stages began to roll.

From Tanney's place to Satank bridge the route was a little more direct than the present one and the Jerome Park road branched westward over Rock Creek at a point (and bridge) about one-quarter mile south of the present bridge. The old bridge was in two parts with an island between them. From Satank bridge to Glenwood Springs the road followed the east side of the river fairly close to the present State Highway No. 82. Traces of it can still be seen on one side or the other.

Barlow & Sanderson ran the first stage coaches semi-weekly, but soon had to change their schedule. Charles Fravert drove the first vehicle over the completed road. Later, Kit Carson's stages traversed the road daily in each direction.

An article in the December 13, 1924, issue of the *Crystal River Empire* of Carbondale, which was written by Charles H. Harris, tells of the development of the roads in the valley of the Roaring Fork.

In May, 1880, Harris and a partner came to Bowman (in Taylor Park) in a wagon. They left the wagon and packed into Aspen. Then, as they

Colorado Midland business car 100, the "Cascade," is now being restored by Del Gerbaz of Woody Creek. When the slow and meticulous task has been finished, this once-beautiful coach will be a joy to behold. This car made hundreds of trips along the Frying Pan River—a short distance away from where she resides at present. Photographed about 1898.

were looking for homestead claims, they went on down the Roaring Fork. They found suitable locations near a point later known as Wheeler (a station on the Colorado Midland Railway) and squatted there. In August, 1881, they went back to Bowman and brought their wagon to the claims over the Taylor Pass road, thence over whatever route they could find between Aspen and Wheeler.

In September they and several neighbors swamped out a rough road to Aspen, crossing and recrossing the river at passable fords. When finished, Harris could haul loads of wild hay weighing as much as 1500 pounds to that town; this hay he sold for $200 per ton. The next year the settlers roughed out a passable road from Wheeler to Glenwood Springs.

In 1883 Pitkin County built a good road from Aspen to Emma (the one mentioned at the beginning of this section). J. B. Wheeler's Coal Company built a toll road from Emma to their mines in the Jerome Park area in 1883 and 1884. And from the toll road at a point near Satank, Garfield County improved the road to Glenwood Springs when the stage line was started that year.

Because this road lay south of the Roaring Fork River, Harris promoted a road down the north side of the stream. On October 14, 1884, he and sixteen other settlers started at Frying Pan and built two-and-one-half miles of road which extended to present El Jebel (so named later). The next year the road was extended downstream to a connection with the stage road below Satank bridge. From El Jebel it ran about midway between the present highway (the old Colorado Midland roadbed) and the river. Along that section it made many right-angled turns as it followed property lines and went south of the Ed Stauffacher ranch house, thence along one side or the other of the present highway.

At some time during these years the Frying Pan, Hook's, Stauffacher's, and Satank bridges were constructed.

38. Dinkel's Stage Station, 1883. When William M. Dinkel and Robert Zimmerman arrived

72

in Aspen in the spring of 1881, they brought in 800 pounds of flour. They had bought it for $4 per hundred pounds in Buena Vista; here they sold it for $50 per hundred. That was a large profit for those days, but the task of bringing it to Aspen had been extremely difficult and they felt that they were entitled to it.

They worked for a few months around Aspen, then started down the valley intending to go to Montana. At the site of present Glenwood Springs they rested and bathed in the hot water. Dinkel once told about being almost scalded when he carelessly jumped into a small pool. The two men then climbed the steep hill and started across the Flattops plateau toward the White River Indian agency. They hadn't gone far till they were stopped by a band of Utes who robbed them of most of their food and ordered them to turn back.

They couldn't do otherwise, so retraced their steps to the site of present Carbondale. This was in August, 1881, and the only persons in that locality were the Yule Brothers, with their cowboys and a large herd of cattle, and Bill Gant, the trapper, who has been mentioned before.

The lands of the Indian Reservation were opened to settlement soon afterward—September 4—and the two men squatted on homesteads about one-and-one-half miles eastward and started to build a log house. As soon as the house was completed, they started hunting game to sell, for that was their only means of getting the food supplies they needed. They easily killed some game and packed the meat to Independence; they sold it there then went on to Leadville and bought their food: flour, bacon, potatoes, salt and pepper. James Zimmerman and Newton Lantz

This unfortunate wreck on the Colorado Midland occured at the bridge just below the Seven Castles. Seven passengers and three employees were injured May 14, 1914, due to a truck on chair car 108 leaving the rail.

The Thomasville area sparkled with pure snow during January 1952. The buildings are an ice house and blacksmith shop on the Mc Laren ranch.

joined them; they made other hunting trips and bought more supplies.

During the summer of 1882 the two men built a larger house and James Dinkel and his wife joined them. About a score of other men, some with families, moved into that locality and squatted on homesteads. In 1883, after the completion of the stage road to Glenwood Springs. "Dinkel's Place" became a stage station and they started a small general store. In 1884, when more stages were put on between Aspen and Glenwood Springs, they erected three large buildings for use

Residents along the Frying Pan River found a way to operate the Colorado Midland even though the line was abandoned during World War I.

Excursionists stop for a view along the Frying Pan River below Ruedi, about 1895. Colorado Midland engine Number 39 heads this train.

as house, store and barn. Dinkels prospered and became a very lucrative boarding-house-restaurant-store business. In 1886 Zimmerman sold out to Dinkel and returned to Virginia, and Dinkel became the sole owner of the business.

In the spring of 1887 my parents visited the store to buy provisions, and fortunately took me along; otherwise I would not have seen the place. For soon afterward, before the Denver & Rio Grande Railroad reached Carbondale, Dinkel moved his business to that site. He undoubtedly moved the buildings, too, for in later years there was no sign of them at the original location.

39. Satank Post Office, 1883. When the stage coaches began to roll between Aspen and Glenwood Springs in 1883, Harvey Tanney, a rancher who lived north of the present town of Carbondale, applied for and secured a post office which was called Satank. He was appointed its postmaster on June 27, 1883.

Satank was the name commonly given by the white settlers to Setanta (Standing Bear), a well-known Kiowa chief. His name, according to Mrs. Sarah Cooper, was prominently in the news at that time and Tanney had been favorably attracted to it.

When this photograph was taken in 1907 this station at Ruedi was a busy spot on the Colorado Midland. The Roaring Fork Plaster Company plant — visible in the right-hand portion of the picture — was served by the Midland by the spur leading in from the right. A caboose and flat car are near the small depot and water tank. Water now covers this area, backed up by the Ruedi Dam.

Tanney's place of residence was later known as the Tom Turpin ranch and still later as the Dan Lyon ranch. It was about a mile north of the stage road and just how he handled the mail is uncertain. He was killed in an accident in 1884 and his wife, Mrs. Ottawa Tanney, became the postmistress.

Before the Denver & Rio Grande Railroad reached Carbondale, she filed on land at that place, moved there and started an eating-house for the stage company. She took the post office with her and ran it in connection with her other business.

40. Ashcroft, 1883. Ashcroft progressed much faster than Aspen in 1883 and 1884, and its population increased to 2,000 people. A telephone line was constructed from Gothic to Ashcroft in 1883 by a locally-formed company. It crossed Pearl Mountain at about 12,500 feet and was a difficult undertaking. Those concerned, however, figured that the results obtained were worth the costs and the hardship of its construction. To obtain a service connection each subscriber had to deliver a pole to the line or hire someone to do it for him.

This connection with the outside world was greatly appreciated and enjoyed by those isolated pioneers.

The production of the Montezuma and Tam

O'Shanter mines was enormous and their wealth attracted much favorable attention to the town. As a consequence it gained favorable recognition throughout the state. A few new business firms which appeared in 1883 were Brooks & Bethusen Company, smelter; Coombs House, Thomas Coombs, proprietor; Hugo Eyssel, druggist; and Traynor & Company, general merchandise.

41. Crystal City, 1883. A road from Schofield to Crystal City was built down the canyon in 1883 and when wagons began to come in, there was great rejoicing among its residents, for theirs had been the most isolated condition of any in the valley. The coming of vehicles put an end to the long jack-trains which had been their supply line up till that time.

During 1883 and 1884 most of Schofield's populace moved to Crystal City and its population increased to about 300 people. Some of its businessmen and concerns were Adams Prospecting & Mining Company, W. Davis, manager; E. W. Fuller, saloon-keeper; E. F. Howell, justice of the peace; Moody Mining Company; Sheep Mountain Consolidated Mining Company, George A. Stone, superintendent; R. R. Sterling, U. S. deputy mineral surveryor; R. Stus, miner; A. A. Johnson,

proprietor of a general merchandise store and postmaster.

42. Glenwood Springs, 1884. The first election held in Glenwood Springs was on November 6, 1883, and the county officials chosen were A. J. Rock, sheriff; N. R. G. Ferguson, clerk and recorder; George Ferguson, treasurer; Gus A. Minor, judge; Frank P. Monroe, surveyor; S. A. Parker, assessor; Pat Tomkins, coroner, and M. V. B. Blood, superintendent of schools. Also, the residents by popular vote chose Glenwood Springs as the new county seat.

Olie Thorson, one of the town's popular citizens, came to that locality in 1883. He was always in the forefront of its progress and development, and served as postmaster for twenty-one years, which is one of the longest terms of postmaster service found in the valley. According to John B. Schutte, the present postmaster, Lyman Mow and William C. Beans were early postmasters who followed Mrs. Garretson. Later ones were Amelia Williams, July 24, 1897; Olie Thorson, July 26, 1906; H. W. Smith, March 7, 1914; Olie Thorson, September 20, 1922; H. T. Hubbard, September 16, 1935; John B. Schutte, May 16, 1939. Schutte's term of service is therefore more than nineteen years.

SUNDANCE BOOKS: RUSS COLLMAN

The old Colorado Midland wood truss bridge near Ruedi was still in use in 1962 before the Ruedi dam was built. Notice the extra trusses on the left end of the bridge which is due to the fact that this bridge was twice the length when in use on the railroad right-of-way.

The Colorado Midland wood truss bridge near the west entrance of Meredith — four miles east of Ruedi — was a favorite spot for fishing for residents of the valley when this photograph was taken, about 1898. Notice the full length of the bridge here in comparison with the previous photograph.

The population of the town was 300 in 1884 and considerable building was in progress. Cooper, Gelder and Anzensperger built the original part of Hotel Glenwood and opened it to public use. It was a two-story building, 50 x 50 feet in size.

Chapter XV

43. Aspen, 1885.   The reader of this narration now stands on the threshhold of a great adventure—the stampede to Aspen—which followed the rich strike in the Aspen Mine in November, 1884.

The population of Aspen at that time, as shown by the official census of May, 1885 (the first one taken in the state), was more than 4,000 people and that of Pitkin County was 4,994. However, it is the opinion of many old-timers that it was almost double that number, for thousands of men were running around in the mountains and could not be, or were not, counted.

The Aspen Mine was located originally as the Twenty-six. H. B. Gillespie and his associates acquired it with other claims, but lost it when they neglected to do the necessary assessment work. It was then relocated by Lewis Stone and Elmer Butler as the Aspen Fraction. The area of the claim was about three-and-one-third acres, a fraction of the ten acres allowed by law, and its size accounted for its name.

Stone and Butler worked the claim for several months, then became discouraged and gave it up. During that time they had bought groceries and lumber amounting to nearly $100 from the Cowenhoven store. Stone offered Dave Brown, the junior partner, his half of the claim if Brown would assume his half of the indebtedness. Brown accepted his offer and the goddess Fortuna undoubtedly smiled at that quirk of fate, which left Stone penniless and made Brown wealthy.

Butler and Brown then leased the mine to J. D. Hooper and Charles Todd, carpenters and contractors, who wanted to try out their luck. At the end of four months they struck a bonanza—silver ore of great value. With only two months to go, they put on three shifts of miners, hired every team and wagon they could get and hauled the ore down to Aspen as fast as possible. Before the lease expired they took out ore valued at

$600,000. The ore was piled up south of Durant Street until it could be hauled to market and men with shotguns stood guard over it. Matthew & Webb purchased it and hauled it away during the months of February and March, 1885.

Before the leaseholders turned the mine back to the owners its fame had spread across the nation, for its enormous output exceeded that of the Tam O'Shanter at Ashcroft. Its daily production was described in a January issue of *The Aspen Times:*

"The Aspen is working 100 men and producing 100 tons of ore worth over $100 per ton, or a daily output of $10,000. Mayor Hooper gets about $3,000, Charles Todd, $1,000, D. R. C. Brown, 1/3 royalty, about $666. E. T. Butler gets $2,000, D. M. Von Hovenberg, $1,333, J. B. Wheeler, $1,666, Harvey Young, $333, per day. When the lease expires Wheeler has one-sixth, Butler one-third, Brown, one-third and Young one-sixth."

When the owners took charge of the mine, Butler became the manager and he had his hands full because its large output taxed all the transportation facilities of the town. Even as late as 1890 the mine was producing 160 tons of ore each day. In 1891 the owners shipped over 39,753 tons of ore—by rail, of course. The lot contained 1,381,148 ounces of silver and 3,039,897 pounds of lead; its value was $1,325,213.03. An 1893 report showed that the total production of the mine was slightly over $7,800,000.

Butler and Brown eventually realized nearly $3,000,000 each from the mine. Butler took his millions and decamped to New York City; Brown stayed on and became the industrial leader of Aspen. To the end of his days he was loyal to the source of his wealth, a criterion not often found in the history of the West. He bought other mines and developed light, water and power facilities for the city.

Other big strikes were made just before and

PHOTO BY DAVID S. DIGERNESS

The Colorado Midland called the "Seven Castles" one of their most spectacular scenic spots. At this point in Red Rock Canyon, seven immense cliffs of brilliant red sandstone rise abruptly from the canyon floor. The railway line was down in the bottom of the canyon along the Frying Pan River — more or less where the automobile road is today.

80

just after the one in the Aspen, but they were not so spectacular. In September, 1884, the owners of the Emma Mine struck paydirt, and according to the March 14, 1885, issue of *The Aspen Times:*

"The Emma Mine shipped ore during the period September 20, 1884-February 18, 1885, worth $377,450.25. It netted the owners $347,989.05. It is estimated by good authority that the mine is still worth $2,500,000."

In 1884, Reumanalor C. Wilson, another carpenter-prospector, made a strike of rich silver ore in his Vallejo claim at the lower end of Spar Gulch. On account of its seemingly poor location, his claim was the joke of the camp. Wilson, however, ignored their jibes and at shallow depth found rich ore. For several years afterward "Wilson's luck" was a much-used expression in and around Aspen. He later bought a ranch and homesteaded another in the area northeast of Carbondale and was active in the affairs of that community.

Those strikes and others in the Spar, Durant and other mines produced more ore than could be hauled out, although there were freighters by the score. Several wagon-trains plied steadily over Independence Pass to Granite, Taylor Pass to St. Elmo, and Pearl Pass to Crested Butte, hauling ore to railroads at those points. One of the freighter outfits to Granite was run by Billy Day and Tom Carlin.

J. B. Wheeler bought an interest in the Emma, Aspen and other good producers, and formed the Aspen Mining & Milling Company. His action in some way precipitated the great apex vs. side-line fight which was carried through the courts for over two years. Injunctions shut down several of the mines when owners of the Durant, Spar and other apex mines demanded one-half of the ores produced by the Aspen, Emma and other side-line mines. They entered suit when Brown and Butler of the Aspen refused their demand. The contest finally ended in a compromise of some sort.

During that time "R. C." Wilson's (no one ever called him Rheumanalor) luck still prevailed, for his Vallejo kept on operating and provided employment for many otherwise idle miners.

As a result of the wide publicity given to Aspen's rich strikes, there were hundreds of new arrivals in 1885. Eighteen of them were S. I. Silvius, transfer and express; W. F. Deaner, mine manager; W. R. Callicotte, school principal; A. F. Bardwell, assayer; A. C. Lockhart, grocer; M. O. Bert, liquor dealer; B. Silver, gents furnishings; Robert Shaw, hay-grain-coal dealer; Harry G.

The public schoolhouse at Thomasville was a simple, but effective structure that provided many kids with education in the Frying Pan area.

Koch, lumberman and sawmiller; Henry Beck, bottling works and liquor store owner; George D. Johnstone, district attorney; Samuel I. Hallet, mine manager; William O'Brien, attorney; T. R. Sanders, justice; T. J. McGlynn, blacksmith; C. I. Glassbrook, under-sheriff; George W. Nyce, county surveyor 1888-94; and Chris Sanders, breweryman.

Seven men who came in 1886 were Edward I. Stimson, attorney; David G. Miller, mining engineer; Theodore G. Lyster, bank cashier; William Wack, rancher; Henry Wurtz, rancher and meat dealer; John Prechtel, blacksmith; and Ed Bonnell, grocer. J. D. Hooper was mayor, and Messrs Pearce, Hopley, Green and Von Hovenberg were trustees, H. L. Harding was clerk.

My father, H. C. Shoemaker, came to Aspen from Rosita in the Wet Mountain Valley in July, 1885. Hearing of the boom there, he, Abner J. Nichols, John Yeoman, John May, John Berrier and Tom Lee moved their families (twenty-one persons interrelated by marriage) and their worldly possessions to that place. They came via Silver Cliff, Hayden Pass, San Luis Valley, Poncha Pass, Maysville, Arkansas Valley, Chalk Creek, St. Elmo, Tin Cup Pass, Tin Cup, Taylor Park, Taylor Pass and Castle Creek valley, a distance of nearly 250 miles. Horses, mules, oxen and milk cows were used to pull the six covered wagons (mountain-schooners). A herd of about 150 range cattle and twenty milk cows were taken along.

No serious difficulty was encountered. Their small cavalcade passed one ex-horse-thief, dangling from a tree on Texas Creek, had hard going across Tin Cup Pass and sometimes met long wagon-trains of freighters which were hard to pass. On the 6-mile grade between Taylor Pass and Ashcroft this happened and it took five hours to get by. Some of the wagons had to be unloaded and set off the road until the others went by, then set back and reloaded.

Aspen was like a bee-hive when they arrived; pedestrians, horseback-riders, and vehicles of all kinds were coming and going on most of the streets. Long jack-trains were packing ore. Hundreds of miners were working around the clock and when they came off shift at midnight and came down Aspen Mountain with their lamps flaring in the breeze they formed a pleasing and unusual spectacle.

Building construction was given a boost by the new mining activity. Edward Rice built and opened the Tivoli Theatre, the first to give operatic performances; it had a seating capacity of 1,500 persons. In later years it was used as a ballroom.

The Armory Hall was built to house the activities of the local company of the State Militia. After the company was disbanded the hall was used as a recreation center. In the 1920's it was the city's main hall for public dinners and dances.

The Rink was also built when the roller-skating craze struck the city that year. It had the largest floor of any in the city and the building was often used to accommodate other large groups.

82

The Aspen Electric Company was formed in 1885 and the Consumers Electric Light & Power Company in 1886 and their plants began to furnish electric lights to the residents.

Joe Sendelbach and Almont opened a brewery in 1885 at the confluence of Roaring Fork River and Castle Creek. The public was invited to attend the opening, and needless to say, a large crowd responded. At a later date, Chris Sanders opened one at the junction of Hunter Creek and the river.

Bonds amounting to $10,000 were sold in 1885 and another schoolhouse, which could accommodate about 300 pupils, was constructed. Later the capacity of those buildings was increased by additions, and they were known as the Garfield and Lincoln schools. Another early teacher was Miss Rosetta Noble (who later became Mrs. Charles Harris). Davis H. Waite was the first superintendent of schools for Pitkin County, and E. M. Scanlan was a later one who served eight years.

A high school was started in 1884. One of the early principals was Henry C. Rogers. In 1901 D. R. C. Brown presented his palatial residence to the school board and it was remodeled into a high school building. From a business bulletin printed in 1893, it is learned that the number of pupils in the several schools were: 50 in 1881, 275 in 1885, 475 in 1888, and 1,165 in 1893. Twenty-three teachers were employed during the year last listed.

Postmaster Connor, who had just been reappointed, moved the post office to a new location in the Brown & Hoag building on Cooper Avenue in the spring of 1885. That building was much larger than the former quarters and had 1,000 locked boxes. The post office remained there until about 1926 when it was moved to the Elk's Building on Hyman Avenue.

On March 11, 1885, the Rev. J. A. Smith was appointed pastor of the Methodist group at Aspen and held the first service at The Rink on March 29. A permanent organization was affected on April 11 and plans for a church building were made. A certificate of incorporation was filed two days later. Meetings were then held in Miner's Union

Heavy studies were taking place in the Thomasville school in 1904. George McLaren is the lad seated to the far right.

Thomasville—on the Colorado Midland—was the starting point for Wood's Lake, a resort that was highly advertized. Around 1905 large quantities of lime and limerock were shipped from here

View on preceding page: The west side of the Busk—Ivanhoe Tunnel (to the far left) is shown here about 1898. The Ivanhoe depot sat near the stock pens. Construction of a covered wye — which extended out into Lock Ivanhoe — was in progress at this time. Behind this the main-line can be viewed climbing to the higher Hagerman Tunnel. In the distance a water tank snow shed and section house can be seen — at 10,944-feet elevation. The foreground buildings were used during the construction of the tunnel.

Hall and in the Episcopal Church.

The church board then contracted with J. W. Atkinson to build a brick building for $6,000. He laid the cornerstone on May 30 and finished the building early in December. Early pastors who followed Smith were J. R. Rader, A. B. Bruner, R. A. Carmine, R. H. Barns, C. Bradford, L. E. Kennedy, J. L. Vallew, C. E. Webb, S. E. Ellis and E. N. Edgerton.

Early Presbyterians held their meetings at The Rink and at other places and then acquired a church in 1886.

Some of the business concerns in 1885 were Aspen Mercantile Company, D. R. C. Brown, president and manager; Aspen Mining Company, E. T. Butler, manager; Aspen Smelting Company, W. B. Devereux, manager; *The Aspen Times,* O. I. Wheeler, proprietor, B. C. Wheeler, manager; J. W. Atkinson, county sheriff; William R. Augustine, photographer; E. J. Barnett, grocer; Belmont Hotel, Wilson & Visino, proprietors;

E. T. Butler, coal mine manager; J. H. Bixby, jeweler; Granite & Aspen Telegraph Company, W. B. Rundle, superintendent; Eugene H. Grubb, blacksmith; H. L. Harding, city clerk; Holbrook & Atkinson, feed store; John D. Hooper, mayor; C. H. Jacobs, county treasurer; John Prechtel, blacksmith; W. B. Root, clerk and recorder; Thomas A. Rucker, attorney; Shilling & Company, dry goods; Frank A. Sheppard, agent Aspen Smelting Company; B. F. Slagle, physician; Smuggler Mining Company, Charles A. Hallam, manager.

On May 9, 1885, *The Aspen Times* printed an itemized list (a sort of inventory) of what Aspen had to offer, to wit:

"Aspen, the Metropolis of the Pacific Slope, in Colorado, has: 5,500 people, 1,500 men hankering for wives, *one* old maid who is marriageable, 500 men who own mines that can produce $15,000,000 in one year, 1,000 exes such as colonels, captains, judges, senators and cashiers.

"One large schoolhouse, 1 school with 5 departments, 5 teachers, 400 school children. One Protestant and 1 Catholic church, 4 church societies, 4 Sabbath schools, 1 GAR post, 1 Masonic Lodge, 1 K of P lodge, 1 IOOF lodge, 1 AOUW lodge, 1 temperance society, 1 miner's union.

"One mayor and 3 ex-mayors, 1 city marshal and 4 deputies, 2 justices of the peace, 8 doctors, 2 dentists, 31 lawyers, 15 civil engineers, 1 undertaker, 2 photographers, 5 dairymen, 5 milliners, 2 jewelers, 2 coal and 1 lime dealers.

"One fire company, 2 brass bands, 1 daily and 2 weekly newspapers, 3 water wagons, 1 electric light company, 1 telegraph exchange, 1 telegraph office, 2 insurance offices, 5 real estate agencies, 1 abstract office, 2 stage offices, 1 express office, 1 freight office.

"Sixteen hotels, 20 boarding-houses, 8 restaurants, 4 bakeries, 3 fruit stands, 5 lunch stands, 5 meat markets, 10 grocery stores, 10 cigar stores, 10 laundries, 1 Wolftone, 6 barber shops, 3 bath houses, 3 drug stores, 1 gun shop, 2 cabinet shops, 2 wagon shops, 2 harness shops, 1 foundry and machine shop, 3 book and news depots, 1 sewing depot.

"One opera house, 1 bank, 5 brick houses, 1 jail, 3 livery stables, 2 lumber yards, 1 brick yard, 2 wood yards, 4 ice houses, 6 assay offices, 3 hardware and stove stores, 3 second-hand stores, 4 boot and shoe stores, 5 dry goods and notions houses, 4 exclusive clothing stores, 2 tailoring establishments, 4 shops, 1 jewelry auction house, 3 grain and produce houses.

"One soda, 1 cigar, 2 jewelry, and 1 mattress manufactories, 3 steam planing mills, 1 sampling works, 1 80-ton daily capacity smelter, 1 brewery, 4 wholesale liquor houses, 26 saloons, 5 billiard halls, 1 variety theatre, 1 dance hall, 15 sporting houses."

March 7, 1909.

2864. 250,000 small trout for Stocking Wood's Lake, Thomasville, Colo.

COLLECTION OF GEORGE MC LAREN

These milk cans at the Thomasville depot contained live trout to stock Woods Lake. This station also served as the dining car stop-over during 1907 so that the car would not be in transit over the entire main-line.

Boating on Woods Lake was the favorite pastime of most tourists at this resort in 1907. The fish probably hid out with all the goings-on.

The charcoal ovens of Sellar were a short distance upgrade from the sand house and water tank, shown here beside the depot

The Sellar charcoal ovens served the smelters at
Leadville for many years. These were well located
in the midst of dense forests on either side of the
Midland main-line. A spur holding about twenty cars,
ran in front of the ovens, re-entering the main-line at
a wye.

Sellar was left standing forlorn after abandonment of the Colorado Midland—shown here in January of 1922. Section houses, coal trestle, station and water tank may be seen in this view. Hell Gate is in the distance—to the left, above the power lines.

A runaway train and engine blowup occurred just above this point on the Midland at Nast, elevation 9,078-feet.

The Norrie school house, built at
the turn of the century, later had
an addition put on—with the help
of George McLaren and his
father. The children of both
Biglow and Norrie attended this
school until the Colorado Midland
ceased operation in August, 1918.

When this photograph was taken—about 1912—a short Colorado Midland passenger train consisting of a caboose and two coaches dropped down-grade at Nast. The Nast Curve and Hell Gate are far above, out of view to the right of the picture.

91

A glimpse through the golden aspen leaves reveals Mount Massive on the Continental Divide—with the abandoned Sellar wye in the foreground and the charcoal oven ruins beyond.

This is undoubtedly a very complete list and the reporter who gathered the data deserved a medal. It is regrettable that he did not give the name of each one.

44. **Tourtelotte Park, 1885.** Tourtelotte Park was merely a prospector camp for a few years, but was slowly developing. In January, 1885, Judge W. K. Taylor finished the construction of his Mountain House the first hotel. He opened it on his birthday with a supper and a ball, and some forty couples came to pay him honor. It was a gala event for the honorable judge and for the townspeople, according to Tom Atkinson, a long-time resident of the town.

Several other buildings were completed that year and a school with twenty pupils was started.

92

Chapter XVI

45. Ashcroft, 1885. Ashcroft reached the peak of its boom in 1885. It had a population of about 2,500 residents and half that many transient prospectors, according to Dan McArthur and Jack Leahy, two of the old-timers.

There were six hotels and four of the proprietors were Thomas Coombs, Morris Johnson, Mrs. William Warner and Fogg & Jones. Other businesses were Ed Nathan, dry goods entrepreneur; Abbey & Hallet, B. Monson and Traynor & Company, general merchandise stores; T. C. Monoghan, John Gavin and George Kinchin, saloon-keepers. There were 17 other saloons in the town at that time.

The Montezuma-Tam O'Shanter group of mines were still producing well and the Castle Peak Smelter was operating. However, the rich strikes at Aspen were drawing men from other camps, Ashcroft included, and the residents began to drift that way. This movement increased as news of a possible railroad into Aspen was circulated. When the arrival of the railroad became a certainty, some of the migrants also moved their houses to Aspen. It was a difficult undertaking, for the 12-mile road was rough and uneven. But despite the obstacles encountered, several people made the move successfully.

In 1886, Felix L. Kinney, who ran a grocery store, was appointed postmaster on June 5. He replaced Teuscher who joined the exodus to Aspen.

In 1889 a group of Ashcroft men organized the Pecos Mining & Milling Company to develop the Pecos and other claims in the vicinity of Pearl Pass. It worked several men there during most of the year, but no ores of value were found and the venture collapsed. Also, during February of that year, W. H. Fogg's hotel at Ashcroft was completely destroyed by fire.

46. Lenado, 1885. Prospectors who searched northward from Aspen found many mineralized outcroppings. The only ones worked were on Woody Creek and on Porphyry Mountain. A small settlement called Lenado developed on Woody Creek in the 1880's when A. J. Varney struck an unusually rich vein of lead and zinc ore.

Varney and his associates formed the Varney Tunnel Company to develop the claim. It started a tunnel on the south side of the stream and soon had about 150 men at work. The claim produced heavily and hundreds of other claims were located in that vicinity. However, no paydirt was found elsewhere.

A settlement of some 300 people grew up around the tunnel. Many log houses were built; also a large log barn to house the company's mules. After the company started a sawmill, several frame houses, a boarding-house, two saloons and a store building were constructed.

About the time Varney began to operate, Pitkin County officials approved and partly financed a road to the Frying Pan valley. It had been considered for several years and was now built by William Koch to Rocky Fork Creek, a distance of fifteen miles, via the Hunter-Woody Creek divide, Lenado, Silver Creek and Larkspur Mountain (so-named later). The road bogged down at the foot of Porphyry Mountain, and the project was abondoned later when it was learned that a railroad was to be built down the Frying Pan valley. A few large log houses and several cabins were built on Rocky Fork Creek by Judge Deane of Aspen and others who mined on the mountain.

The small settlement had no name officially, and was referred to as "Deane's Camp" by those with whom I talked afterward. In 1915 when I first saw the place, Frank Henry was the only resident and there it was that he told me the tale about the Smuggler Mine and the mule.

After the road reached Lenado, the company built a large lead mill near the tunnel entrance. Mansfield Brothers of Leadville were the con-

PHOTO BY H. H. BUCKWALTER – COLLECTION OF R. A. RONZIO

This passenger special of about 1900 had stopped at Hell Gate to view the spectacular abyss. Only the bravest passengers stepped out of the coaches to peer over the cliff.

94

Colorado Midland Number 1—a trim Consolidation—waited patiently at Ivanhoe for the photographer before returning to Leadville after having helped a train up the east side from Arkansas Junction.

tractors and builders. Some ore had been packed out to the mill at Aspen and now the concentrates from their mill were hauled out and shipped to Leadville and other markets.

47. **Glenwood Springs, 1885.** The population of Glenwood Springs was over 300 people in 1885. George Arthur Rice & Company opened the first bank that year. Cooper, Gelder and Anzensperger started to enlarge the Hotel

Glenwood to a 3-storied building, 75 x 100 feet in size. It was opened to the public on August 9, 1886. In 1891, the property was sold to R. J. Bolles. Several decades later it was completely destroyed by fire.

The town was incorporated on August 25, 1885, and the first town election was held on September 21. J. E. Schram was elected mayor and J. H. Pierce, Thomas Kendrick, R. P. Malaby, W. E.

Colorado Midland engine Number 2 "split the switch" at Ivanhoe depot and laid over on her side in the chill waters of Loch Ivanhoe in 1908. A freight train may be seen entering Busk-Ivanhoe Tunnel just above the derailed engine.

Shaffer, E. M. Carlton and William Young trustees.

The first newspaper, *The Ute Chief,* appeared that fall, and it did much to publicize the town. Its publishers were J. S. Swan and W. J. Reid, and they continued its publication well into the 1890's.

One of the men who came to Glenwood Springs that year was George S. Swigart, who arrived in January by stage via Granite, Independence Pass and Aspen. He had come to pay a short visit to two old friends, Arthur and Sally Poe, who had preceded him by several months, but he liked the town so well that he stayed.

At that time many of the residents still lived in tents, because house construction hadn't kept up with the demand. Professor Poe was teaching the town school at that time, "which was held in a brick building down by the creamery" as Swigart once described it. The school board had leased the building from Henry Moell.

Olie Thorson was planning to put on a local talent minstrel show that summer in order to start a school library fund. So one of the first things Swigart did was to help Thorson and Poe with the show. He had a hearty, booming laugh which added much fun to the performance. They charged a fifty-cent admission fee and took in about $100, which was given to the school board.

George had been a cowboy before he came to the valley and he, later, went into the stock-raising business in the vicinity of Carbondale. He once told the following tale about one of his cowboy experiences: He and a few companions were working a herd some distance from town and all of them ran out of chewing tobacco. So he sent one of the number to town to get a few plugs and told him to made the trip as hastily as possible.

Two days passed and the errand boy did not return. By that time all of the group had begun to

View on following page: This rare action photo, taken in 1902 at Hell Gate, illustrates what high-country railroading is all about. This Leadville-bound Colorado Midland 18-car freight train was pulled by road engine Number 19, followed by reefers, coal cars, a helper engine, box cars, another helper engine and a caboose.

96

Colorado Midland engine 301 exploded on October 9, 1912, while helping a livestock extra up the hill from Basalt to Ivanhoe. The accident happened above the Nast curve when the boiler suddenly joined the birds and landed on a stock car just behind the road engine. The "remains" of the engine—shown below at Leadville—were then taken to Colorado City and rebuilt for service in 1913. Both the engineer and the fireman were killed in the blast.

COLLECTION OF GEORGE MC LAREN

chew sage and other substitutes. On the third day a rider appeared and approached. With a joyous whoop they left the herd and rode pell-mell to meet him. The rider stopped a minute and watched their approach, then turned and rode away as fast as his horse could go. The cowboys followed and—after a two-mile chase—caught the rider, only to discover that he was a total stranger.

"What do yuh—want—of me?" he stammered. "I hain't done nuthin."

George explained and told him that they had thought he was their errand boy. He then asked, "Do you have any chewin' tobacco?"

The man burst into tears. "My gosh, no!" he wailed. "I ain't had none for a week. That's why I was comin' over to see you!"

Some of the Glenwood Springs businesses in 1885 were F. A. Barlow, hotel operator; Dr. D. E. Baldwin, druggist; M. Carr, saloon-keeper; H. R. Cain, grocer; John McKeavey, saloon keeper; G. W. Ragland, blacksmith; E. E. Thomas, hotel operator; Schram & Company, general merchandise; E. C. Stuart & Company, groceries; Carson's Stage-line to Aspen, Granite and Leadville—two stages sometimes required—daily mail service.

48. **Crystal, 1885.** Crystal City residents dropped the word "City" from its name about 1885 or 1886. By that time it had a population of about 400 people. W. D. Parry located the Black Queen lode claim in 1885 and the mine became the best producer in that locality. The Sheep Mountain tunnel was also producing well and mills were built at both mines.

Some new business concerns were George L. Chalis, mine superintendent; A. J. Edgerton, saloon-keeper; G. D. Griffiths and F. C. Johnson, mine contractors.

In 1886, the *Crystal River Current*, a weekly newspaper, appeared. It was published by A. A. Johnson, James A. Bray and Thomas O'Brien, with Johnson as editor, and it existed until 1892. Its use of the term "Crystal River" is the first appearance of the name that supplanted "Rock Creek" and undoubtedly suggested the change.

During 1886 the wagon road from Schofield was constructed on downstream about nine miles to where a man named McClure had settled. He had built a large house and he fed and lodged those who passed by. He called it McClure House and it became well-known throughout the valley. The locality was referred to as McClure Flats.

From the end of the road a trail was developed by use (not constructed) across the Rock Creek-Muddy Creek divide. It was used for thirty years and was known as the McClure Pass trail. The

wagon road was constructed from McClure's place to Carbondale in the 1890's, and in the 1940's a road was built across McClure Pass. It has become a part of State Highway No. 133.

Some of the concerns and businessmen at Crystal in 1888 were Anderson & Company, marble; A. W. Brownell, justice of the peace; A. R. Burnett, construction; *Crystal River Current*, newspaper; C. J. S. Hoover, attorney; A. A. Johnson, postmaster and general store proprietor; W. F. Mason & Company, marble quarries. The population of the town was still about 400 people.

49. **Prospect, 1885.** In the mid-80's a town called Prospect was started about three miles below Clarence and Marble. A few of the early settlers were Y. B. Ford, H. W. Anderson, J. Anderson, J. R. Sterling, W. W. Wood, and Mrs. Melton. The lady ran a boarding-house there and she and others staged a big celebration on Christmas Day, 1889.

Other residents were William Robinson, Patsy Ryan, Allen Hodges and T. H. Wigglesworth. Hodges was a freighter and hauled ore to the mills. Later he hauled mail and supplies between Marble and Crystal.

Wigglesworth acquired coal and anthracite claims in that vicinity and sparked a boom in the early 1890's which resulted in a population of about 200 people. He was associated with the Colorado Coal & Iron Company and was the manager of their auxiliary, The Crystal River Railroad Company, when it attempted—unsuccessfully—to build a railroad into that region in 1892. He was socially inclined in those days and gave dinners and dances which many of his Carbondale friends attended.

50. **Jerome Park, 1886.** Jerome B. Wheeler and James J. Hagerman, president of the Colorado Midland Railway Company, organized the Grand River Coal & Coke Company in 1885 to develop the coal mines at Sunshine, Marion and Spring Gulch, which had been opened in 1883 and 1884.

This action, according to Miss Ruth Guest of Denver, was completed on May 13, 1886, when the company was incorporated under the laws of New York. Those identified with its control were R. K. Terry, W. B. Devereux, James F. Sutton, Samuel S. Sands, J. J. Hagerman, J. B. Wheeler and Frederick F. Thompson. Wheeler was president, Hagerman, vice-president and Sands, secretary-treasurer of the company.

In 1885 and 1886 a contest for possession of those coal lands took place between the Colorado Fuel Company and the Grand River Coal & Coke

SUNDANCE BOOKS: DELL A. MC COY

Fall colors, the Continental Divide and the Colorado Midland grade near Hell Gate combined to make a striking scene of high country beauty.

Company, but the land was held by the latter company until it was properly filed on and the dispute was settled. Many men filed coal claims along that coal field. Charles Reuter of Aspen once told that he was one of a group of about 200 men who acquired claims and sold them to the company. W. M. Dinkel once told that he supplied much of their food and clothing during that time from his store at present Carbondale.

The Glenwood Springs newspaper, *The Ute Chief,* in its December 31, 1887, issue commented on activities in the Jerome Park area as follows: "Here individuals hold possession of an extensive area for and in behalf of Colorado Coal & Iron Company, which is composed of men allied in interest to the Midland Railway." In the light of the information mentioned above, the reporter had named the wrong company. It seems that he should have said: "in behalf of the Grand River Coal & Coke Company"; its officials were the men who were interested in the Colorado Midland Company.

To substantiate this statement, it may be recalled that General William J. Palmer and his associates, after forming the Denver & Rio Grande Railroad Company, formed the Colorado Coal & Iron Company in 1880 by consolidating the Central Colorado Improvement Company, the Southern Colorado Coal & Town Company, and the Colorado Coal & Steel Works Company, which they had previously formed in 1871, 1876 and 1879, respectively.

51. Thompson Creek, 1887. From available records it appears that the Colorado Coal & Iron Company's holdings lay south of Jerome Park in the Thompson Creek-Coal Basin country. In 1886 it purchased some 2,500 acres of coal land from the government on a cash per acre basis.

One of their draftsmen mapped that land and a reporter for *The Ute Chief* described it in the December 31, 1887, issue of that newspaper in great detail. Incidentally, he stated: "The Company has assigned a new name Crystal River to Rock Creek to distinguish it from the numerous streams of that name." That statement clarified the uncertain origin of the new name for the stream.

To open that field, in the summer of 1887 the Coal Company built through an auxiliary company—The Aspen & Western Railroad Company—a 13-mile narrow gauge railroad from the survey line of the Denver & Rio Grande's on-coming track at Carbondale to Willow Park on Thompson Creek. That point was relatively five miles south of Spring Gulch.

Many local men worked on the Aspen & Western Railroad project and three of them were Edwin White, as a foreman, Charles Sewell, as a blacksmith and George Swigart, as a stable boss.

The railroad was completed in December, 1887, and the mine tunnel was bored for several hundred yards. However, both projects were shut down early in 1889, because the mine was too poorly located to compete with the Jerome Park project of the Grand River Coal & Coke Company. With its three mines and its coke ovens closely adjacent to the broad-gauged Colorado Midland railroad, it held an advantage which Colorado Coal & Iron Company could not overcome.

Records show that the Willow Park mine produced only 113 tons of coal in 1888. George Phillips, the superintendent, and a few men were left in charge of the mine, but early in 1889 they were withdrawn and Ed White was hired to look after the improvements. He was retained till about 1895, when both projects were abandoned. With them went Carbondale's hope for a coking plant, which the Coal Company had intended to set up there.

The Aspen & Western Railroad had crossed the Charles Sewell ranch at the mouth of Thompson Creek and in later years Robert O. Sewell heard a lot about it from his father. Also, he remembers the old roadbed, the mine and the buildings at Willow Park camp. The store buildings and the houses were log structures with dirt roofs and many of them had outdoor baking ovens, a custom which prevailed among foreign-born workers at many camps. Mervyn E. Swigart, now deceased, knew the location of the camp and the mine, as he rode herd on his father's cattle in that country for several years. Once, in the heat of the chase, a wild steer ran into the mine tunnel; he dismounted and followed to bring it out, but had to give up when it grew too dark for him to see the animal. A few tumbled-down shacks now mark the spot.

Chapter XVII

52. Aspen, 1887. Aspen had become a booming city in 1885 as shown by the state census and the list of business concerns shown in a previous statement. In 1886 and 1887 it grew more rapidly as it became known that two railroads were being built towards it. According to an item in *The Aspen Times* of 1887, Aspen had a population of 6,000 people, 2 public schools, 2 banks, 2 theatres, 5 churches, 3 second-hand stores, 6 real estate offices, 2 bottling works, 13 express wagons, 3 lumber yards, 1 plumbing shop, 1 dance hall, 1 variety, 14 billiard and pool tables, 1 bowling alley and 38 saloons. Other businesses were not listed. Considering the list given two years previously, this reporter was either too stingy or too lazy to do justice to the subject.

Some of the men who arrived in 1887 were David W. Brunton, engineer and mine manager; Al S. Lamb, druggist; Lou D. Sweet, railroad employee, county treasurer; William G. Cox, Mollie Gibson Mine superintendent. Four men who arrived in 1888 were J. J. Warnack, county clerk; J. T. Stewart, county sheriff; J. A. Hall, justice of the peace; and J. S. Thorn, hay and grain dealer. Five men who arrived in 1889 were Elias Cohn, mine manager; P. Frank Irving, county sheriff; Dr. E. P. Rose, mayor; L. A. W. Brown, insurance and real estate agent; and Dr. W. R. Wilson.

The First National Bank was organized in May, 1886. The officials were W. S. Cheesman, president; H. P. Cowenhoven, vice-president; T. G. Lyster, cashier; O. S. Moore, assistant cashier. The directors were Cheesman, Cowenhoven, Lyster, Moore, D. H. Moffat, D. R. C. Brown and J. B. Wardell. The bank was reorganized in 1898 and incorporated as the State Bank of Aspen with Moffat as president, Cheesman as vice-president and Lyster as cashier.

In that year H. P. Cowenhoven and D. R. C. Brown secured a franchise from the town board to supply water to the town. They formed the Castle Creek Water Company, laid mains and piped in Castle Creek water. Having water always on tap was a decided improvement over the former way of taking it from the town ditch or securing it from one of the water wagons.

At about that same time Brown and his associates organized the Aspen Electric Company and the Consumer's Electric Light & Power Company. In 1887 those companies united and formed the Roaring Fork Electric Light & Power Company. It was incorporated on April 25, 1887, by D. R. C. Brown, Horace K. Devereux and James M. Downing.

There, under the direction of W. B. Devereux, was developed the first hydroelectrical power in the nation. Its capacity when first installed was close to 3,000 horsepower. The Smuggler Mine (one of twenty customers) which was sunk to the 1,800-foot level, contributed $50,000 annually for power purposes only. In 1927 that company and the Castle Creek Water Company were combined as the Roaring Fork Water, Light, & Power Company, with Harry A. Brown as president and manager. That company contributed to Aspen's welfare for more than twenty years. C. E. Doolittle was plant superintendent for many years.

The worst fire in Aspen's history, up to that time, occurred during the summer of 1887. It burned six store buildings in the business section of the town.

In August, 1887, when Chief Colorow and his Ute band left their reservation and made their hunting foray into the White River country, Captain Goslin, who was in command of Company F of the Colorado National Guard, at Aspen, took his troop to Meeker to help drive out the trespassers. In a fight with the Utes at Cedar Hill on August 25, Lieutenant Frank Folsom of Aspen and under-sheriff Jack Ward of New Castle were killed. Their bodies were brought to Glenwood Springs on the 28th and the troop returned to Aspen on

September 2.

A wagon road had been built previously up Maroon Creek to the junction of the West and East Forks. During 1887 some company built a toll road from that point to Copper Creek in Gunnison County. It extended up the East Fork and across East Maroon Pass. Frank Stewart had charge of the construction job. During the fall, four of the workmen were killed by an avalanche. Just why the road was built, or the need for it, is uncertain. It has been said that it was an outlet to the Gothic smelter, but with the expectation of the railroad's arrival that year, that motive seems unlikely. Whatever the reason, it was a dismal failure financially for it was used only a short time.

The road was soon rendered impassable to all but foot or horse travel when someone burned a large bridge which spanned a deep canyon about midway up the East Fork. In 1920 I cleared the old road and added it to the trail system of that district.

53. Glenwood Springs, 1887. News of the approach of the railroads also sparked the development of Glenwood Springs and it grew rapidly. In 1886 its population was 700 and in 1887, 1,200.

In 1886, W. B. Devereux, one-time manager of the big Aspen Smelter at Aspen, promoted and organized the Glenwood Light & Water Company. It provided the town with electric lights that year. He also organized the Colorado Land & Improvement Company, which began the development of

This view of 1898 illustrates the winter conditions found at the west portal of Busk-Ivanhoe Tunnel. Leed engine number 51 and 49 wait for orders on the covered turntable lead track. To the right, the tunnel entrance is being exhausted of smoke, while in the trees above may be seen the old grade leading to Hagerman Tunnel.

PHOTO BY H. H. BUCKWALTER -- COLLECTION OF R. A. RONZIO

ROTARY SNOW PLOW. COLO.

Two of the Colorado Midland 300-series locomotives are shown here battling the snowed-in line during the winter of 1911.

Wid Herwick and Mate Bradley perform their duty on Spy Peak lookout, the first in the area in 1912.

the natural hot springs. A swimming pool, 600 x 150 feet in size, a large bathhouse and a sweat cave were constructed at a total cost of $400,000. The bathhouse cost one-half of that amount.

After the bathhouse and pool were completed and the railroads arrived, the town gained wide recognition as a leading health resort. It was called The Spa and several other hotels—among them being the Yampah, Williams, Star, Denver, and Kendrick Cottages—were built to take care of the tourist trade which came to The Spa for pleasure or for the benefit of their health.

The First National Bank was started in 1887 with James J. Hageman as president, Walter B. Devereux as vice-president, and J. H. Fessler as cashier. The company erected a 50 x 100-foot, 3-story building to house its business. On June 1 the Glenwood National Bank was opened by John L. McNeil with C. N. Greig as cashier. On December 1 The Glenwood National bought the Rice Banking business, previously mentioned, and in 1891 it was combined with the First National Bank.

Another newspaper, *The Glenwood Echo,* appeared that year. It was originated by B. Clark Wheeler of Aspen and was managed and edited by James L. Riland.

In July, 1887, the town board accepted Isaac Cooper's offer to lay water pipes in the city and on October 10 he started to work on the Banning Ranch in his effort to bring water to the city from Noname Creek. His death delayed the construction of the project, but in 1888 the Glenwood Light &

Dropping down from Hell Gate, the Colorado Midland ran through this rock cut near the short Mallon Tunnel. Notice the cinders on the road—still providing evidence of the hard work performed by Midland engines many years ago.

Lunch time in the Rockies

Water Company took hold and finished it.

Five churches were founded in the last half of the decade, the Presbyterian, in 1885; the Catholic, in 1886; the Christian, in 1887; and the Methodist and Episcopal, in 1888. In August, 1887, the town voted to build a new schoolhouse. It was constructed quickly at a cost of $25,000.

The city was comparatively free of crime, even in its beginning. The first shooting affray occured in September, 1885, when Elijah Cravens and George Ford quarreled and fought. Cravens went home, got his gun, returned and shot and killed Ford. In December, 1887, Chester Baker, known as "Texas Kid," fought with another gambler in Hawley & Reese's saloon and fired two shots which missed his opponent, but killed two onlookers—Joseph Mathison and F. M. Smith. In July, 1888, Herman Babcock shot and killed James Riland. All of those miscreants were tired, but each got off with a light sentence.

John H. "Doc" Holliday, the notorious gambler and gunman of the West, came to Glenwood Springs in 1887. On November 8, he died of tuberculosis in Hotel Glenwood and was buried in the local cemetery. In 1955 the town council raised a descriptive headstone over his grave.

Some of the businessmen and concerns of Glenwood Springs in 1887 were Hotel Glenwood, William Gelder, proprietor; Denver & Rio Grande Restaurant; Fred C. Schram, general merchandiser; E. B. Everett, staple and fancy grocer; Meadow Brothers, meats and vegetables; W. P. Woodruff & Company, candies, cigars and tobacco; Napier & McClure, dry goods; Parks & Company, building materials; F. J. Wood & Company, books and stationery; F. H. A. Lyle, Sunshine coal and Jerome Park blacksmithing coal; T. R. Williams, gents furnishings goods entrepreneur; Hotel Barlow, proprietor; George C. Banning Stables, livery and feed; Schwartz & Johnson, undertakers; First National Bank, Capitol stock, $100,000; Rice & Hopkins, real estate and insurance; Rice, McLean & Company, real estate and loans; Monroe & Trumbor, civil engineers; John T. Shumate, attorney at law; George Bennett, sawmill operator; A. W. Dennis, photographer; George Edinger, general merchandiser; James H. Kerwin, postmaster; A. E. Stafford, marshal; *Glenwood Echo,* Echo Printing Company, B. Clark Wheeler, manager; Western Stage Line to Aspen and St. Elmo; D. W. Rees, J. B. White, J. L. Hayes, G. A. Rice, R. P. Malaby, town trustees.

A. W. Dennis was the best or one of the best photographers in Western Colorado in those days. He ran his studio for many years—well into the 1890's—and most of our early family photographs were taken by him.

Some of the business firms of 1888 were American House, Putnam & Dumont, proprietors; Anna Anderson, restaurant; F. A. Barlow, grocery and clothing store proprietor; A. L. Beardsley, attorney; J. H. Bixby, jeweler; L. G. Clark, physician; *Daily News,* H. J. Holmes, editor and publisher; Colorado Midland Railway, C. H. Marsh, agent; Denver & Rio Grande Railroad, C. J. Feist, agent; Colorado Land & Development Company, W. B. Devereux, manager; J. R. DeReamer, D. & R. G. passenger and freight agent; Grand River Coal & Coke Company, W. B. Devereux, manager; H. R. Kamm, groceries and hardware W. S. Parkinson, druggist; *The Ute Chief,* H. L. J. Warren, manager.

Chapter XVIII

54. The Railroads Arrive. The main event in the valley in 1887 was the arrival of the Denver & Rio Grande Railroad in October and the Colorado Midland Railroad in November. Their arrival put an end to the numerous stage-lines and wagon-trains that plied across the mountain passes to outside railroad connections, and rescued the region from the isolation which had retarded its growth.

Much praise is due to those faithful public servants who made the complete development of the valley possible. The fate of the Colorado Midland is regrettable, but it served its purpose well—the exploitation of the Western Colorado coal fields. The Denver & Rio Grande's continued operation under adverse circumstances is commendable. Its service over the years should be, and is, I believe, appreciated by the people it serves.

55. Denver & Rio Grande Railroad, 1887. The Denver & Rio Grande Railroad Company had completed a narrow gauge railroad line to Leadville on July 20, 1880. Commencing in December, 1881, it built across Tennessee Pass, arriving at Rock Creek (later Belden) in March, 1882.

Expansion westward from that point began in 1885. During that summer Paul Blount, a long-time resident of Glenwood Springs and clerk and recorder of Garfield County, made a survey from Leadville to Grand Junction. This survey showed that there was an abundance of natural resources in that area. In 1886, hearing of the hot springs, the coal seams and the rich ores of the valley, four companies put engineering corps and grading crews to work.

For a short time competition was keen, but in 1887 the Colorado Railway (a Burlington company) and the Union Pacific withdrew and left the field to the Denver & Rio Grande and the Colorado Midland companies.

Starting from its railhead at Rock Creek (near present Gilman) in January, 1887, the Denver &

Rio Grande Railroad Company built down the Eagle River and Grand (Colorado) River canyons to present Glenwood Springs and up the Roaring Fork River valley to Aspen. This was a fairly accessible route and permitted that company to easily outdistance its competitor, the Colorado Midland.

The company officials expected to reach Glenwood Springs by October 1, but construction of the Jackson Tunnel (just above town) took longer than they had planned. The track-layers spiked down the rails through town on October 4 and on the 5th the first train, a 20-car special, arrived.

The train brought several-hundred visitors, foremost of whom were Governor Alva Adams, his staff and some of the railroad officials. Among the last-named group were D. H. Moffat, president; W. S. Cheesman, director; S. T. Smith, general manager; E. O. Wolcott, counsel; J. Gilluly, treasurer; A. S. Hughes, traffic manager; and S. K. Hooper, general passenger agent.

The train was a double-header and the lead engine, No. 187, was piloted by Engineer O. B. Gutshall. Trailing the passenger cars was President Moffat's special car, Maid of Erin. As the engines emerged from the tunnel, the engineers blew their whistles loud and long, and pulled into town at 7:45 p.m., amid a flare of electric lights, the music of a brass band, the roar of 3,500 voices and the terrific din of blasting giant powder.

After about fifteen minutes the clamor subsided and Mayor P. Y. Thomas welcomed the visitors cordially and pleasantly; then he and his committees escorted them up town with the band leading the procession.

At 10:00 o'clock a banquet was spread in Hotel Glenwood by proprietor William Gelder and his staff, and all of the visiting dignitaries and the local officials gathered around the board. Honorable J. W. Taylor acted as chairman and Judge H.

T. Sale as tostmaster. Many speeches and toasts were delivered and much merriment prevailed. Following the banquet, a grand ball was held for those socially inclined, while outside there was a street carnival for the hilarious crowd. Both lasted till dawn.

As part owner of the hotel, Isaac Cooper—although in poor health—helped to spark the entertainment, as shown in an article in *The Ute Chief* of October 8, 1887. "The arrival of the train at the foot of Grand Avenue was the supreme moment in the life of Captain Isaac Cooper. *The Ute Chief* expresses the hope that he lives long enough to see the country as it is pictured in his mind's eye. It was eminently proper that the founder, pioneer and benefactor of Glenwood Springs should ride the first train, and be greeted with music, cheers, exploding fireworks and giant powder."

In the meantime the trackmen were "scratching gravel" toward Aspen. The work train, pulled by engines No. 83 and 403, arrived in Carbondale on October 13 and at the depot flat at Aspen at 4:00 o'clock on October 27. The members of the train crew were Conductor C. S. Lake, Brakemen Charles Thomas and M. F. Masden, Engineer George Cordon and Fireman Thomas Smith, on the lead engine, and Engineer Beecher Dynes and Fireman Peter Clauson, on the rear engine.

Most of the residents of Aspen, including the school children, went to meet the train, and the teachers and children were given a short ride. The local brewery took a wagonload of beer to the workers. Whistles tooted, bells rang and according to Judge Deane, "the miners set off enough giant powder to bore a mile of tunnel."

On the following Saturday afternoon a large barbeque was held for the railroad workers and the townspeople generally. The menu consisted of two beeves, two mutton, 100 pounds of weiner-worst, 300 loaves of bread, a barrel of pickles, 100 pounds of bologna and fifty barrels of beer.

The demonstration continued for several days and climaxed when the first train arrived at 8:22 p.m., on November 1. It was a 25-car special and aboard were Governor Alva Adams, his staff, most of the officials of the railroad company and

Loch Ivanhoe is in the center of this view of the Colorado Midland grade as it enters the Busk-Ivanhoe Tunnel (to the left). The older grade up to Hagerman Tunnel climbs across the hillside behind the lake, circles around back and appears again in the trees above the wye at the edge of timberline. In this view the photographer was looking to the southeast.

SUNDANCE BOOKS: DELL A. MC COY

several hundred visitors. They were met and welcomed by Mayor Harding, his committee, and about 5,000 other citizens. Governor Adams responded with a short address. Then a procession formed, and with the governor and railroad president riding in Kit Carson's finest stage coach, the long parade led by a brass band traversed the business section of the town for an hour.

During the parade the miners again set off many kegs of black powder and the cannonading continued well into the night. Fireworks and flares lit up the town and the surrounding hills for several hours. The parade ended at the Clarendon Hotel, but later at The Rink the state and railroad

The east portal of Hagerman Tunnel viewed here was 11,528-feet above sea level. The Colorado Midland's right-of-way leading to the tunnel was finally dismantled in 1899 after the Midland had purchased the lower Busk-Ivanhoe Tunnel.

PHOTO BY SANDFORD - DU BALL --
COLLECTION OF DAVID S. DIGERNESS

PHOTO BY SANDFORD - DU BALL -- COLLECTION OF DAVID S. DIGERNESS

This view is just inside the east portal of the abandoned Hagerman Tunnel as it looked in 1940. The Colorado Midland was forced to re-open this tunnel for a couple of years prior to 1899 because of their dispute with the owners of the then new (and lower) Busk-Ivanhoe Tunnel. This move nearly bankrupted the Midland due to the unusually harsh winter of 1899.

110

A gravel slide caused engine 33 to go into the Roaring Fork River about one and one-half miles below Basalt. Engineer Danielson was a staunch prohibitionist and caused considerable unhappiness to the "wet" crowd when they learned that he escaped.

officials were entertained at a banquet prepared by Aspen's best chef. Judge James M. Downing presided over the affair which sparkled with witty speeches, toasts and merriment.

A grand ball followed the banquet; It was attended by the visiting officials, Aspen's elite, and, in fact, everyone who could secure an invitation. It was a glamorous affair and was considered a social success of the highest order by Aspen's four hundred.

In constrast to and probably in opposition to that decorous social gathering, a hilarious jamboree was held at Ben Dixon's dance hall. At that hijinks the dance hall girls, the demimonde, the gamblers, card sharks and other riffraff tried to outdo the more sedate affair. The saloons—all thirty-eight of them—held open house and at many of them the drinks were free.

Aspen's two bands played continuously at one place or the other throughout most of the night.

The theatre, the variety, other places of entertainment, and the restaurants and hotels were jammed to capacity.

If one wanted to go in a direction opposite to that of the crowd, he had to get out into the middle of the street. However, as one old-timer aptly expressed it, that didn't happen often, because everyone was going wherever the crowd went.

All in all, it was a jubilee which those who attended never forgot. My mother, Elvira Shoemaker, and my sister, Mamie Nichols, rode the special train from Carbondale to Aspen, saw the crowd, and enjoyed the public demonstration. To them it was a spectacle beyond words, or *for* words, for they seldom if ever quit talking about it for several years.

However, throughout the whole run of events, the people of Aspen did not forget the railroad company whose action had fulfilled their dreams

111

Looking west near Loch Ivanhoe—a summer shower soaks the mountains in this scene—where trains once slowed down before entering the smoky hole of Busk-Ivanhoe Tunnel, a short distance to the left.

and their hopes. Many expressions of appreciation were made to the visiting officials, but the real sentiment of Aspen's citizenry was expressed by Judge Downing at the banquet, when in response to a toast, he raised his champagne glass and said:

> Then, here's to our Aspen, her youth
> and her age;
> We welcome the railroad, say farewell
> to the stage;
> And whatever her lot and wherever we
> be,
> Here's God bless, forever, the D. & R. G.

The Denver & Rio Grande Railroad Company extended its line from Glenwood Springs to Rifle in 1889, and to meet the stiff competition of the Colorado Midland Company, during 1889 and 1890 it broad-gauged its entire line from Denver to that point. According to an 1889 issue of the *Carbondale Avalanche,* its first broad-gauged train passed through that town on August 13.

During 1888 the Colorado Midland Company had extended its line westward from Glenwood Springs to New Castle, arriving there on October 20. And soon after the Denver & Rio Grande reached Rifle the two companies got together and formed a company—The Rio Grande Junction Railway Company—to build a jointly-owned line to Grand Junction. Each company paid one-half of the costs and each owned one-half of the stock.

PHOTO BY THE LATE JOHN B. SCHUTTE

Elk forage in the lower valleys of the Roaring Fork district during the winter. Big game was present in great numbers until white man arrived on the scene and killed wildlife in a senseless, malicious fashion.

The railroad was completed on November 14, 1890. The Denver & Rio Grande then granted the Colorado Midland trackage rights over their rails from New Castle to Rifle and both used the same rails from there to Grand Junction. Thus, the railroad from Glenwood Springs to Aspen became a branch line.

Two well-remembered conductors on the Aspen branch line were Ed Wolf and Harry Hill. One day shortly after the Aspen-bound train had passed Carbondale, Wolf came into the passenger car and shouted, "Catherine!" The train slowed to a stop and a woman got off. The train proceeded for several miles and Wolf again entered and called,

"Emma!" When the train stopped another woman got off. The train went on for several more miles and a third time Wolf entered and yelled, "Woody!" Immediately a man arose and left the train.

As Ed turned to leave the car, another woman passenger arose, faced him, and somewhat angrily exclaimed, "Mr. Conductor, my name is Mary, but I want you to know that I am going to Aspen and I don't intend to leave this train until it gets there." Momentarily mystified, Wolf was stumped, but quickly grasping the situation he smiled, bowed, and said, "Have no fear, madam. I think the engineer can now pull the remainder of

113

us safely into town."

In later years when Hill was conducting a Glenwood-bound train, it ran into a mudslide. Harry investigated, returned to the passenger car, and told the passengers that they probably would have to spend the night there. One male passenger immediately began to complain and curse the railroad company. In a pleasant way, Hill tried to pacify him, but the man still continued to rant. Pleasantly but a trifle sarcastically, Harry said, "I'm sorry, mister, but it can't be helped." Then banteringly, he continued, "Why, man, you ought to consider yourself lucky. Few men have the chance of sleeping between Emma and Catherine, as you have. Why don't you take advantage of it?"

56. Colorado Midland Railway, 1887. The Colorado Midland Railway Company was organized on November 23, 1883. Its charter authorized it to construct a standard-gauge railroad from Colorado Springs westward to Leadville, Aspen, Glenwood Springs and Elk Creek (New Castle). Then, if desired, it could build onward to the Colorado-Utah line.

After several attempts, early in 1886 the company raised enough funds to build the 250 miles of road. President James J. Hagerman, in his annual report dated April 4, 1887, made this statement: "On June 1, 1886, the Colorado Midland Railway Company entered into a contract with the Colorado Midland Construction Company, whereby the latter would construct the road. However, prior to that date, under a preliminary agreement work had already started on May 17, 1886."

By authority of the stockholders, the company issued 6 per cent bonds in the amount of $6,250,000 and filed a mortgage deed of trust to assure their payment. The deed of trust, dated July 15, 1886, revealed that work on the road was already in progress between Colorado Springs and Leadville *and* between Leadville and Aspen.

The construction of the railroad across the Sawatch Range was a masterful feat of engineering. After making several switchbacks up the east face of the range, the company bored the Saguache (later the Hagerman) tunnel through the Continental Divide. It was 2,164 feet in length, 11,528 feet in elevation, and cost $2,000,000.

The route then followed the Frying Pan River to its junction with the Roaring Fork. At that place the company established a division point across the river from the town of Frying Pan and called it Aspen Junction. The new town soon replaced the old one when railroad employees and businessmen began to build homes and business houses.

The railhead reached Aspen Junction on or about November 5, a few weeks after the Denver & Rio Grande had passed Emma, the corresponding station on that line across the Roaring Fork River. The distance they had covered was much less than that crossed by the Denver & Rio Grande, but the Hagerman tunnel and the generally rough terrain they had encountered had delayed them.

The exact dates when the railroad reached Aspen and Glenwood Springs are uncertain. From newspaper accounts of that period it is known that the track-layers reached Maroon Creek, one mile from Aspen, on December 2, 1887, and the Roaring Fork bridge at Glenwood Springs on December 9. At those points trackmen were held up by the construction of the two bridges (Maroon and Castle) near Aspen and the one (Roaring Fork) at Glenwood Springs. However, trains were run to the end of track and passengers, mail, express and freight were transported back-and-forth to the towns by stages and wagons, until the bridges were completed many weeks afterward. Statements by other writers say that the railroads reached Aspen and Glenwood Springs in January, 1888. In the early 1920's Judge Deane told me that the first train pulled into Aspen on February 4, 1888. That is the only specific date that has been found.

Both towns staged celebrations when the first trains arrived, but they were not so jubilant as those which followed the arrival of the Denver & Rio Grande trains. Nevertheless, mine owners and businessmen generally welcomed the arrival of the Colorado Midland whole-heartedly, as the competition it provided immediately lowered transportation costs of ore shipped out and goods shipped in.

The competition of the Colorado Midland, in part, forced the Denver & Rio Grande to broad-gauge its tracks, as previously mentioned, but this reacted against them in a business way as the rival railroad could then haul more tonnage.

Each railroad ran week-end specials between Aspen and Glenwood Springs, the round-trip fare being $1.50. The competition, naturally keen, at times became rivalry. At one time the Colorado Midland ran the specials without charge to the passengers. The Denver & Rio Grande retaliated by giving free rides and a swim in the hot-water pool "to boot". The local people called them "laundry trains" and enjoyed them greatly as long as they lasted.

Chapter **XIX**

57. Railroad Towns, 1887. The arrival of the railroads created a generally prosperous condition throughout the valley. Building and business activities at Glenwood Springs and Aspen expanded and the population of each increased immediately. New towns sprang up, and those with minor station sites and sidings brought many new names into existence. Red Canyon, Cattle Creek, Satank, Carbondale, Emma and Woody Creek appeared along the Aspen branch of the Denver & Rio Grande. Snowmass, Watson and Rathbone were sidings or stations on the branch line of the Colorado Midland.

The stations or sidings on the main line were Busk, on the east side of the Divide, and Ivanhoe, on the west side. Thence westward were Mallon, Sellar, Nast, Norrie, White Sulphur Springs, Ruedi, Sloane, Howbert, Aspen Junction, Wheeler, Sands and Cardiff. Some of those places were named for railroad officials or stockholders of the company, to wit: J. R. Busk, W. D. Sloane, J. B. Wheeler, S. S. Sands, Mallon, Gordon Norrie, D. P. Sellar, Howbert, Watson and Rathbone.

On the Jerome Park coal branch the old names of Sunshine, Marion, and Spring Gulch, and two new ones — Pocahontas and Black Diamond— appeared.

Gradually over the years new names appeared along the main line of the Colorado Midland: Hell Gate, Quinn's Spur, Muckawanago, Calcium, Meredith, Hopkins, Wilson's Quarries, Seven Castles, El Jebel, Catherine, and Carbondale. And some of the names were changed: Quinn's Spur to Biglow, Muckawanago to Orsen, Calcium to Thomasville, Sloane to Sloss, Wilson's Quarries to Peachblow, Aspen Junction to Basalt and Sands to Bryant.

58. Satank, 1887. The first of the new towns was Satank which was located near the confluence of the Roaring Fork River and Rock Creek. In 1884 Captain Isaac Cooper and F. C. Childs picked the site and Mrs. Sarah F. Cooper

filed on the land on January 26, 1885. They laid out a townsite which they called Cooperton, but soon changed the name to Rockford presumably to harmonize with Rock Creek.

Cooper, who had an interest in the Denver & Rio Grande Company either as an official or a stockholder, arranged for a station or possibly a division point at their town, and on the first railroad map issued (in 1887), Satank is the only place named on the branch line.

Childs built a large store and started a general merchandise business. Cooper contrived to have Satank post office moved from its location at present Carbondale to Rockford and Childs was appointed postmaster. Rockford thus became Satank. Incidentally, Childs housed the post office in his store and placed his daughter Hattie (later Mrs. James Zimmerman) in charge of it. I first saw the store in the fall of 1887.

The transfer of the post office from Carbondale to Rockford started a rivalry between the towns which lasted for several years. The residents of Carbondale called Satank "Yellow Dog" and the Satank group called their town "Hogmore." The conflict was mostly a war of words and seldom went further than banter or raillery, except among the boys who sometimes "scrapped" about it.

In the summer of 1887, as the construction of the railroad advanced, the town boomed. Cooper started to build a large brick hotel which he called Hotel Moffat in honor of D. H. Moffat, the president of the Denver & Rio Grande Railroad Company. Then, in October he changed the name of the town to Moffat, although the post office was still called Satank.

Several businesses were started: Captain Davis ran a large restaurant-hotel establishment, which did a thriving business. John Killian ran a real estate office. Frank Page had three stores. J. J. O'Boyle was a building contractor; he was constructing the Cooper hotel. There were seven saloons; one was operated by Thams, another by

Kinney. Kinney opened on December 9 with a free dance which, according to a Glenwood Springs newspaper, was a very successful affair.

On December 31, 1887, the residents welcomed the New Year with a grand ball at Hotel Moffat, although the building was still in the course of construction. For the occasion the Colorado Midland Railway ran a special train from Glenwood Springs to their siding across the Roaring Fork River. Judge Childs and other prominent men of Moffat and Glenwood Springs had charge of the affair.

The first school was held in a log building which was located in the northwest corner of the town. School was then held in one of Page's buildings on Main Street and one of the teachers there was Charlotte Cooper. In 1889 a brick schoolhouse was constructed in the north end of town, under the supervision of Luther K. Crane, secretary of the school board. Annie Hendrie (later Mrs. Samuel Eubanks) was the first teacher there; she had seventeen pupils. Edna Denmark (later Mrs. Frank Sweet) taught there for several years and guided me on my quest for knowledge. She was a lovely and gracious woman, a talented and capable teacher, whose kind assistance and friendship were appreciated. Other teachers remembered were Mrs. Osburn, Loren Phillips (the only male teacher), Nora Lydick, Elizabeth Mullin, Alma Leonhardy and Bertha Silver.

Although its beginning was auspicious, before the railroad reached town the plans of its promoters were wrecked. Officials of the Colorado Coal & Iron Company, who were planning to exploit the Thompson Creek coal field and establish a large coking industry in the Roaring Fork valley, induced the railroad officials to by-pass Satank and build their station about one mile farther southeast. They started to build their coal-branch railroad there and the town of Carbondale resulted.

The proposed industry was never carried to completion, but its allure at the time was sufficient cause for the Denver & Rio Grande Company to select the site the coal company wanted. Cooper died on December 2, 1887, and his plans for Moffat died with him. Mrs. Cooper's attorneys, Ross and Bennett of Denver, tried to carry out Ike's plans, but were unsuccessful.

59. Carbondale, 1887. When it became known that the Denver & Rio Grande Railroad Company was going to place its station southeast of Moffat, a group of town promoters came in and acquired a part of the land that had been filed on by Mrs. Ottawa Tanney, John Mahnken, William Moore and others. They formed the Carbondale Town & Land Company and surveyed and platted a townsite which they named for their home town, Carbondale, Pennsylvania.

Mahnken and Moore wanted the place called Dinkels and Mrs. Tanney wanted it called Satank (for her post office), but their wishes were ignored by the town company. Ellery Johnson was the surveyor and principal promoter. William E. Johnson, president, and William Kopfer, secretary-treasurer. The company filed its papers for record on August 13 and made a request for incorporation on January 30, 1888. Approval was granted on April 26.

Before the railroad arrived many men bought lots and several houses and store buildings were constructed. Most of those buildings were at the east end of the present Main Street, where Mrs. Tanney's eating-house and Satank post office was located. As previously mentioned, William M. Dinkel moved his store from its former location and set it up near Mrs. Tanney's place. E. R. Alexander built and opened a grocery store across the street from them.

Other early businesses were Tommy Graham's hotel and restaurant, George Alcorn's hotel, Mrs. Alcorn's millinery, Tucker & Swigart's livery stable and Jack Chaney's saloon. It was one of thirteen which were started that year. Dinkel applied for and secured a Carbondale post office and became its postmaster. A school was started with eighteen pupils and with Miss Josephine Woodward as teacher.

The railroad company's track-laying crew reached the town on October 13 and a station and a section-house were soon constructed. The first agent was J. H. Shuckhart. The Aspen & Western Company's roadbed to Willow Park was half-completed, and its rails and rolling stock soon arrived.

A. H. Danforth, who was manager of the Colorado Coal & Iron Company, was also president of the Aspen & Western Company and on his visit to inspect completion of the railroad in December he told Carbondale citizens of the company's plans to develop the town. He said that they intended to build a large coal and iron plant there as soon as they could get to it. His statement added momentum to the boom already in progress.

Marshall H. Dean and William S. Camp were the first doctors. Dean arrived during 1886 and Camp moved in from Rosita sometime in 1888. Dean

This view looks out over the townsite of Schofield, the fourth town to be established in the region. Independence, Ute City (Aspen) and Highland were established first. Several likely-looking veins of ore were located here by prospectors in the early 1870's, however, they soon played out. Avery Peak looms in the background.

The first road to be built into Crystal City was completed in 1883. This road came over the pass, by way of Schofield, making travel to and from Gunnison much easier. A few buildings still remain here in this isolated region, far away from the populated areas of Colorado.

pulled my first aching tooth. He moved to Glenwood Springs later and thence to Denver. There he became active in the Masonic fraternity and in 1902 became the Most Worshipful Master of Masons in Colorado.

The first newspaper, *The Advance*, was started in 1887 by Frank Beslin, who had lost his sight in an explosion at Red Cliff. He published the paper for about two years, then sold it to Henry J. Holmes. Holmes renamed it the *Carbondale Avalanche* and put out the first issue on July 12, 1889. He later moved to Glenwood Springs.

In August, 1887, two trackmen on the Aspen & Western project, John O'Connor and Hayden, quarreled and Hayden shot and killed O'Connor.

On February 20, 1888, the town held its first election and the following officials were chosen: Dr. M. H. Dean, mayor; E. R. Alexander, Ward Tucker, J. E. Chaney, J. A. Workman, W. F. Scott, and Y. B. Ford, trustees.

Charles Williams built a large hotel midway along Main Street in the late 1880's and he and his wife, Mrs. Ellen Williams, ran it for a few years. It was the town's principal hostelry until, unfortunately, it was destroyed by fire. Mrs. Williams was widely and favorably known for her good meals. She was also the author of a book entitled *Three and One-half Years in the Army, or the History of the Second Colorado* (Cavalry).

Charlie had been a bugler in that troop and she had ridden with him during the time of his enlistment.

Mount Sopris Lodge No. 75, I.O.O.F. was organized in 1888 and built a frame hall shortly thereafter. It was opened on a Fourth of July with a grand ball which was attended by people from all parts of the valley. George Swigart and Clara Finch (a visitor from the East), who where each over six feet tall, led the grand march. Prior to that time they had held their dances in Campbell's and Scheue's halls. In 1906 the lodge members replaced that building with a two-story brick. The lower floor was used for shows, dances, dinners and other forms of entertainment.

Mount Sopris Post No. 68, G.A.R. was also organized in 1888. It took an active part in civic affairs, and held parades and annual balls. The *Carbondale Avalanche* of December 25, 1889, stated: "The boys in blue will hold their annual New Year's Ball at Campbell's Hall. Alex (E. R.) Alexander, Hy (H. C.) Shoemaker, and Doc (W. D.) White are the committee on arrangements." According to the next issue, the dance was well-attended and the music was furnished by Owen Williams, Al Skaar and Winnie Alexander. A list of those who attended (too long to show) was also given.

Carbondale Lodge, U. D., A. F. & A. M. was

organized in 1889 with B. B. Hill as worshipful master and George T. Millner as secretary.

The early business section of the town was a busy place in the late 1880's. I especially remember the crowd at Alexander's store in 1889 or 1890, when Alec generously passed out candy to everyone. He had won it from Jake Saunders, his clerk, on an election bet, and he gleefully made much ado about the incident.

In later years I learned more about the incident. Jake, it seems, had offered to bet Alec $5 that a certain candidate would be elected. Alec in return had offered to bet a half-interest in his store that he wouldn't be. Jake said he didn't have the amount of money necessary to cover the bet, whereupon Alec said he'd stake his bet against Jake's promise to marry a certain young lady whom both knew. Jake agreed, provided the young lady was willing, and the bet was sealed.

Alec then went to the young woman and asked her cooperation if he won the bet; together they would have some fun with Jake. She agreed to help him carry out the joke. Jake's candidate lost and he tried to beg off, but Alec insisted that he pay the debt. As the young woman seemed to be willing, even anxious, Jake felt compelled to go through with the agreement.

On the day when Jake was supposed to pay his debt a large crowd assembled, probably by invitation, as my parents were. Jake and the minister showed up but the young lady didn't and after waiting for nearly a half hour Alec told Jake he would release him from the bet if he would treat the crowd. Jake, amid much raillery and laughter, set two 20-pound buckets of candy on the counter and told everyone to help themselves. Alec personally filled my pockets and those of all the children present. Jake, whom everybody liked, kept urging each newcomer to have some candy and the two buckets were soon emptied.

The climax of the affair was reached when the young woman appeared and apologized for being late. And her concern when she learned that the bet had been called off was seemingly very distressful. However, she told Jake that she forgave him and hugged and kissed the bashful fellow much to the crowd's delight, then paraded him up and down the store. As Jake was a small man and she weighed up towards 200 pounds, their performance was, to say the least, ludicrous. The whole affair was probably an advertising stunt, but if so, it was a good one. Everyone enjoyed it and I still have a pleasant recollection of it after 60-odd years.

60. Emma, 1887. Emma was the next station above Carbondale on the Aspen branch of the Denver & Rio Grande Railroad. The corresponding station on the Colorado Midland Railway was Aspen Junction which lay about two miles northeast. It began with a station, a sectionhouse and a water tank; then a few buildings were constructed. Robert M. Morrison opened a post office there on February 15, 1888; he possibly ran a small store in connection with it.

Charles H. Mather supplanted him as postmaster on June 12, 1889, and opened a general merchandie store which he ran for about twelve years. He housed the post office there. In 1898 he replaced his frame building with a large brick and built a fine brick residence beside it.

In 1901 Mather sold out to Harry A. Pinger of Aspen and he operated that store and one at Basalt under the firm name—Pinger Mercantile Company—until 1904. J. F. Sloss acquired the Emma store at that time and ran it until 1907. He then moved his business activities to Basalt and Edwin Powell took over the store.

61. Aspen Junction, 1887. A new town, Aspen Junction, developed across (north of) the Frying Pan River and Frying Pan town when the Colorado Midland Railway reached the Roaring Fork River valley in November, 1887. D. R. C. Brown of Aspen and representatives of the railroad company had purchased land from Lucksinger Brothers for their tracks and buildings in advance of its arrival and had planned for a townsite. The residents of Frying Pan moved to the new location and most of that town disappeared. Only parts of the charcoal kilns are now visible.

As this new town was to be a division point on the main line of the railroad, the company set up a roundhouse and an inn, in addition to its usual station buildings. Also, to supplement its tracks and sidings there was a wye for turning engines between the main line and the Aspen branch.

Many of the railroad employees bought lots and built homes. A row of business houses was gradually built up on Main Street (facing the railroad tracks) and that became the principal business section. Dennis Barry and Red Duggan moved their businesses from Frying Pan to the new locality. Duggan later moved to Thomasville, but Barry's fate is lost in the unknown.

Some of the first business houses were those of Basil L. Smith & Company and the Tienery Company, who handled general merchandise; Zimmerman Drug Store, drugs and sundries; W. W. Frey, grocer; Matt Hanson, boot and shoe store owner. Two of several saloons were run by E. B.

SUNDANCE BOOKS: RUSS COLLMAN

The Devils Punch Bowl was probably the most dangerous section of the road between Schofield and Crystal City because of a very steep grade above the falls. Several people have been killed here after loosing control of their vehicles. President Grant probably viewed the Devils Punch Bowl while on tour of the West in 1880.

Kelly and Epperson. Smith's store was about midway in the block and the others were on either side. In addition to the railroad hotel and inn (across the tracks) there was a boarding house west of Smith's store, which was first set up as the Gould Hotel. At one time it was run by Charles Lucksinger.

Smith later had the post office in his store and put up the first "Basalt Post Office" sign. Later he was a newspaper publisher and still later he moved to Denver. R. H. Zimmerman, the druggist, was also a notary public, an agent for J. C. Johnson, an Aspen undertaker, and the head of a real estate agency. The name of that store was changed later to The Basalt Pharmacy. Frey survived longer than the others mentioned and ran his business well into the 1900's.

A post office was secured in 1890 with M. B. Louthau as postmaster. He took office on February 13, but was replaced by Arthur J. Kibby on June 21. He had the post office somewhere on Main Street. Basil L. Smith succeeded him on January 12, 1894, and then housed the post office in his store.

In 1890 J. P. Jones was elected justice of the peace and Frank Hotchkiss constable. Jake Frison and Fred Hotchkiss were two of the several who built new homes. The second bridge was built across the Frying Pan River. M. McNeilan and P. T. Rucker were the early doctors; W. G. Fleming, the railroad agent; Grant Ruland, the school principal; and Colonel Stiffler, an auctioneer.

In December, 1892, the Colorado Midland Railway's depot building was completely destroyed by fire. The whole populace turned out to fight the blaze but were unsuccessful. A new building was erected soon afterwards.

View on preceding page: In 1880 a large mill was built near this waterfall in Schofield. President Grant road a mule from Gothic to see Schofield at that time and was warmly greeted by the town officials who promptly tried to sell him mining claims. One day they took him to a brink of a deep, dark canyon north of town and told him it was known as Sonofa-B-Basin, and when Grant learned its name he laughed and said: "You Westerners certainly name things appropriately!" Grant probably viewed the Devils Punch Bowl while on tour of the West in 1880.

SUNDANCE BOOKS: DELL A. McCOY

121

Chapter XX

62. Jerome Park, 1887. A branch of the Colorado Midland Railway reached the Jerome Park mines in December, 1887. Its completion was well-described in the December issue of *The Ute Chief,* the Glenwood Springs newspaper:

"The Branch line of the Midland road is already completed and in operation to Sunshine and Jerome Park. Cardiff is on the main line on the Roaring Fork, 2.6 miles from Glenwood Springs. Here the branch line goes up Fourmile Creek 8½ miles to Sunshine Junction. A spur line runs to the mine. Continuing 4½ miles, Marion is reached and 2 miles beyond is Spring Gulch mine. This is the end of the line, but it is planned to construct it on to Coal Basin about 6 (10) miles further south."

However, the extension to Coal Basin was never built and that camp was reached in 1900, via Crystal River and Coal Creek, as hereafter recounted.

The Grand River Coal & Coke Company owned and operated the three mines at that time. Marion and Spring Gulch were located on the steep slope of Coal Mountain, but both were active camps despite that handicap. Both of the mines were managed by James P. Morgan, who lived at Marion.

At that time the company built fifty coke ovens at a siding called Union, one-half mile south of Marion, to coke the Spring Gulch coal. After Cardiff was chosen as the coke-oven center, those ovens were abandoned. The February 26, 1890, issue of the *Carbondale Avalanche* stated: "There is a possibility that the coke ovens at Marion (Union) will be moved to Cardiff." However, that was not done, for they are, in part, still there. Recently, a few of them were repaired and used temporarily in a test of the coal from a newly opened North Thompson Creek mine.

In August, 1892, the Grand River Coal & Coke Company sold their mines and the coke ovens at Cardiff to the Colorado Fuel Company, which had been organized in 1884 by John C. Osgood, Julian A. Kebler, Alfred C. Cass, Henry W. Wolcott, Paul Morton and David C. Beamen, and incorporated on July 18, 1884.

On October 31, 1892, the Colorado Fuel Company and the older Colorado Coal & Iron Company were consolidated as the Colorado Fuel & Iron Company, and through this association the new company gained control of most of the coal land of that region. It started extensive development of the Spring Gulch and Sunshine seams and boomed the camps at those places and at Cardiff. Spring Gulch and Cardiff became the main camps, for the former produced much of the coal and the latter coked it. The Colorado Supply Company opened stores to supply the miners at each camp and they prospered for over twenty years.

As early as January, 1888, the coal output from the area was over 200 tons daily and four trains of coal were shipped each day to Leadville and other markets. After the new company took over in 1892, the output was enormous in comparison to those figures.

The reports in the office of the State Inspector of Coal Mines at Denver show these facts: In 1891, 231 men mined 53,995 tons of coal at Marion. Tim Tinsley was the superintendent. In 1892, only 1,700 tons were mined; mine shut down. In 1893, mine not operating; 1895, mine abandoned; 1898, old mine reopened by Harry J. Elliott, superintendent at Spring Gulch, 1,375 tons of coal mined.

In 1892, 170 men mined 77,576 tons of coal at Spring Gulch. It produced 53,019 tons of coke. C. H. Stephenson was superintendent. In 1895, the output was 36,980 tons of coal—65,617 tons of coke. H. J. Elliott was superintendent. In 1898, 120 men at work, 143,348 tons of coal mined; in 1899, 168,412 tons mined.

In 1892, the Sunshine mine worked 70 men

who mined 43,780 tons of coal. The superintendent was Crist Cristenson. The mine was abandoned. In 1898, mine reopened, 29,136 tons mined, in 1899, only 6,000 tons mined. B. L. Davis was superintendent.

63. **Marion, 1887.** Marion was the largest of the three coal camps in 1887, and was growing rapidly. By 1889 over 100 men were working and the company was steadily increasing the force. There was a live labor organization called Black Diamond Assembly No. 978, Knights of Labor, with a membership of 300 men recruited from the three camps. They had a hall in which they held weekly meetings, week-end dances, dinners, programs, and other forms of entertainment whenever they wished to hold them. In fact, it served as a general recreation center for the camp.

There was a Marion Glee Club which staged a Christmas celebration that year. A large number attended the entertainment and a long program was put on by local talent. Some of the performers were Mesdames James Morgan, S. L. Crouse, George Williams and E. G. Thomas (who acted as organist); Misses Bertha Perham, Laura Evans, Mary Morgan, Bertha Bruce and Bertie Morgan; Messrs. David E. Abbott, Charles Burns, Avery Wayman, Joe Hoofnagels, David Burns, Charles Darlington and Smith Ludlow. Abbott acted as Santa Claus in a highly satisfactory manner.

Early that year James Anderson supplanted Morgan as superintendent and W. S. Sheery was his manager there. Frank Myers of Carbondale bought out an Italian's butchershop at Marion and started shops at Marion, Spring Gulch and Carbondale. The Knights of Labor staged a big celebration on July 4 and held a dance in the evening. In the fall the company constructed four frame houses. A larger force of men was employed in the mine. However, despite all of those favorable indicators, the mine was closed early in 1892.

When the Colorado Fuel & Iron Company acquired the mine in 1892, Tim Tinsley was the superintendent in charge and he undoubtedly nursed it along for a while. At least the camp survived, to some extent, for several years. A State Inspector of Coal Mines' report shows that the mine was abandoned in 1895. The records of the Colorado Fuel & Iron Corporation show that the company did some work there in 1898. M. E. Swigart, then of Satank, went there often with his father who sold meat and produce to the Dalrymple boarding-house. In 1905, when I first saw the camp, all of the frame houses were gone; only the log cabins remained.

Two years later, in December, 1907, a new drift was opened in Marion Gulch (also known as Edgerton Creek) about one-half mile below, or north of, the old camp and mine. A new camp was started on level ground just above the point where the railroad crossed the creek. It consisted of three large frame buildings: a residence for the superintendent, a boarding-house and a store building with living quarters attached for the store manager. The store was No. 47 of the Colorado Supply Company's chain of supply bases for the miners.

Richard Malloy was made superintendent, I was made store manager, and Mrs. Mike McKeown and her daughter, Annie, ran the boarding-house. The project, however, was short-lived. About mid-June 1908, the company shut down the mine because the coal wouldn't coke well. Most of the workers were sent back to Spring Gulch; the merchandise was transferred to that store. A few men, under the direction of August Marchetti, were left to work the mine. In 1909 and 1910 the mine and store were opened for short periods. John Nash was superintendent and J. N. Graham was store manager. Afterwards, Jim Marchetti (and probaly others) ran the project as a wagon-mine for an indefinite period.

64. **Spring Gulch, 1887.** Spring Gulch was just about as large as Marion in 1887, but soon outstripped it. Gus Larson, the mine superintendent, was working over 100 miners in 1890. They were mostly Italians or Austrians and they lived in a compact mass of log cabins in the gulch below the mine adit. Larson once described the mine as a stope which branched into several tunnels, one of which extended a mile toward North Thompson Creek.

John Renstrom ran a saloon and W. M. Dinkel ran a general store at that time. William (Fate) Girdner (an employee, later a partner) ran a daily supply wagon to Spring Gulch and to Marion. He was appointed postmaster on September 10, 1891, and had a contract to carry the mail to the camps. As he couldn't readily distinguish the foreign names, when he reached Spring Gulch he dumped the pouch and let the women (who always came out to meet his wagon) help themselves. There was always a wild scramble and much merriment, which helped to increase the store's popularity.

During the fall of 1890, the company built four frame houses. On October 1, Ed Wald and his partner "Frenchy" took charge of the boarding-house. At Christmas-time they gave a dance; it was well attended, many coming from the lower valley. From a newspaper account of the affair, it is learned that it was one of the most successful social events that the camp had known.

Fall colors and a small lake form a pleasant vista above Geneva Lake along the trail leading out of Crystal. This area has been set aside as the Snowmass Wilderness Area.

Pete Lispon, later a merchant at Aspen, peddled dry goods to both camps. He had several burros on which he transported his merchandise. Many ranchmen ran supply wagons and sold meat and vegetables. John Larson, who had a ranch-dairy in Jerome Park, delivered milk and butter to the residents.

W. M. Dinkel once said that much of his business at Spring Gulch was with the locators of the coal claims and that his business at Carbondale was increased very much by the miners from the camps who came down on week-ends to trade. Often-

times, he sold them a thousand dollars worth of goods on a Saturday night.

Girdner was replaced as postmaster by Abraham Cohn on September 28, 1892. Over the years the Colorado Fuel & Iron Company's superintendents were Charles Stephenson, Harry Elliott, W. G. Deck, Tim Tinsley, Dick Malloy, A. H. Robinson and again, Elliott.

The Colorado Supply Company store, No. 4, was opened on January 1, 1893, with Frank X. Rickelman as manager. Other managers who fol-

In the morning sun aspen provide a heartwarming back-lit view on the road above Crystal.

lowed him were Joshua H. Espey, James B. Bowen Collis O. Redd, John E. Chambers, Charles Ambrose Williams, Chester L. Hudson and J. N. Graham.

On April 19, 1895, the name of the post office was changed (shortened) to Gulch and Rickelman was appointed postmaster. Following him, other store managers were likewise appointed: Espey, September 16, 1895; Bowen, February 28, 1898; Rickelman again, December 1, 1900; Redd, January 22, 1902; Chambers, January 18, 1903; Williams, February 13, 1904; Hudson, December 7, 1907. Raleigh Guye, who was not a store manager, was the last appointee, on May 6, 1916. His service' was limited to about seven months as the office was discontinued on December 15, 1916.

65. Sunshine, 1887. Sunshine was almost as large as the Jerome Park camps in 1887. Griff Williams was mine superintendent under James Morgan and later under James Anderson. He was followed by Smith Ludlow who had previously worked at Marion. In the late 1880's, after Moffat had withered on the vine, Fred Childs moved his stock of merchandise to Sunshine and ran a store there until the Colorado Supply Company took over; his son William had charge of it and John W. Jett was some kind of an assistant. George Geriken had charge of the boarding-house.

After taking over the mine in 1892, the Colorado Fuel & Iron Company operated it for a short period during 1892-93. It was then shut down because, it was claimed, the coal seam had played out. However, in 1897 the mine was re-opened and it was operated until some time in 1904. During that time H. J. Elliott, James Stewart, J. H. Whitsill and John W. Allen were superintendents.

The Colorado Supply Company opened a store, No. 13, and ran it until March 1, 1900. They then rented it to the Rocky Mountain Stores Company until September 1, 1901. After that date they again ran it until December 20, 1908. During those two periods seven men served as store managers; they were H. A. Thompson, E. B. Wise, C. S. Tindall, P. H. Smith, C. A. Williams, J. H. Wilson and H. C. Clancy.

A post office called Sunlight was established at about the same time as Gulch post office. The camp eventually became known as Sunlight, but Spring Gulch always retained its original name and only postal authorities called it Gulch.

According to Arthur Gregory, Sr., of Denver, his father, Victor Gregory, and Mike McKeown settled at Sunshine in 1883 and worked in the first coal mine opened at that place. Arthur was the first boy born in the camp, arriving on June 14, 1889. Mike's daughter Lizzie was the first girl born there.

The Rocky Mountain Fuel Company operated the Midland Mine at Sunlight from 1907 to 1921, on land which they leased from the Colorado Fuel & Iron Company. The Rocky Mountain Stores Company ran a store there, probably for the same length of time. I worked in their store at Carbondale in 1909, and went to Sunlight for a 10-day period when the manager, H. C. Clancy, was ill. At that time, A. A. Shumway was manager of the mine and probably of the company. For a while the company leased and operated the Pocahontas Mine, north of Sunlight.

About 1912 Charles Coryell was mine superintendent, Harry Cummings was store manager. Fred Hamm was blacksmith for the company and Ed Starr ran a saloon. The camp lasted until the Colorado Midland Railway shut down its railroad in 1918. But according to the State Inspector's report the company was working only 56 men in the Midland mine in 1916 and their daily output was about 350 tons of coal.

66. Cardiff, 1887. In September, long before the Colorado Midland Railway reached the present site of Cardiff, the Grand River Coal & Coke Company had selected that point as the location of a coal-coking industry. When the railroad reached the spot in December, 1887, a townsite was laid out and the town of Cardiff was soon a reality. The coal company began the construction of fifty coke ovens, and the railroad company started to build its station buildings and its roundhouse. The work on the coal branch was in progress and it was pushed to the limit, for the company wanted coal to coke as soon as the ovens were ready. Many railroad employees built homes there and the town eventually became a division point.

The ovens were completed and they were fired in January, 1888, when the first coal was delivered. Later the number of ovens was increased to 240 and a large supply of coke was soon available. Many men were employed to man the ovens and handle the coke and they increased the population of the town threefold. In 1890 the coke-boss, as he was called, was M. E. Strickler.

As a result of the industry Cardiff blossomed into a thriving town, but its pretty cottages were usually shrouded by a pall of smoke from the ovens. That, however, didn't hinder its development. In 1890 there was a Railroad Inn, a Hotel DeCardiff run by a man named Fanning, and several mercantile establishments, and the population of the camp was more then 150 people.

Chapter XXI

67. Aspen, 1888. In 1887 and 1888 the Aspen mines were producing enormous quantities of ores. Within two weeks after the arrival of the Denver & Rio Grande Railroad its engines were hauling twenty-five to forty carloads daily. After the Colorado Midland railway arrived the average output was fifty-nine cars each day and the number eventually ran up to eighty cars daily.

In 1888 the local telephone company extended its Gothic-Ashcroft line to Aspen, thus bringing its citizens closer to the outside world. In 1890 the line was extended to Tourtelotte Park.

In January, 1889, John Frazier opened the European Hotel on Cooper Avenue; it had sixty rooms and free baths. The rates were $6 and $8 per week. Yes, that's right, *per week.* That rate and not the opening of the hotel is the important point.

The following city officials were elected in February, 1889: J. C. Carson, mayor; H. C. Kennedy, John O'Reilly and C. I. Glassbrook, trustees; Louis Jennett, treasurer.

In April of that year members of the Aspen Park Association opened a one-half mile race track and ball park in west Aspen. It constructed a grandstand which was 120 feet long and seated 800 people.

Postmaster J. C. Connor was replaced by Josiah A. Small on August 2, 1889, and he was succeeded by Moses Bradshaw on December 21.

Horse-drawn street cars were operated on Main and a few other streets during that summer. The lines were lengthened and the cars were electrically powered in 1891. The street cars were operated for a period of about five years.

The old Clarendon Hotel was turned over to J. H. Bixby, who held a mortgage on it, according to an 1889 issue of the *Aspen Times.* It was still going in 1892 and 1893 under the management of J. W. Blake. He kept a chained bear at its rear entrance on Durant Street as an added attraction. The bear created a lot of excitement one day when it got loose and attacked some pigs nearby. The *Times* stated that the pigs were saved, but failed to tell the fate of the bear.

On April 23, 1889, J. B. Wheeler finished constructing and opened the Wheeler Opera House, then one of the finest buildings in the state. Its cost was nearly $100,000. On the opening night the Conried Opera Company presented *The King's Fool* to an audience of about 800 people. It was a gala occasion and was considered the most brilliant affair in the city's history. The following day Theodore Rosenberg of Glenwood Springs and Miss Jageman, a member of the opera troupe, fenced in the opera house for a purse of $150. Rosenberg won the match, then gave the prize money to Miss Jageman. In later years two fires gutted the interior of the theatre building and it lay idle for a long time. However, it had been overhauled recently and is being used again.

Wheeler also opened the Jerome Hotel on November 27th of that year. It was one of the largest hotels in the state at that time, 110 x 100 feet in size, three stories high, ninety rooms and fifteen baths. T. J. and S. Ellis constructed the building for $70,000. They bought in a carload of red sandstone from Peachblow and contracted for about one million bricks from the Atkinson yards. The large ball which was held on the opening night was attended by people from far and near and proved to be another rung in Aspen's social ladder.

The Washington schoolhouse was built that year at a cost of $30,000, and additions were made a little later to the Garfield and Lincoln buildings.

The returns from the 1890 census showed that Aspen had a population of 6,645 people and Pitkin County a population of 8,804.

In the early 1890's Aspen had the best volunteer fire department in the state and held the state championship belt for the proficient operation of its team in annual competion. It was composed of

The ghost town of Crystal City warms in the noon sun on a beautiful autumn day. This town once had newspapers, saloons, hotels and various business buildings.

one hook and ladder and three hose companies, and had one hook and ladder and five hose carts. The city had a fire engine drawn by horses in 1898, which it used for several years.

D During the summer of 1890 Otto Kappele and Ed Weber bought a large U. S. flag and raised it on the skyline of West Aspen Mountain. They or someone else kept a flag flying there for many years.

Gould Brothers and Grover opened the Mesa Grocery Store and meat market on West Main street in July, 1890.

In November, 1890, the J. D. Hooper Hook & Ladder Company held its Thanksgiving Ball at the

Tivoli Theatre. Those in charge were B. Clark Wheeler, W. R. Phillips, P. E. C. Burke, S. D. Potter, S. Wachtel, J. E. Slagle, Joe Leonard, W. E. Rhode, F. S. Snell, F. H. Belden, L. Flamm, Isaac Johns, Frank Cordriss and T. E. Bean.

The Presbyterians planned for and started to build a new church in early 1890. The cornerstone was laid on April 17. The builders used red sandstone from the Peachblow quarries and an unusually beautiful building resulted. In October The Rev. Beavis, the then pastor, preached the farewell sermon in their little church on Cooper Avenue and they moved to the new building on

View on preceding page: Deadhorse Mill at Crystal City, just six miles east of Marble. This mill was probably built in 1890 and has withstood the extreme weather conditions found near timberline throughout the years.

PHOTO BY DAVID S. DIGERNESS

129

Aspen and Bleeker Streets. It was dedicated at Thanksgiving time.

In later years the Methodists and Presbyterians combined forces and formed the Aspen Community Church; they used the Presbyterian building and the Methodist conference furnished the pastor. In the 1920's the members used the Methodist-building as a play-house; once a week they met there, talked, sang and played games. The Rev. T. J. Trammel fostered and led the movement—a practical application of Christianity to everyday living—which brightened the lives of his pastoral flock. Several years later the building was torn down.

The members of the Catholic Church also replaced their building in 1890 with a fine large brick, their present St. Mary's church. The Lutherans and the Episcopalians built churches at that time but they were razed many years ago.

The Community Church members had their building overhauled recently. It is now a lovely restful place of worship. Undoubtedly the other church buildings have also been reconditioned.

Henry P. Cowenhoven, Aspen's first merchant, organized the H. P. Cowenhoven Company; then in 1886 he helped to organize the First National Bank, and on July 29, 1889, he and J. B. Wheeler organized the Cowenhoven Mining, Transportation & Drainage Company, capitalized at $250,000. Cowenhoven was president, Wheeler, vice-president and Thomas Little, secretary-treasurer. That company, managed by F. M. Taylor and D. W. Brunton, civil engineers and mining experts, drove a two and a half-mile tunnel under Smuggler Mountain to tap the lower levels of some of the mines and drain the whole area. It also afforded an easy outlet for transportation of the ores. The cost of the project was $500,000.

In 1890 Cowenhoven was also president of the Della S. Consolidated Mining Company. During that year Taylor & Brunton built, incorporated and operated a sampling works for the better handling of ores.

David M. Hyman, the Cincinnati capitalist who had backed B. C. Wheeler's venture, acquired the Durant and other mines and engaged actively in their development. For many years he and D. R. C. Brown were opponents, each striving to gain control of certain mines in that area.

During the contests over the apex and side line issues in 1887, Henry Gillespie and Byron Shear obtained control of the Mollie Gibson and the other mines of that group. They formed the Mollie Gibson Mining & Milling Company, with Gillespie

as president. In 1889 they interested James J. Hagerman in their company and reorganized it as the Mollie Gibson Consolidated Mining Company, with Hagerman as president. He deposited $100,000 for development funds and sparked Aspen's loudest boom.

The company made its first big strike on December 9, 1890, and two years later declared a cash dividend of $200,000. The ores averaged 600 ounces of silver per ton. One car of twenty-three and a half tons netted $44,000; one of twenty-four tons, $76,000; one of twenty-eight tons, $64,100; one of twenty-two tons, $60,400; one of twenty-two tons, $60,000; and another, the richest, $118,000.

Gillespie bought a large ranch below present Basalt and built a mansion on it. He called it El Jebel and the Colorado Midland Railway put in a spur or a siding. The locality was usually referred to as "Robinson's" as the Robinson family took over the management of the ranch. Late in 1890 they obtained a post office which was called Sherman, but further details are lacking.

Charles Dailey came to Aspen in 1890 and started publication of the *Aspen Democrat*, a weekly newspaper. For a while there was considerable rivalry between Dailey and W. S. Copeland, who was then the manager of the *Aspen Times*, but in the course of time the two papers were combined as the *Aspen-Democrat Times*, and it became a daily. Dailey later reduced it to a weekly and it was known locally as "The Little Humdinger." As the *Aspen Times* it still serves Aspen and Pitkin County, and is one of the live newspapers of the state.

On January 1, 1956, the *Aspen Times* began its 75th year of publication. In an issue of that date it disclosed these facts: B. Clark Wheeler assumed control of the newspaper in 1883 and was later assisted in its publication by Davis H. Waite, his law partner. Charles Dailey owned the *Democrat* and the *Times* (and combined them) during the period, 1900-1932. During the last part of that time, Charles Dailey, Jr., was his assistant.

The changes which occured down through the years were as follows: First issued as a weekly April 23, 1881; first issue as a daily, February 19, 1885; *Democrat* issued as a daily, August 6, 1890; *Democrat* and *Times* merged as the *Daily Democrat Times*, June 6, 1909; changed to the weekly *Aspen Times*, January 14, 1926; continued as such to the present time—a remarkable record.

Aspen had several shooting frays and one of the first was an accidental killing. Frank Jones, a drunken gambler, raised a disturbance in a saloon by making threats and flourishing a gun. Two officers tried to disarm him and in the ensuing scuffle the gun was discharged and Jones was killed. In the 1890's Leo Pinger, a merchant, was shot one night while going from his store to his home. The killer was never apprehended.

In 1890 and 1891 many fine structures were completed and opened for use. Some of them were the Cowenhoven Building, the City Hospital, which was built by Truman Case, the County Courthouse, whose cornerstone was laid in September, 1890, the Holden Lixiviation Works, the Telephone Building, and the new State bridge across Castle Creek, which was dedicated by Governor Routt in December, 1890, while attending some kind of a meeting in Aspen.

Those sumptuous buildings, the schools, churches, the large commercial brick blocks, and hundreds of substantial residences added much to Aspen's growth and glory. They earned for her the glamorous title—Crystal City of the Rockies—a title which she still proudly bears. Incidentally, that name was bestowed on her by Edward L. Ogden, one of the leading merchants.

68. Tourtelotte Park, 1888. A rich strike was made at the Silver Bell Mine in Tourtelotte Park in 1888. Almost overnight a town developed when the miners opened a 6-foot vein of 300-ounce silver ore. In 1889 its average daily output was worth $24,000. For about six years the town vied with Aspen; it had a post office, many stores, and according to Tom Atkinson, who lived there during the boom, "more voters and more saloons than Aspen had."

The town's population built up fast and many businesses were started. Two boarding-house proprietors, I. R. Weamer and W. K. Taylor, constructed additions to their buildings to take care of the trade. Other lodging houses were opened, and in 1889 Weamer constructed the Weamer Block, the largest edifice in the town.

In the fall election a voting precinct was established and more than 200 votes were cast. A little later, rich strikes were made in the Edison, O K and Silver Star mines, and so much ore was taken out that its transportation to the railroad became a problem. Fifty ore-wagons and several jack-trains couldn't keep up with the output, and plans for a bucket tramway were considered.

During 1889 E. T. Hendrickson ran a bakery, a restaurant, and a boarding-house; he was also a justice of the peace. W. H. Nichols set up an assay office. A schoolhouse was constructed. Mrs. Hattie

Findley was the teacher and she and her pupils put on a fine entertainment that fall in Weamer's Hall.

A post office (shortened to Tourtelotte) was established, and Mrs. Louisa Coll was appointed postmaster on March 19, 1889. Austin E. Schooley followed her; he was appointed on September 27, 1892. On August 17, 1894, F. Nash was appointed postmaster, but he declined the appointment and the office was discontinued on November 5, 1894.

Early in 1890 a cable bucket tram was built from the railroad in Aspen to the mines. It served the Silver Bell, Edison, O K, Silver Star, Last Dollar, Little Rule and other mines. It afforded quick, easy transportation of the ores, cleaned up the accumulated supply and put some of the ore-haulers out of business. A few passenger buckets were added later and the round-trip fare was $1.25. After the price of silver declined in 1893, it ceased to operate because the business was unprofitable. Some work in the mines continued until 1920, the last to close being the Park Tunnel, managed by Ed Turner. In 1918 another tram was built from Aspen to that tunnel, but it was shut down before it was well started, at a considerable loss to the stockholders.

In those days the settlers often formed "literary societies" where they got together for local entertainment. Those meetings and their dances were favorite forms of recreation. In 1892 the citizens of the Park organized a society and had many pleasant gatherings that winter. The officers were A. G. Groh, president; Samuel Rogers, vice-president; T. E. Castle, treasurer. There were thirty-five members and one of its debating teams was composed of the following members: John Bean, J. A. Curry, J. F. Fulkerson and M. A. Callahan.

Water for the town came from the Justice Mine; a small reservoir was built and water was pumped from it to the several parts of the town. The Justice Company gave the service free, but in 1892, because of so many complaints, their manager, Peter Lux, shut down the plant. Until the matter was ironed out, water was packed by burros to the several homes.

It is said that Hank Tourtelotte made a fair stake from the Buckhorn, but was unhappy and disconsolate because his wife (a beautiful woman) would not live in the town and went back East. In his old age Hank lived with Gene Grubb (they had married sisters) at Gene's Mount Sopris ranch near Carbondale. He died in 1919, but his name is fixed to the spot where (to quote his own words) "he camped in 1880, so that his jack would have plenty of good water and grass."

William Zaugg was the last resident of that locality, having lived there for many years at the lower limits of the camp.

Little trace of the town is now visible. The old mine dumps have been leveled or sloped by bulldozers to provide better terrain for ski runs. And skiers who ride the aerial tram to the Sundeck on Ajax Mountain (so-named for the Ajax Mine there) find it difficult to visualize the former existence of a city of several thousand people in the basin below them.

This breathtaking view is a part of the Snowmass Wilderness Area— showing Geneva Lake surrounded by Meadow Mountain to the left, Capitol Peak in the middle and Snowmass Mountain to the far right. This was one of Len Shoemaker's favorite areas to patrol.

SUNDANCE BOOKS:
DELL A. MC COY

Chapter XXII

69. Independence, 1888. Independence had about 100 residents in 1888, but most of the business firms were gone; the loss of the stage-runs had sounded their death knell. Theodore Ackermann had closed Sparkill post office on October 18, 1887, and at sometime near the first of the year he closed his store and moved his restaurant to Aspen. Con Hansen still ran his saw-mill; J. R. Connor was constable.

Previously, Charles Moore, who had surveyed the route of the Independence Pass road, had moved to Aspen. There he made other surveys, one of which was a road up Aspen Mountain and another, the line of the Salvation Ditch.

The residents of the town then changed its name to Mammoth City and later they called it Mount Hope, when the Mammoth and the Mount Hope mines were being exploited. Neither of those names took and eventually the original name of Independence was again used. Mail was secured at Aspen.

The town survived and the mill was operated occasionally for several years. It was active during the period 1897-99 and for a short time in 1900, but the mine and mill were closed that year. During that revival Walter S. Ritchie secured a post office called Chipeta and became its post-master on April 20, 1899. He ran the office until it was discontinued on October 17, 1899.

Jack Williams had acquired a ranch on Snowmass Creek in the 1880's, but he returned and acted as caretaker of the mill until 1912. He did a little mining on the side and occasionally brought some gold to the Aspen Bank. He was thus the last resident and the only one for several years. The old stamp mill was torn down in the 1920's.

Jack was typical of the prospector-settler of the 1880's; he knew much about the early happenings in the valley and liked to tell about them. Much of the material included in this record came from him. Before he went to the mill he acquired

land at the northeast corner of Aspen, a part of which became the Williams Addition in May, 1889. The adit of the Cowenhoven Tunnel was on this land and his sale of that portion of it netted him more profit than his prospecting had done.

Today the traveler over State Highway 82 can still see several of the old cabins built in 1879 and 1880 at Independence—the first erected in the valley. They afford a good picture of that often-used term of the present day, "a ghost town."

70. Janeway, 1888. Hugh C. Pattison, who later settled at Carbondale and ran a blacksmith shop, prospected on Avalanche Creek (a tributary of Crystal River) in 1880. He found evidence of prospecting which had been done many years earlier. His findings might have been signs of work done by the Richard Sopris party in 1860, although it is not known definitely that the party went that far south.

Mrs. Mary Jane Francis and Harry Van Syckel, long-time residents of Carbondale, acquired the Skobeloff claim on Avalanche and the M J claim on Bulldog Creek in 1882. Van Syckel did a lot of work there but found no valuable ore. Clark Edwards had a claim on Avalanche and lived there for many years.

Ed Gift, Andy Anderson, and H. D. Penny located claims near the Penny Hot Springs on Crystal River. Penny developed a pool and built a bathhouse over it; the springs took his name and it was attached to that part of the valley for many years. A small stream near Gift's location, took his name.

In October, 1899, Harry Van Syckel and Charles Scheue opened the Silver Queen Mine on Avalanche Creek and worked a force of men there for about a year. However, it, like the other claims in that locality, proved to be worthless.

As the turn of the century deer were very scarce in that part of the valley and local game wardens were vigilant. One of them visited Ed Gift's cabin and found a haunch of venison hanging in his shed. He arrested Ed and took him (and the venison) to Aspen for prosecution of the case. Enroute they stayed overnight at Carbondale and put their wagon in Hugh Pattison's shop, Pattison being a mutual friend. During the night Hugh took the venison from the wagon, carried it to the local meat market, and matched it as nearly as possible with a haunch of veal.

Next morning he told Gift to claim, when the case came to trail, that the meat was veal, not venison. This Ed did. Men were called in to look at the meat and all agreed that it was veal, so, much to the warden's chagrin, his prisoner was released. Ed went back to Carbondale, hunted up Pattison and asked, "What did you do with my venison, Hugh?"

Pattison laughed gleefully and rubbed his tummy. "What do you suppose, Ed, what do you suppose!" he exclaimed.

When John Mobley gave up his claim at the Clarence townsite, he moved down to the junction of Rock and Avalanche Creeks. There he started a small settlement which was known as "Mobley's Camp." Later it was named Janeway, for Mary Jane Francis, when she became interested there in some way. Mobley secured a post office under the name of Janeway and was appointed postmaster on August 16, 1887. In 1888 the town had a population of fifty people. W. D. Parry ran a general merchandise store.

Four channeling machines are in sight in this view of one of the Colorado Yule marble openings. Some blocks were broken out by first drilling the holes in line and then filling them with water. The water then froze, expanded and broke loose the marble.

Treasury Mountain, at 13,464-feet elevation, glistens in the morning sunlight on a fall day. This view is on the road between Crystal and Schofield.

When the Crystal River Railroad was built from Carbondale to Redstone in 1898, Janeway became a railroad station. Mobley sold out and moved to the vicinity of Meeker, and Mrs. Mary Rowan was appointed postmistress on May 21, 1898. She served as such until the office was closed on November 30, 1900.

71. Calcium, 1888. The first (or one of the first) town settlements in the upper Frying Pan valley was Calcium, a station on the Colorado Midland Railway. It was situated at the confluence of Lime Creek with the Frying Pan where there were large deposits of limestone. Those, of course, were the source of the names of the creek and the town.

In 1888 a group of men formed the Calcium Limestone Company and built several lime kilns there. They quarried and burned limestone and a small settlement grew up around the kilns. There was a boarding-house, a store, two saloons and several log houses, most of which lay across the stream on the closest suitable location.

Mrs. Nellie Daugherty, who ran the boarding-house, secured the Calcium post office in 1888. She became its postmistress on March 10. She later married Charles V. Noble and he became the postmaster on July 13. He held the post for six-and-one-half years.

Little is known of the town's people or their activities. It thrived and survived till about 1890

In this view Sheep Mountain rises to the left. The photographer was looking west near Crystal.

137

This view looks north along the first Colorado-Yule Marble Company quarry works in 1907. The tall boom would lift the marble blocks from inside the quarry, up and out over the hillside to a waiting tram motor on flat cars below.

when it gave way to a rival settlement, Thomasville, which was located about one-half mile downstream.

One item of unusual interest occurred in 1898 when a workman named Breen accidentally pulled some hot lime onto some dynamite which someone else was thawing out. The resulting blast killed Breen, wrecked some of the kilns, and rattled the windows of the George McLaren house nearby—according to George McLaren, Jr., of Basalt.

72. Sellar, 1888. Sellar was only a railroad station, but it had the second post office in the upper Frying Pan valley. It was obtained by Mrs. Rose Kirk who was in charge of the Inn which the railroad company maintained for travelers and employees. She became postmistress on April 12, 1888.

Besides the railroad buildings, a few other structures were built. Several loggers lived at or in the vicinity of the station, but these did not add much to the settlement as they were somewhat scattered. Charles Isola was one of the loggers; he harvested mine props from an old burn and shipped them to the coal mines on Fourmile Creek. He employed quite a crew of men. Harry Davis settled on a homestead claim east of the station and patented 130 acres in 1890.

Seventeen postmasters followed Mrs. Kirk, and supposedly they were railroad agents who came and went during the 30-year period that the office existed. Their names and the dates of their appointments were Edward W. Little, December 9, 1889; Austin B. Buck, March 15, 1890; Clarence W. Garrett, September 28, 1892 (he declined); Leon F. Tyler, May 10, 1895; Willard G. Fleming, August 21, 1896.

The office was closed on December 4, 1896, but was reopened January 18, 1897, with Austin B. Buck again the postmaster. Milton Y. Crutchfield was appointed on March 21, 1898, but the office was again discontinued on May 28, 1898. It was reestablished and Horace G. Oliver was appointed postmaster on January 25, 1901. After him came Otto B. Kirkpatrick, May 22, 1902; Charles A. Cooley, July 28, 1906; Charles H. Weible, December 2, 1907; Leslie G. Kay, December 10, 1908, (he declined); Charles G. Peterson, February 23, 1909; Robert H. McConnell, May 11, 1910; John E. Leary, September 6, 1910; Clark Bugbee, March 2, 1915; Bernard T. Benton, April 6, 1915. The office was finally closed on August 10, 1918.

73. Ivanhoe, 1888. Ivanhoe was the first station that the Colorado Midland Railway Company established in the valley. It had several railroad buildings and a wye for turning engines.

COLLECTION OF ROBERT A. LE MASSENA

Treasury Mountain locomotive Number 1 shows her dainty profile at the end-of-track where she was abandoned between 1912 and 1946. This railroad and quarry operation probably folded due to the lack of funds to continue after the construction costs had piled up to excessive amounts.

This merry group stopped for a view overlooking Marble while on their way to the Colorado-Yule Marble quarry for a picnic. Notice the whistle and headlight on this tram motor.

COLLECTION OF THE LATE WILLIAM MC MANUS

In 1971 the largest quarry opening of the Colorado-Yule Marble Company still afforded an awsome view at the brink overlooking the huge chasm cut from living marble. The openings are connected by large tunnels inside the mountain.

There was a long snowshed at the entrance of the Busk-Ivanhoe tunnel. Ivanhoe Creek which had its source there, was dammed and a small lake was formed. In 1913, when I first saw it, many large mackinaw trout swam in its waters and defied all efforts to catch them.

It also had a post office in the station building and, like Sellar, it had a long list of postmaster-agents. Their names and the dates of their appointment were Patrick J. Doody, April 26, 1888; Frank Skinner, August 4, 1888; Shadrach L. Smith, November 20, 1889; Albert S. Crawford, December 24, 1890; William H. Brenton, January 2, 1892; William L. Taylor, March 11, 1890; J. H. Patterson, June 20, 1893. The post office was closed on June 30, 1894, but was reopened on July 31, 1899, with Israel G. Beverlin as postmaster.

Others appointed were John W. Errvin, February 29, 1900; Wilbert G. Cole, April 2, 1900; Charles

A portion of the Treasury Mountain Railroad may be seen running toward the power house at the end-of-track. The lines little Shay locomotive was stored here for many years. Climbing up the mountain to the left and through the trees was the Funicular tram grade that lowered the marble to the loading dock of the Treasury Mountain Railroad. Several quarry openings had begun. A glimpse of the Colorado-Yule marble quarry is in the upper valley along the route leading over Yule Pass.

A train-load of marble waits for orders to proceed into Marble at the Colorado-Yule Marble quarry end-of-track. This 1908 view shows Superintendent William McManus keeping a close watch of the work in 1908.

E. Criswell, December 5, 1905; Luke G. Campbell, April 4, 1906; E. H. Blough, November 5, 1906; Burrell I. Sipes, May 25, 1907; Bert G. Farrar, September 7, 1907; Clark Bugbee, February 2, 1910; Forest B. Rose, August 22, 1913; Charles S. Lively, March 2, 1915; John H. Harris, January 19, 1918. The office was discontinued on August 10, 1918.

74. Ruedi, 1888. When John Reudi settled on the Frying Pan in 1880, he didn't expect to have a railroad in his front yard some day. But that was what happened when the Colorado Midland Railway built down the Frying Pan in 1887. The company named their siding for him, and later

put up a station building and a section-house. Reudi secured a post office and was its postmaster. There was a school which Miss Mattie Stiffler of Basalt taught in 1899.

William Henderson later acquired his holdings and built a large house near the depot. William Smith had another large house close by; in 1917, he or his wife was the postmaster. Henderson and Smith were very friendly and cooperative when I worked there in 1917 and 1918; their wives were hospitable and I have pleasant recollections of good times at their homes. Rial Clay and Burns Biglow lived on Ruedi Creek north of the station and Swan Nelson lived east of it.

142

About February 1, 1931, the 56-ton block of marble for the Tomb of the Unkown Soldier began it's journey from the quarry. A great deal of care went into transporting this block down to Marble, nearly three and one-half miles away. The crew is shown making a flat car ready to receive the load. Later the block was simply skidded along on the track, having being placed on top of an oak timber and two small wheels because the tram motors were not able to hold back the weight on the 12-percent grade along the lower part of the tramway.

75. Peachblow, 1888. A man named Wilson opened a stone quarry at a point about eight miles east of present Basalt in 1888 and began to cut and sell red sandstone building blocks. As his business grew a few houses were built by his workmen and a little settlement developed. It was first known as "Wilson's Quarries"; then the railroad company built a loading spur connection and called it Peachblow.

A store and a schoolhouse, and possibly a post office, were started. One of the teachers was Roaldo D. Strong, and a few of the workmen were

L. M. Larson, Gus Anderson, Albert Downey and Dave Hull.

Wilson increased the size of his quarries as his business developed. He furnished building blocks to Aspen, Glenwood Springs and all other local markets; then expanded to markets throughout the country. He used the trade name "Peachblow Sandstone" with success for the name became widely known within and without the state. In 1890 he sold 3,000 carloads of stone to one buyer in Chicago.

This pile trestle served the tram motors as they crossed the Crystal River at the edge of Marble on their way to the quarry. The grade then crossed to the right, gaining elevation as it passed by snow-tipped White House Mountain.

Chapter XXIII

76. Colorado Midland Railway, 1890. During the summer of 1888 the Colorado Midland Railway Company extended its tracks westward, and as previously mentioned, then cooperated with the Denver & Rio Grande Railroad Company in building a jointly owned railroad to Grand Junction. However, on October 25, 1890, the Atchison, Topeka & Santa Fe Railroad Company purchased all of the Colorado Midland stock and took control of the road. The purchase price was $4,905,500 in stock and $1,900,000 in cash.

For some time before that transaction was completed, plans had been made to bore a tunnel through the Continental Divide at a lower level, and during the summer of 1890 the Busk Tunnel Company was formed to do just that. It began the job on August 1 and spent over two years and nearly $4,000,000 in doing it. During that time several lives were lost in the course of its construction.

When completed the Busk-Ivanhoe Tunnel, as it was called, was 9,394 feet in length, 15 feet in width, and 21 feet in height. It was 581 feet lower than the Hagerman tunnel and saved a rail distance of 6.9 miles.

The Aspen Short Line Railroad Company was then formed and it laid track through the tunnel. It might have been the same company as the one which bored the tunnel but the two names were used. Whatever its name, it began immediately to charge the Colorado Midland a fee for everything it transported through the tunnel. The fee was twenty-five cents per passenger and twenty-five cents per ton for freight. This was a steep charge but less costly than the upkeep of the high line had been.

Later, the Colorado Midland Railway Company bought the tunnel, and it and the Aspen Short Line Company were consolidated as the Colorado Midland Railroad Company. The railroad had now cost about $20,000,000, and though the new route through the lower tunnel had relieved the drastic conditions caused by the weather during each winter, its cost so weakened the company's economic stability that by 1892 it was in sad distress financially. During the panic of 1893 both companies went into receivership. The Colorado Midland was again sold, this time to eastern capitalists, and it struggled along for years under the management.

77. Thomasville, 1890. The St. Louis & Colorado Smelting Company, headed by a man named Thomas, built a smelter a half-mile below Calcium in 1890. A town called Thomasville developed at and below the smelter. The Colorado Midland Railway Company built a station and put in a siding and a spur to the smelter. A store, three saloons, a boarding-house, several houses and a building known as Alhambra Hall were constructed. That part of the valley boomed for about two years.

The June 11, 1890, issue of the *Carbondale Avalanche* stated: "Calcium is now called Thomasville for a man, Thomas, who is making so much improvement there." According to further statements, Editor Holmes didn't like the change in names at all.

The railway company is credited with naming the town for Thomas, whose name or initials, by-the-way, were not known by anyone with whom I made contact. He had a daughter who married B. H. Hopkins, who had a photographer's studio in Daniels & Fisher's tower (in Denver) for several years.

Thomas was interested in several mining ventures, some of them along the Lime-Brush Creek divide, and an 11,991-foot peak there bears his name. His mine (or mines) produced some ore, some was obtained from the Bessie Mine near town and some was shipped in. Those ores kept the smelter going for some time, but the venture was unprofitable and the smelter was shut down in 1892. It is said that it was reopened again in 1893 and 1894, but this was not confirmed.

The Crystal Bridge crossed the Crystal River here at the edge of Marble where the tram motors began their long pull up the hill. White House Mountain dominates this scene flanked in fresh snow.

During the boom Lige Thompson enlarged his boarding-house and it became the Thompson Hotel. His wife ran it while he ran a sawmill on Deadman Creek. The hotel existed for many years; however, according to Keith Biglow of Denver, the Thompsons once sold it and moved to a ranch near Ruedi. But after a year or more there they returned to Thomasville and repossessed it.

Charlie Noble moved the post office from Calcium to the new town and its name was officially changed to Thomasville on March 31, 1890. Just where he housed the office is uncertain, but it was housed later in the Irions house, a large building which stood near the hotel.

Russell M. LaPree replaced Noble as postmaster on January 14, 1895, and held the post for more than six years. He also ran a general store.

78. Hopkins, 1890. Hopkins was a siding on the Colorado Midland about midway between Ruedi and Sloss. It was put in about 1890. The railroad company kept a track watchman there for many years to patrol the track through the 3-mile canyon which lay upstream.

Frank Blair, the watchman, and his wife lived in a house beside the track, far removed from other people. Mrs. Blair was known to all the railroaders as "Mother Blair," and she was loved by all of them for her kindness and affability. She was ever ready to listen to their troubles and to feed them if they were hungry. Cake and hot coffee were always on tap for every trainman who had to stop at the siding, and many of them found that their engines needed a brief rest when they neared the place.

One engineer, running "wild" towards Basalt, once facetiously remarked that he always had to stop there and build up steam before he could go on to his destination. The joke may be more readily understood when one learns that the engine could have gone on to Basalt without any steam.

146

This 1909 view of Marble shows activity in the railroad yards as a tram motor shunts three flat car loads of marble into the mill and the second motor waits for orders to go to the quarry. Notice the electric tramway bridge crossing the Crystal River—and above this, the marble-lined turntable pit with the converted horse barn engine-house. Number 6, a CR&SJ 2-6-0 is at the far left.

The traveling crane has just lifted a 25-ton block of marble off the flat car to process it in the mill. Later, wire cable was used around the blocks in order to cause less damage to the chain. Photographed in 1909.

147

The "Black Bull"—Number 99—was an electric rotary snowplow built in 1915 for use on the electric tramway between the Yule quarry and the finishing mill at Marble. She is shown here spotted on her own spur in 1941, sadly in need of paint. The operator could enter through the side doors and both ends had blades for snow removal.

79. Muckawanago, 1890. Harvey Biglow and Robert Reed first settled in the Frying Pan Valley at a point above Calcium, and in 1889 or 1890 the railway company built a loading spur for their use in shipping out the timber they cut and milled near by. The company called the spur Muckawanago, an Indian word which meant "the place where the bear walks." According to rumor the trainmen or some traveler on the trains had seen a bear near the track at different times.

During the 1890's and the early 1900's, the railway company ran special trains to the place to accommodate the large groups who picnicked there each summer. The company built a large open-air pavillion across the stream from the track and a bridge whereby they could cross to it. Church groups from surrounding towns went there. I attended one of their picnics in 1895 and I have a record of an Aspen group who picnicked there on July 16, 1903. Swedish groups from Leadville also patronized the place, but their picnics were very unlike the church affairs; there was always a lot of beer on tap.

In the late 1890's a group of Grand Junction people, one of whom was the well-known writer and poet, Dr. Edward F. Eldridge, established a summer camp there. They built floor-foundations and pitched tents over them. There was a long one which was used as a dining-hall and several smaller ones which were used for living quarters. The length of the camp's existence is uncertain. Some people have said that Dr. Eldridge bestowed the name Muckawanago, but that is not definitely known. If he did, it was before he and the group set up the camp, for that name had been applied to the railroad spur previous to that time.

A siding called Orsen was built in that vicinity and the euphonious "Muckawanago" disappeared. In recent years a resort called Riley's has been set up at or near the point where the pavillion stood. It is regrettable that he didn't use the old name, for the bear still walks there—I saw one last summer (1957).

80. Biglow, 1890. As previously mentioned, Harvey Biglow and Bob Reed settled on land between Norrie and Calcium in the 1890's. They first had a sawmill in the vicinity of Muckawanago and later had one on Miller Creek where A. J. Dearhamer was associated with them. Still later, Harvey filed on land at the confluence of the Main and North Forks of the Frying Pan River. He built a lodge and several houses and started a tourist resort which he and his wife ran for many years.

Previously, the Midland Company had put in a loading spur for George Quinn, a logger. It was called Quinn's Spur, but the railway company

St. Paul's Episcopal Church in Marble looks like a Christmas card in this 1972 view. This church was brought into Marble on a flat car from Aspen in 1909 and the first couple married were William and Maude McManus. The bell tower was added once the church was in Marble.

changed the name to Biglow soon after Harvey settled there.

When Francis Johnson gave up the post office at Norrie, Mrs. May E. Biglow took it to their resort, still under the Norrie name. She was appointed postmistress on June 5, 1905, and held the post until the office was closed on June 15, 1906.

Bob Reed maintained a cabin home there all through the years. John W. Irions, who had been a Land Office surveyor, settled on land on the North Fork east of Biglow. He had four sons, one named Charles, lived on the ranch in 1913.

81. Frying Pan Road, 1890.
A newspaper item of 1890 stated that a wagon road would be built through the Frying Pan valley that year, but the road failed to materialize. In 1899 the State legislature appropriated $2,500 to construct a bridge across the Roaring Fork River at Basalt and $7,000 to construct a wagon road from Basalt to Ruedi. The bridge was built that year and the road might have been started, but it wasn't completed till about 1905.

The bridge was constructed by M. J. Patterson whose contract was $1,998 for the steel section, $620 for the wood section, and $4 per foot for fill. B. C. Fuller had charge of the work and completed the job in May, 1899.

The first bridges in that locality were the County and Hook bridges across the Roaring Fork River, above and below present Basalt, and the early residents there sometimes followed that circuitous route when they went to Aspen, instead of fording the Frying Pan River. A bridge was built across that stream in 1885, according to an item in the *Aspen Times*. And according to an item in the *Carbondale Avalanche* another bridge was constructed across the stream in 1890. One bridge possibly supplanted the other at the location east of town.

When the road through the valley was eventually constructed it was a winding track high on the mountainside, and because of that location it was called the "High Line." When the Colorado Midland railroad was abandoned, that wagon road was also abandoned and the railroad grade became the present highway into that delightful part of the valley.

The business pursuits of the Frying Pan region are ranching, stockraising and tourist-resorting; its recreational values, hunting and fishing. Large herds of elk and deer abound and many trout live in its lakes and streams. All in all, it is a sportman's paradise, for hunters and fishermen find game and fish enough to satisfy their desires—to many of them it is a place where dreams come true.

82. Ashcroft, 1890.
After the railroads reached Aspen, there was some talk of a branch line to Ashcroft, but nothing was done about it. The operators of the Montezuma Mine built a large mill and an aerial tram from it to the mine. It was a losing proposition and was soon shut down. With its collapse all hope of a railroad vanished. Several attempts were made later to open the mine, but each attempt failed. As the operation of the mines was Ashcroft's only chance of survival, each failure was a heartbreaking crisis to its few survivors.

The town slowly declined and by 1890 most of the business firms had moved out. Felix Kinney, the postmaster, still ran his grocery store, and Mrs. W. R. Warren her restaurant. In 1894 Ferdinand F. Reiner was appointed postmaster on November 19, but was replaced by Daniel McArthur on November 25, 1895. He ran the post office on one side of the street and Dan's Bar on the other, until 1912. On November 30 of that year the office was closed.

In 1916, when I first worked in Aspen, the residents of Ashcroft were Peter Larson, Calvin Miller, William Lipps, Paddy Sweeney, Dan McArthur, Jack Leahy and three other men. Each of those men was still doing some mining with but little success. McArthur was keeping (without remuneration) a weather observation station for the U. S. Weather Bureau, which he had started on February 20, 1901. He reported weather conditions regularly until August 11, 1923, four days before his death—a term of twenty-two and one-half years.

Dan was very hospitable and his cabin was a stopping place for all who came that way. He had a second cabin which he rented to visitors, a convenience which many transient travelers appreciated. He had an old phonograph and more than 1000 cylindrical records and on any occasion he would play as many of them as was desired.

One night in 1921 I rented Dan's cabin and visited with him until 2:00 a.m. He told me much about the early days of the camp and played about 200 records. Among other things he told me of the steep descent of the early wagons from timberline to Castle Creek. The next day we climbed the mountain and he pointed out the trees that had been used and the ruts made by the wagon-wheels.

Leahy was the last resident in the town. He died April 27, 1939, and then Ashcroft became a ghost town. In the early 1880's Jack (in conjunction with Tom Walsh and Phil Harrington) had owned the Columbia mine. He and those partners had led the movement to organize the Columbia Mining

District. He located a forest homestead later, which adjoined the Ashcroft townsite, and prospected intermittently. He called himself the mayor of Ashcroft, wrote good verse and could deliver a good oration on any subject at any time. The large natural basin at the head of Pine Creek (on the Panorama Trail) has always been known as Leahy Basin, because Jack had a cabin there for many years and dwelt there part of the time.

Two other old prospectors of that vicinity were George Brum, on Difficult Creek, and John Stubeggar at Montezuma. They were typical of that clan who overran the mountains of the region searching for rich ore, then settled down in their favorite Eden to wait out the remaining years of their lives when they failed to find it. Without them this enchanted land would have lacked much of its glamour and romance.

83. Ashcroft's Auxiliary Camps, 1890. During the years in which Ashcroft started, boomed and declined, several small settlements grew up around it, flourished for a few years, then faded into obscurity. Some of them have been previously mentioned. The exact time of their existence is not known, but each added its bit to the settlement and development of that area.

Haunley Addition was started by a man of that name in 1880 and the St. James Hotel was built. It was operated by Mrs. Farrell in 1881, but it was destroyed by fire in August and her two children

This early photo shows Marble (formerly Clarence) about 1908 as it looked when most of the buildings were made of wood. Main Street is in the center, with the business buildings running left to right. Notice the many tents that newcomers were living in until they could build houses.

This pond is above the Crystal River—which flows past in the valley beyond and Chair Mountain rises in the background the high elevation of nearly 10,000-feet.

barely escaped death. A few houses were constructed and the Castle Peak smelter was erected on, or at the east edge of, the tract.

Several cabins, a few houses and a large boarding-house were built around the large mill below Montezuma mine. And at the Kellogg mill, two miles downstream (to which the ore from the Montezuma was first packed), there were about twenty buildings. In 1916, when I first saw the place, only the foundations of the buildings and a lot of scattered debris remained.

About one mile south of Kellogg a small settlement called Cooper's Camp existed. It was started when Cooper discovered iron ore nearby. He and other prospectors filed on claims and built cabins in which to live while securing patent title to the claims. They sold their claims later to the Colorado Fuel & Iron Company who planned to open iron mines there. For some reason the company did not open the mines and eventually relinquished title to the land. The hump where the ore lay was called Iron Mountain; the site of Cooper's camp, Cooper Basin; the stream, Cooper Creek, and the peak to the south, Cooper Peak.

On the east fork of Castle Creek a group of mines was developed by the Express Mining Company. The mines produced well and a mill was erected. It ran for several years and a small settlement of log cabins resulted. Many of the old cabins were still there in 1934. During the years

The Marble City Hotel was always a favorite gathering place for townspeople to hear the latest local news (and gossip) as this view of about 1909 portrays. Main Street was illuminated at night with the then new electric street lights — most unusual for a small "backwoods" town located in the remote Elk Mountains of the west-central Colorado.

in which the camp existed the name East Castle Creek was changed to Express Creek and the long ridge between the forks became known as Express Ridge.

Near the head of Express Creek on the Taylor Range divide some one put up a sign in 1880 on the Bowman-to-Aspen trail which read: "This Way to the Roaring Fork." The place became known as Roaring Fork Pass although it was eighteen miles from that stream at Aspen. Just east of that sign, prospectors found pockets of gold ore and though the hump was 12,400 feet in elevation they called it "Gold Hill."

Some of those men started a small settlement north of the hill in the head of Difficult Creek canyon. They built several log cabins and dug a long tunnel. When the Taylor Pass road was constructed a branch road was built across Difficult Pass to the camp. Jack Williams found ore on Gold Hill and built a mill to treat it, but the ore played out and he abandoned it. Frank Barr later lived there for several years and it became known as

Barr's Mill. The mill still existed in 1934.

In Brum Gulch, about one mile east of Barr's Mill, George Brum worked in his tunnel each summer. He was grubstaked by Dr. F. S. McKee of Aspen, who took George and a load of supplies to the mine, via Ashcroft, each spring. They had agreed that George would come out on November 1 each fall, but in 1923 he didn't show up.

Doc waited two weeks, then asked me to check up on George. I told him that George could take care of himself and did nothing about it. However, when he hadn't come in by the 20th, I told Doc I would go after him. Accordingly, on the 22nd I rode, via Ashcroft, to Barr's. The snow was deep on Difficult Pass but I got through, stabled my horse, Whistler, in the tunnel, fed him oats and went on to Brum's on snowshoes.

I found George safe and sound at the cabin and spent the night with him. Next morning I tramped back to my horse, fed him more oats and started back to Ashcroft. When I attempted to climb back over Difficult Pass the snow was crusted hard

153

This early photo shows the Colorado-Yule Marble Company plant during construction. The office extension was yet to be built and marble was being hauled in by tractor from the quarry because the tram line did not yet exist. The Crystal River & San Juan Railway was in it's infancy, having only begun operations one year earlier; even so, the marble business was making great strides. Near the edge of the mill may be seen engine Number 6 pushing the side-door caboose-combine that was used to carry passengers, baggage, mail, l.c.l. freight and provide space for the rear-end train crew.

enough to hold me, but not the horse. We fought it for nearly two hours, then got stuck in a 5-foot snowdrift.

My only recourse then was to go down Difficult canyon which was difficult to travel even in summertime. However, after resting awhile I tackled it, and all day without food, I bucked snowdrifts, swamps, windfalls, brush, rocks and timber. Ten long miles I tramped on webs, with Whistler plodding along behind me. And at times it was more difficult for him than for me, especially to get over or around some of the windfalls.

We reached the Roaring Fork at about 4:00 p.m. Fortunately there was a bridge across that stream at that time. I then rode on to the highway and reached Aspen and home about six o'clock. And ever after I knew why those early prospectors had called the stream "Difficult Creek."

And, by-the-way, Brum came into town shortly after noon the next day. He had followed my track to Aspen without a bit of trouble (he said).

154

The powerhouse dominates this scene in Marble—with the railroad grade of the Treasury Mountain line under construction on the hillside beyond this structure.

This unusual view is of the Colorado-Yule Marble Company plant, C. 1914, when the finishing mill reached its full length. Gang saws, diamond saws and rubbing beds filled this structure. The large separate building was built especially to create the magnificent stonework for the Lincoln Memorial. Company houses run the length of the mill and the railroad terminal is in the distance with the town of Marble in the trees (at center).

155

Chapter XXIV

84. Glenwood Springs, 1892. The population of Glenwood Springs in 1890 was 2,000 people and it was growing rapidly.

In 1889 the state decided to build a better bridge across the Grand (Colorado) River and contracted the job to the Bullen Bridge Company of Trinidad, for $37,469. It took that company more than a year to do the work, but the bridge was finished in 1891 and dedicated on April 25.

Editor Holmes of the *Carbondale Avalanche* commented frequently about the construction of the bridge. On April 23, 1890, he said: "The State Bridge at Glenwood Springs is beginning to assume shape under the direction of Engineer Theodore Rosenberg." A May issue stated: "an extension of time has been granted for the completion of the Glenwood bridge." And on September 10 he grumbled: "The Glenwood State bridge is going to be completed when Bullen gets good and ready."

Holmes moved his newspaper to Glenwood Springs on March 11, 1891. He bought the *Glenwood Echo* and combined the two papers as the *Avalanche Echo,* and as such it was published for many years. He later started the *Daily News,* which shortly afterwards became the *Ute Chief News.* That newspaper was reduced eventually to a weekly and finally folded up.

In August, 1892, the Devereux Brothers, Walter, Henry, and Horace, who were heavy stockholders in the Hot Springs Company, induced that company to construct a large hotel north of the pool. It—Hotel Colorado—was rapidly constructed, completed in May, 1893, and opened on June 15. The Denver & Rio Grande Company ran a special train from Denver and the Colorado Midland Company ran one from Colorado Springs. Both companies ran trains from Aspen. Thousands of visitors attended the brilliant affair.

The hotel building cost $850,000. Besides the many rooms for general use, there were 200 bedrooms. A court between the east and west wings had a fountain which spouted a stream of water 100 feet into the air. At the time of its construction it was the second largest hotel in the state, the Brown Palace of Denver being the largest, according to a newspaper statement at that time.

The Devereux Brothers eventually left the town and ownership changed hands several times. At one time it was managed by F. H. A. Lyle, who had been associated with the Devereuxs, and who had helped to establish a polo field near town. Through all its changes of ownership and management the hotel has maintained its original standard of excellent service to its patrons. And one reason why that excellence has not waned during the last decade is the watchful care exercised by its able, efficient housekeeper, Mrs. Grace Brock.

In 1898 A. J. Dickson started another weekly newspaper, the *Glenwood Post,* and continued to publish it for 30-odd years. It was a newsy "sheet" and the present management has kept it to the high standard of excellence set by Mr. Dickson. It is now the city's leading newspaper.

Also, in 1898 the townspeople staged two new, interesting, and entertaining events. One was an annual Strawberry Day, which was held in June. Strawberries and cake were served to all who came. The celebration was a big success and the practice has been continued throughout the years. The other event was an annual bicycle race in July. It was sponsored by the Glenwood Wheel Club in cooperation with the Colorado Midland Railway. The 23-mile course was from near Basalt to the city, a $1 fee was charged, and many local men participated. Each time, the railway company ran a special observation-hospital train. William Broughton won the first race in one hour and twenty-six and one-quarter minutes.

The Citizen's National Bank was opened in 1903 with B. T. Napier as president, George Yule as vice-president, George H. Bell as cashier and

The Colorado-Yule Marble Company mill was a most impressive sight as this 1914 view illustrates. The blacksmith shop beside a storage shed (to the left) had just burned down.

M. Waesall as assistant cashier. After a successful operation over a 30-year period, it was closed in 1933.

Several Presidents of the United States have visited Glenwood Springs while on cross-country speaking tours or for other reasons. Two instances known were President Benjamin Harrison in May, 1891, and President Theodore Roosevelt in March, 1903. My parents made wagon trips from Satank to see those illustrous visitors and to hear them speak.

President Theodore Roosevelt made at least two hunting trips to Colorado and stopped at Glenwood Springs each time. During the period January 11 to February 14, 1901 (while Vice-President), he hunted in the White River country. And from April 15 to May 8, 1905, he hunted in the area between East Divide Creek and Redstone on Crystal River. The hunting party went southward from their first camp to Muddy Creek, thence eastward to Redstone where the hunt ended. The

President had killed six bears and a few other animals.

From Redstone the hunting party returned to Glenwood Springs and the President entertained his companions and guides at a banquet at the Hotel Colorado. They were Phil B. Stewart of Colorado Springs, Dr. Lambert, Secretary Loeb, Secret Service escorts Frank Tyree and Jimmy Sloan, guides John Goff and Jake Borah, and assistant guides Jack Fry, Elmer Chapman, Galatia Sprague, Brook Wills, Charles Allen and Al Anderson (who still lived in Glenwood Springs in 1956). The Next day the President left for Washington, D. C., in his special car, The Rocket.

Some of the businessmen and concerns in Glenwood Springs in 1905 were A. L. Beardsley, county judge; William Cardnell, county clerk and recorder; Alice B. Clark, county superintendent of schools; L. G. Clark, physician, county coroner; R. M. Haddon, justice of the peace; C. H. King, school principal; Everett McPhee, county treas-

Crystal River & San Juan Railway 2-6-0 Number 6 is pictured here attempting to plow open the line to Redstone about 1908. This was on the present-day air strip at Marble and shows White House Mountain (to the left) and Ragged Mountain. The Crystal River Railroad combination coach-caboose Number 02 is behind the "6 spot."

urer; R. P. Malaby, marshal; Charles Messik, night marshal; H. M. Rudisall, clerk of the district court; John T. Shumate, district judge; W. H. Trumbor, city engineer, county surveyor; J. F. Squire, register, and J. W. Ross, receiver, U. S. Land Office; Charles M. White, county assessor; A. Williams, postmaster; James Zimmerman, county sheriff; *Avalanche Echo,* H. J. Holmes, editor and proprietor; Charles D. Barnes, druggist; Charles Beck, contractor; George Bennett, sawmill operator; C. E. Bingham, baker; J. H. Bixby, Jeweler; Borst Brothers, boots and shoes; Henry Bosco, saloon-keeper; A. J. Bray, contractor; Broughton & Axe, contractors; Ed Burnaugh, owner of transfer business; Joe Claudon, plumber; William Conagon, liveryman; Daniel Connor, blacksmith; Al Coulter, meat market proprietor; William Cresman, construction contractor; W. W. Crook, physician; C. W. Darrow, attorney; M. H. Dean, physician; S. J. De Lan, attorney; J. W. Dollison, attorney; Victor Dosogne, shoemaker; W. W. Dunn, physician; W. H. Ennen, restaurateur; A. H.

Foreman, expressman; C. C. Graham, furniture store owner; Thomas Hayes, taxidermist; George Heisler, baker; T. M. H. Hotopp, physician; James Howe, painter; S. Hymes, tailor; H. B. Ikeler, plumber; B. Lynch, operator repair shop; C. C. McKissick, construction contractor; O. L. McCartney, dentist; Clint Marvin, saloon-keeper; George W. Moore, carpenter; William Dougan, mayor, hardware and lumber dealer; James C. Gentry, district attorney; John P. Rittmyer, hardware and implements dealer; Charles W. Taylor and Edward T. Taylor, attorneys; Olie Thorson, book store proprietor; Rev. A. J. Voight, Methodist Church; Father O'Dwyer, Catholic Church; Rev. H. Bullis, Episcopal Church; Mrs. Katie C. Bender, Commercial Restaurateur; Glenwood Hot Springs Company, F. H. A. Lyle, manager; *Glenwood Post,* A. J. Dickson, editor; Glenwood Springs Opera House, Thomas Harkins, manager; Grand Hotel, J. P. Phillipi, manager; Hotel Colorado, M. Elmendorf, manager; Hotel Glenwood, W. R. Lee, proprietor; Hunn Brothers, meat market

Crystal River & San Juan Railroad engine Number 2 is shown here with Cookman Chidester at the throttle-heading for Marble on September 6, 1941. Placita, the end of the Crystal River Railroad, was just behind the hill in the center of this view. After 1916 the CR&SJ operated the entire railroad from Carbondale to Marble under a lease arrangement. This trainload was about all one engine could handle on the steeper grade just ahead.

proprietor; W. W. Livingstone, grist mill operator; Kendrick Cottages, Thomas Kendrick; John L. Noonan, attorney; W. S. Parkinson, druggist; E. L. Peiser, jeweler; L. A. Robinson, physician; Mrs. J. C. Schutte, rooms; J. C. Schwarz, furniture dealer, undertaking; Troy Laundry, R. J. Witteman; Cross & Baker, taxidermists; George Edinger, real estate agent; L. Anderson, carpenter; F. A. Atkinson, brick mason; John Bagett & Company, saloon-keeper; Ernest Barlow, owner of transfer company; Mrs. Anderson, restauranteur; Mrs. E. Austin, milliner; Caldwell House, Mrs. M. Caldwell, proprietor; Mrs. M. Blowers, rooms; O. B. Brady, rooms; A. Cohn, grocer; Colorado Livery & Feed Barn, Thomas King, proprietor; Citizen's National Bank, G. H. Bell, cashier, M. Waesall, assistant cashier; City Bottling Works, James Sheridan, manager; Colorado Telephone Company, R. R. Rhoda, superintendent; A. J. Connelly, saloon-keeper; County Hospital, T. M. Schwartz, in charge; *Daily Avalanche; Glenwood Springs News*, W. J. Wills, editor; First National Bank, J. H. Devereux, presi-dent, Louis Schwarz, vice-president, C. C. Parks, cashier, Sherwood Crocker, assistant cashier; Andrew Gallo, shoemaker; Peter Dapro, saloon and rooming house owner; M. Demaestri, saloon keeper; A. H. Gamble, agent Denver & Rio Grande; Miss Sarah Dildine, rooms; De Remer Water Wheel Company, J. R. De Remer, manager; Miss I. G. Doty, confectionery and cigar store owner; J. E. Eitel, saloon keeper; Glenwood Lumber & Manufacturing Company, R. P. Davie, manager; Glenwood Springs Bottling Works, Ed S. Hughes, proprietor; Globe Express Company, Otto Barton, agent; George E. Hawkins, contractor; George Jorgenson, blacksmith; Miss Margaret McCartney, dressmaker; J. S. Manly, physician; Leadville Restaurant, J. J. Ryan, proprietor; M. Lewis, meat market proprietor; Law & Fisher, taxidermists; Charles H. King, photographer; Logan Investment Company, W. R. Logan, proprietor; August Mellor, furniture dealer; Agnes Moulton, rooms; Mirror Saloon, Charles Lang, proprietor; Nelson House, Mrs. C. French, proprietor; Napier

159

The last CR&SJ train left Marble in the summer of 1942, pulling out what remained of the Crystal River & San Juan Railroad, and the Yule Tram motors and flat cars. Engine Number 1 is under steam, pulling Number 2, followed by coach Number 9 and the tram cars.

Dry Goods Company, dry goods and clothing; W. E. Nogal, harness shop owner; Palace Hotel, S. G. Smart, proprietor; F. H. Oldenburg, blacksmith; F. F. Park, surveyor; Pulman Bar, H. O. Yewell, proprietor; Raymer House, Charles Poole, proprietor; William Richards, guide; Delmer Pletcher, dentist; Mrs. Etta Rodgers, furnished rooms; J. L. Preville, painter; Hugh Showalter, barber; Theodore Rosenburg, civil engineer; K. C. Vorhees, livery stable owner; J. G. Silver, tailor; T. I. Webb, barber; B. Silver, clothing dealer; West Glenwood Hot Springs Hotel & Bath House, R. W. Ware, proprietor; Frank Walter, furnished rooms; G. A. Webb, owner of novelty works; Western Union Company, Miss Pearl M. Lord, manager; Wulfsohn Department Store; A. E. Yewell, book seller and stationer; George Yule, banker; Richard Grant, rooms; John P. Thomas, district superintendent, Colorado Fuel & Iron Company.

Glenwood Springs is the largest settlement in the valley. It nestles at the confluence of the Colorado and Roaring Fork Rivers, a beautiful location. Its hot springs, caves, and mammoth pool are unequaled anywhere and add distinction and luster to that delightful city. I never lived there, but went there frequently, and have found recollections of the town and its people. Its population is now about 3,500 residents.

85. Cardiff, 1892. When the Colorado Fuel & Iron Company assumed control of the mines and coke ovens in 1892, Cardiff, like all of the coal camps, became a company town. Charles Myers was superintendent and held that position until 1893, when he was succeeded by Thomas Lawton. He bossed the camp until 1899 when John Breen became superintendent.

On April 1, 1894, the Colorado Supply Company started its store No. 8 with James B. Bowen as manager. During the twenty-four years of its existence fifteen other men served in that capacity. They were A. M. Ross, A. Frazier, W. L. Patchen, M. M. Manning, E. B. Wise, W. P. Brewer, H. A. Thompson, E. T. Hind, Joseph H. Wilson, Felix J. Young, B. G. Rodda, E. S. Wilson, Chester L. Hudson, Herman Wolfe and James Donaldson. The store was closed on June 1, 1918.

In 1901 the town's population was 250 people; Breen was also the postmaster; A. L. Hulls was the company clerk. The Colorado Midland Railway officials there were L. H. Harding, agent; R. W.

Hays Falls are a delightful sight, but a short distance from the highway, south of Redstone.

The Redstone Inn—shown here C. 1912—was constructed in 1901 and has since been enlarged. J. C. Osgood built this lodge as the bachelor quarters for workers, since families each had a house in Redstone.

Rubensdale, cashier; William Fipps, bill clerk; and W. J. Herrington, night operator. In 1902 Miss Linda O'Boyle was the schoolteacher and Mrs. Henry Heichimer ran the company boarding-house.

The coke output at Cardiff was enormous, and here where coal was more plentiful and the railroad company had easier access to it, the coking industry which the Colorado Coal & Iron Company had planned for Carbondale became an actuality. Year after year the ovens produced thousands of tons of coke which went to the Colorado Fuel & Iron Company's blast furnaces at Pueblo, or elsewhere.

For many years from the Carbondale-Glenwood Springs wagon road, across the Roaring Fork River, the long rows of blazing ovens was to night drivers a pleasing spectacle. Many trips were made from various places in the valley to see them. Today they lie cold and drab and almost unnoticed as one passes along the present road. Some activity, however, kept the place alive and it still retains its identity as a town.

As the Colorado Supply Company played such an important part in the development of the west end of the valley, this data concerning it is recounted here. According to N. K. Martin, manager of the Colorado Supply Division of the Colorado Fuel & Iron Corporation at Pueblo, it was organized in the 1880's, shortly after the Colorado Fuel Company was formed. It opened its first store at Sopris, Colorado, on July 6, 1888. It eventually opened fifty-three stores (thirty-seven in operation at one time) and had, at different times, two warehouses and two ladies' ready-to-ware shops. Its large store at Pueblo burned in 1953 and most of its records as well as the store were lost.

During 1901-03, S. Z. Schenck was its vice-president, and during 1903-08, W. H. Howell was traveling auditor. In 1902 a man named Kendall was an auditor. In 1905 C. M. Schenck was president and S. B. Foote was treasurer. From August 1, 1899, to December 31, 1906, W. H. Billington was general manager. Foote now lives in Denver.

86. Satank, 1892. As the town of Moffat declined, the name "Moffat" gave way to "Satank" because of the post office. Many of the residents

moved away. As previously mentioned, F. C. Childs moved his merchandise to Sunshine and opened a store there. Frank Page went to ranching near Cardiff.

By 1892 the Davis Hotel, Tham's saloon, Child's and Page's stores, and the uncompleted Moffat Hotel buildings were all that was left of the business section, and all were empty. The Moffat Hotel building stood for many years before it was razed, and it became a gathering place for all of the young folks of the town.

At that time Ben Davis ran the only store and had the post office there. He carried the mail to the Denver & Rio Grande track below town, about one-half mile away, and when the train went by he threw his pouch in as the baggage man tossed another out. Later, H. C. Shoemaker carried the mail from and to Carbondale six days a week. He lost the job and Satank, the post office, when Rural Free Delivery began on July 14, 1904.

Some of the other residents were Frank Huff, David Strohm, Frank Anzenberger, Mrs. C. E. (Julia) Denmark, Stewart, Billy Spellman, Wise, George H. Rummel, David Hammer, Edson Banning, George Swigart, Tom Anderson, "Uncle Dick" Beeson, John Silverhart, John Sievers, Elbridge Perham, Charles Gerkin, Abner J. Nichols,

Mrs. James Fatkin, Oscar Shoemaker, Minnis Shelton, John Weaver, John Patrick and Frank Dickens. Dickens had first come to that locality before the town was started, July 9, 1886. He did not settle there at the time, but worked at several places in the valley. Gerkin came to Colorado in 1887, but soon went East and returned in 1906. Perham had previously lived on a ranch on Perham Creek, to the south.

While Dickens was living in Marble in 1909, he and his bear-hunting partner, Jim Downing, helped E. S. Porter of the Edison Picture Company make *The Big Bear Hunt*, the first motion picture filmed in the Rocky Mountains. It was staged on Muddy Creek and other residents of Marble (and a few outsiders) completed the cast. The film was shown at Marble, then at Glenwood Springs sometime afterwards.

Dickens and George Swigart went to see the film when it was shown at Glenwood Springs. At one point Frank whispered to George, "When the bear shows up, watch closely; we forgot to take off the collar." He explained later that that particular bear was one they had caught and kept chained to use in an emergency.

I lived six of my youthful years at Satank and later courted and won my lovely Augusta there;

This photo was probably taken in 1899, just after the Redstone depot had been built. The yard trackage had not been built at this stage and electricity had not yet been installed in the depot.

COLLECTION OF JOHN L. JEROME — COURTESY OF STATE HISTORICAL SOCIETY OF COLORADO

PHOTO BY D. E. ROGERS

This narrow gauge outside-frame 2-8-0 was purchased new in 1903 for use on the Crystal River Railroad between Redstone and Coalbasin. She was a husky little engine rated to pull 10 empties up a 4.5-percent grade. She was pictured here in Durango in 1939, classed C-25 on the Denver & Rio Grande Western.

consequently I hold many fond memories of the old town and consider it the seat of Romance in that historic valley. A few families still live there and several of the original buildings are still being used.

87. Carbondale, 1892.   In November, 1891, a large fire destroyed almost all of the business section of Carbondale. However, the safe of the Bank of Carbondale which had been started in the Dinkel store in 1888 was saved and the bank was operating the next day.

Most of the business houses were then erected farther west on Main Street. Dinkel put up a brick building and built up a large mercantile business. He was appointed postmaster in 1887, and as the bank and post office had been housed in the burned building, he now moved them to the new location. Sam B. Eubanks was the cashier and Susan Dunlap was the post office attendant. Frank E. Sweet was bookkeeper and general salesman, Louis Silling and Jake Saunders ran the grocery department. B. B. Hill, then or later, became the deliveryman.

Dinkel started a branch store at Spring Gulch with W. L. Girdner in charge. He built a long row of stables and sheds at the rear of his store, and Fate ran a daily-supply-mail stage to Marion and Spring Gulch for about two years.

In 1892 he enlarged his store building, making it two stories high. He formed the Dinkel Mercantile Company with Sweet and Girdner as partners. He added a lumber yard later with Frank Huber as the attendant. They bought land on East Mesa, built a large ditch and Girdner took charge of it. They called it the Big Four Ranch. Several years later Sweet withdrew from the company, bought land on West Mesa, built another large ditch and established the Sweet Seed Farm. His partners in that enterprise were Lou D. Sweet of Denver and H. Clay Jessup (who built the ditch).

In 1891 Charles Scheue started a general store across the street, east of Dinkel's. A druggist named Kaibeccis ran a drug store in a part of the building. Scheue also ran a coal office; coal was supplied by George Comrie, who hauled it from Sunshine. About that time Oscar Ittleson and

The page opposite shows Chair Mountain to the south, as the Crystal River carries off water from melting snow and rain. The crispness of fall is in the air near Redstone.

SUNDANCE BOOKS: DELL A. MC COY

This was Coalbasin after abandonment in late fall of 1909. The town stood vacant for many years until speculators gradually hauled off houses, furniture and everything else except for a few outhouses. The Mid-Continent Coal & Coke Company now had re-opened this mine. The trestle led to the original mine in this photo, and coal was loaded into railroad dump cars to the left.

Moses Cohn opened a dry goods store; Willis Scheue, a jewelry store; Edward D. Tandy, a drug store.

Meat markets were opened (about in this order) by Reese Tucker, Frank Myers, J. C. Barber, Del Weant, R. L. Sherwood, and John Bennett. Livery and feed stores were run by Ward Tucker, George Young, Clay Jessup, Harrel & Hinkel, and Bert Hinkel & Son (Darryl). Price Wycliffe and George Swigart were, at different times, associated with Tucker in the livery business.

In the early 1890's saloons were operated by Jack Cheney and John Calnan. In the 1900's, Yank Walden & Phil Moore, Skidmore, Price Wycliffe, Sheridan and James Leggett were the operators.

Some of the doctors who followed Camp and Dean were W. F. Farrar, W. J. LeRossignol, J. M. Braden, W. R. Tubbs, and O. F. Clagett. Early carpenters and builders were John Murfitt and Charles Lehow; they built the brick schoolhouses

at Satank and Carbondale. Julius Hart was an early blacksmith; Dan Flynn and Hugh Pattison, later ones. John Hartman was a painter and paper-hanger. Hardy Graves was an early barber; he was followed by Frank Bradley. Two other station agents were V. T. Brown and Robert Jeffers.

A few of the town's mayors were Dean, Dinkel, Tandy, Murfitt and Jessup. Postmasters (as I remember them) were Mrs. Tanney, Dinkel, Mrs. J. F. Woodward, Mrs. Alberta (Winters) Sebree, William Thurston, William Pings, Harold Schwartzel and Glen Norton.

After H. J. Holmes moved his *Carbondale Avalanche* to Glenwood Springs in March, 1891, the town had no newspaper for several years. In 1898 Charles Johnson started the *Carbondale Item*. He ran it until 1912; then Verne Moore gained possession and published it until his death a few years later—January 2, 1912-March 7, 1918. Roy Shadle, Moore's assistant, took it over on

March 14, 1918, and ran it until about 1924, when it was discontinued.

Two of the schoolteachers in 1889-90 were Lizzie Woodward and Berti Smelcer. Lehow completed the large brick schoolhouse on November 1, 1890. During the winter of 1895-96 I attended school there and finished the eighth grade. E. R. Phillips was the school principal and Annie Hendrie, the teacher.

In January, 1892, two ranchers, John C. Morris and Frank Chatham, who lived south of town, quarreled and fought over the ownership of some land. A few days later they met and Morris struck Chatham on the head with a six-shooter. Chatham fought back and Morris shot him in the abdomen. Chatham, although mortally wounded, then shot Morris three times. Neighbors called Sheriff Thomas and he and Dr. Clark came up and took the wounded men to Glenwood Springs. Chatham died the next day and Morris, soon afterward.

Mrs. Mary Jane Francis might be considered the town's fairy godmother. She came to the valley in 1882 to look at some mining property which she had purchased and liked the country so well that she returned in 1883, bought some land at the south edge of town, and later built a lovely villa which she called Bide-a-wee. She was wealthy and generous and helped the poorer people of the community in many ways.

On July 4 each year, she had a large fireworks display for the pleasure of the townspeople and at Thanksgiving time she distributed many turkeys. On one occasion she had beautiful gold four-leaf-clover pins made for each of the charter members of the local Ladies' Aid Society. My mother and my mother-in-law cherished their pins as long as they lived. Among her many assets were a matched team of black horses and a shiny spring wagon in charge of a uniformed coachman. To many of the country folk, who knew and loved her, it was always a pleasing sight to see her go whizzing by in the gleaming equipage.

Mrs. Alberta Sebree is remembered as Carbondale's "grand old lady." She was postmistress for seventeen years and a member of the town council for six years. At one time or the other she was the head of every woman's organization in the town, serving in some of them for many years. She was loved by everyone in the community, and was ninety-one years of age at the time of her death.

This was how the Coalbasin Club House looked when in use in 1904. The camp employees took great pride in their club and had a variety of leisure-time activities, including games of pool and cards, and theatre.

Chapter XXV

88. Crystal, 1892. Crystal was a prosperous town up to 1892, although its most active period was in 1887 and 1888. Its mines were still producing and several jack-trains and a few wagons were transporting the ores to Gothic and Crested Butte. Oliver Thomas was one of the freighters and Ward Tucker and Frank Bogan were running jack-trains. At one time they had 100 animals packing ore from the Black Queen.

In 1889 the Black Queen was inactive, but Editor Johnson of the *Crystal River Current* was predicting a boom. He was still the postmaster and Ed A. Cook delivered mail regularly to him three times a week from Carbondale. Mrs. G. W. Melton, assisted by her husband William (Billy) and son Charles, still operated her hotel.

At that time the Elk Mountain Railroad Company was seriously considering the construction of a road between Carbondale and Crystal. In August, 1889, three of its officials, F. O. Wood, G. H. Stone and S. F. Hazelhurst of Colorado Springs, visited both towns and made an inspection of the right-of-way that had been selected. They told the residents that Senator N. P. Hill intended to construct a smelter at Carbondale as soon as they had completed the road.

Two residents, A. B. Fish and Charley Smith, gave a dance at the Fish cabin in August. Three women, Mrs. Steinmeyer, Mrs. Usher and Miss Mollie Bruce, attended. Presumably, they were the only women there at that time. In order to make up a square dance set Al Johnson donned an apron and acted as the fourth lady. By his antics, he added much merriment to the affair.

The townspeople were trying to get the wagon road to Carbondale completed. The road had been partly built three years earlier, but the Pitkin County commissioners had refused to build a three-mile section through that county until a resurvey was made of that county's south line across Crystal River Valley.

In the fall James N. Bennett, a resident of the Rock Creek district, was elected a Pitkin County Commissioner and he got some action. The survey was made in October by Surveyors George Nyce of Pitkin County and E. E. Warren of Gunnison County, with W. H. Trumbor of Glenwood Springs acting as arbitrator. Incidentally the survey line fell 400 feet south of the old McClure House (then owned by Ed Barthel) and it was marked by a large monument of stones.

In November Bert Young substituted for Ed Cook as mail carrier. He found a lot of snow in Crystal but few people. Jim Usher was in charge of the Black Queen properties; two sourdoughs, Cline and Flannigan, were working their claims; Tim Ring was somewhere about and Jim Jennings was holed up at his ranch near the junction of Coal and Rock creeks.

Crystal's first town council began offciating on January 1, 1890. Jim Usher was mayor, Al Johnson, clerk and Dan Lyons, marshal.

In March Editors Johnson of the *Current* and Holmes of the *Avalanche* argued in their respective papers about the advisability of using the name Crystal River instead of Rock Creek. Holmes was against it; the name Rock Creek (he said) had been given to the stream in 1870 by D. L. McGlouthlin and his party; F. V. Hayden had put it on his map and it had been approved by proper authorities; therefore, it shouldn't be changed. Johnson was quite determined that it should be changed and as time has proved, he was right; it could be and was changed.

In May, Morris & Bogart contracted with Pitkin County to build the piece of wagon road through that county and finished it about July 1. They did such a good job that the residents then began to clamor for better conditions on each end of the road. As soon as the road was completed there was considerable travel over it; several freight wagons and a stage began operating.

Medio—on the abandoned narrow gauge branch of the Crystal River Railroad—still had several buildings standing in 1960. The Huntsman Hills rise in the background where Coalbasin is located. From here the track looped back and forth, as if it were a giant step ladder.

In November C. C. McCoy was awarded the mail contract and used a wagon. Later some ore was hauled to Carbondale and shipped to smelters. However, the outlet had come too late to benefit the miners at Crystal, for the price of silver had dropped so low that they couldn't afford to haul it out.

The Williams Brothers, Horace, John and Ambrose, played an important part in the business life of Crystal and Marble for about forty-seven years. Horace and Ambrose went to Marble in 1894, then went on to Crystal where Ambrose worked for the Colorado Trading & Development Company. After a short time Horace took over and operated that store and in 1900 Ambrose began working for the Colorado Supply Company in their new store at Placita. Subsequently he was the store manager for that company at Sunlight, Spring Gulch and Crested Butte.

John Baroni, one-time resident of Aspen, lived at Crystal during the 1890's and early 1900's. He prospected the surrounding area far and wide but never found paydirt. At various times he worked in the Ajax Mine which was the big producer at Schofield, the Lead King Mine in the basin of that name and the Black Queen at Crystal. At that time Latelle Brothers operated the Lead King.

John's daughters, Mary McHugh and Josephine Kissel, of Denver, who were born in Crystal, remember the early days there. They sometimes walked the four miles to Schofield where their father had another house on his original mining claims. Although but a small girl then, Jo recalls the names of these Crystal residents: Henry Rosetta, Pete Mattivi, Ward and Al Ferris.

About 1907 the family moved to Marble and the five Baroni children went to school there. At a later date Mary worked as a postal clerk for postmaster McWilliams.

M. E. Swigart worked in Crystal in 1907. At that time mining was at a low ebb. The Greater Canada Mining Company was trying to operate the Black Queen properties, but the operation was so unprofitable that they had to shut down. Paul

169

Tischhauser ran a general store, Jack Starr, O. F. Tracy and T. O. Kirke ran saloons, Barnett ran the hotel.

In 1915 he worked there for a few months with a survey party that was retracing property lines for another mining company. This one was also trying to revive mining conditions there. Porter Nelson was doing some mining and Henry Thode was operating a sawmill. There was very little activity and less than a dozen residents. The new company opened some of the old mines and during 1916 they employed nearly 100 men. However, they failed after that season and the town was soon deserted. Some of the old buildings still exist and a few people sojourn there each summer although the road from Marble to Crystal is only barely passable to automobile travel and the road from Crystal to Schofield is a "jeep" road.

89. Crystal River Railroad, 1892. As previously mentioned Rock Creek became Crystal River in 1886, and in 1890 a wagon road was completed which linked the towns of Elko, Schofield, Crystal, Marble and Prospect, in the upper part of that valley, with Carbondale and the Roaring Fork Valley.

In 1892 two attempts were made to construct railroads into that region, but each was doomed to failure by the silver panic of 1893. From the Denver & Rio Grande Railroad at Carbondale the Crystal River Railroad Company graded about twelve miles of track up the east side of the stream and laid a few miles of rails. From the Colorado Midland Railroad, at a point near Sands, the Elk Mountain Railroad Company graded about sixteen miles up the west side. At the beginning of their operation they laid out a townsite on the Louis Lang ranch which they called Wilkesbarre. Neither the town nor the railroad was continued beyond the one season.

In 1897 and 1898 John C. Osgood, president of the Colorado Fuel & Iron Company, began the development of his coal camps, Redstone, Placita and Coal Basin, and his palatial mansion, Cleveholm. During those years he revived the old Crystal River Railroad project and completed the road to Redstone, a distance of eighteen miles.

90. Aspen, 1892. Aspen reached the·peak of its development in 1892 and 1893. The Aspen National Bank was organized in March, 1892, with J. J. Hagerman as president, R. J. Bolles as vice-president, and A. A. Denham as cashier. The directors were Hagerman, Bolles, Denham, W. W. Cooley, W. E. Newsbury and E. L. Ogden. That bank successfully weathered the panic of July, 1893, when eighteen other banks in the state were compelled to close. However, the J. B. Wheeler Banking Company was one of the unlucky eighteen which were shut down.

The Webber Block was constructed that year. Company C of the Colorado National Guard, which had been organized from Company F of Ute War fame, was active in 1893 and had fifty-six members. It was commanded by Major M. M. Smith and Captain Hills. The city had two brass and one string bands at that time. Winfield Scott Post No. 87, G. A. R. was then a very active organization and on October 16 gave its anniversary ball at the Tivoli Theatre. The tickets were fifty cents each.

The People's Party (Populist) developed unusual strength throughout the state in 1892. At their convention in Denver on July 28, they nominated Davis H. Waite of Aspen for govenor, he having gained popularity on account of the stand he had taken on the silver issue. At the fall election Waite and the entire Populist ticket were elected, and he was inaugurated as governor on January 10, 1893. He had a stormy, controversial two years in Denver and then returned to private life in Aspen. The highlights of his term were his occupation of the new State Capitol building and the authorization of Womens' Suffrage—their right to vote in Colorado.

Pitkin County's population was estimated to be about 14,000 people in 1893 and Aspen's about 11,000 by census authorities, but those figures were possibly low. Judge Deane, who saw Aspen's rise and decline, estimated its peak population at 12,000 and a transient population of 5,000 more.

Pitkin County, during the period 1880-92, contributed about $14-million in silver and lead ores. Most of it came from Aspen's mines, with a fair percent from the mines at Ashcroft, Lenado and Tourtelotte Park. Although Aspen's minerals were largely mined out, its other natural resources remain, and through them it is likely to become as glamorous and more substantial than it was in the days of the silver stampede.

In 1895 the Mountain States Telephone & Telegraph Company built a telephone line across Independence Pass to Aspen. That line furnished telephone service to the community and the lower valley until 1939. Being a hard line to maintain, it was then dismantled and service was rerouted via Glenwood Springs.

Only a few of the pioneers who served Aspen or Pitkin County officially have been mentioned. A few more are here named: Henry Webber, Dr. E. P. Rose and Dr. W. H. Twining, who were mayors in 1888, 1893 and 1905, respectively. County offi-

Penny Hot Springs was located about two miles north of Redstone. A small pool was built and covered with this shack for year-round pleasure. The bridge led over the Crystal River to the Crystal River Railroad, where a telegraph shack stood.

This photograph shows Crystal River & San Juan Number 2 rattling downgrade into Janeway on September 6, 1941. During this last year of operation for the CR&SJ business was good—requiring both locomotives to be used almost daily to handle marble shipments. On many runs, the engine ran short on water before reaching Marble, so the fireman would kill the fire and the engineer would nurse the engine into Marble on whatever steam pressure remained. Strangely enough, the only water stand-pipe on the route was at Nettle Creek near Janeway.

171

These beaver ponds—located about midway on the narrow gauge branch of the Crystal River Railroad—were a delight to many of the residents of Coalbasin. They provided a good living for water fowl (such as ducks) as well as affording an ample water supply for trout and other game fish. This view looks eastward toward Redstone, down in the valley several miles away.

cials in 1893 were, in part: James J. Warnack, county clerk and recorder; Lou D. Sweet, treasurer; Jasper W. Johnson, judge; James T. Stewart, sheriff. Thomas A. Rucker was district judge and John F. McEvoy, district clerk.

Postmasters who followed Moses Bradshaw were James Garrahan on June 26, 1893, and John C. Allen on January 30, 1895.

91. Lenado, 1892. About 1888 the Denver & Rio Grande Railroad Company graded an 8-mile roadbed from Woody Creek station to Lenado. However, for some unknown reason, it did not lay track.

A post office was established on February 4, 1891, with Frank W. Mead as postmaster. Because of the slump in ore prices the mill was shut down and Mead gave up the office on September 8, 1893.

The Varney Company resumed operations in the early 1900's. In 1904, according to James Vagneur of Woody Creek, who cut timber thereabouts that

winter under the direction of Foreman Archie Sinclair, it was operating the mine, mill and sawmill. About eighty men were at work. The milling of the ore wasn't very profitable and only one freighter was hauling concentrates to the railroad at Woody Creek over the old abandoned railroad grade. Ed Grover was running a store and a boarding-house; two saloons were going. Mail was brought in daily from Aspen over the Hunter-Woody Creek divide by a horseback carrier.

The post office was reopened on October 2, 1905, with Ellie Johnson as postmaster. But the mill was again shut down in 1906 and the office was closed on December 6.

In 1917, during World War I, the Smuggler Leasing Company of Aspen reopened the tunnel to mine much-needed lead and zinc ores. Harvey Hinman was in charge of the operation. The ore was trucked out and shipped to market from Woody Creek. A new boarding-house was built and

172

Crystal River & San Juan 2-6-0 Number 2 came into Carbondale with a northbound livestock extra, July 4, 1940, hauling 12 cars. Stock trains amounted to almost more business for the CR&SJ than the regular marble shipments near the end of the railroad's operations.

some of the old houses were put in habitable condition. Nels Eklund started and ran a sawmill.

Hinman and George Work, a truck driver, were severely injured when their truck went over the bank into Woody Creek. Since that time the U. S. Forest Service has widened and improved the road.

Three of the later residents were Wilbur, Bill Casady and "Gunnysack" Brown. The names of Wilbur and Casady are still attached to the gulches where they eventually squatted. In 1916 Brown raised a few plants in his garden, which spread to the surrounding country. It was identified later by C. A. Kutzleb of the U. S. Forest Service as spotted hemlock, a poisonous plant dating back to the ancient Socrates. Fortunately the plant was non-poisonous to stock, for it overran that area. In 1933 a Cibilian Conservation Corps crew, directed by Harry Halleck, eradicated much of it, but it spread again.

Several men have operated sawmills at the camp. Jack Flogus, the present sawmiller, has operated there for many years.

A few of the settlers in the area west of Lenado were Victor Natal, Frederick Clavel, Jeremie Vagneur, Benedict Bourg, Pat Monoghan, Dr. Tierney, Charles Rouse, Al and Ed Gray, Sam Letey, Melvin and George Steinberg, William Collins, William Ritch, Ferdinand Vevey, E. K. Torrence, Donald McLean, Sam McCormick, George Zweibel, C. S. Lloyd, Dick Pierce, Mark Karde, Horace Gavin, Frank Frasson, James Goodwin and Charles Savage.

92. Norrie, 1892. Frank E. Gowen started a sawmill and a general timber business at Norrie in the Frying Pan Valley about 1889. He and some of his workmen built houses and he opened a small store to accommodate his lumberjacks, some of whom had hewed ties for the railroad company in 1887.

He enlarged his business in 1890, and soon thereafter (about 1892) he constructed a very large building which covered his store, sawmill and lumber yard. Upstairs there was a large dance-hall, nicely furnished and appropriately equipped. Al Garvin managed his store and Charles Teas was his mill man and sawyer. In 1894 he applied for a post office which he opened as postmaster on November 16 in his store. About that time he started another sawmill on the Frying Pan-Woody Creek divide. He employed about seventy-five men and also bought logs from the other loggers. He shipped his lumber to Grand Junction where he operated a lumber yard.

Gowen was lame and it was difficult for him to

173

Janeway, shown in this view, once was an important rest stop for prospectors on their way into the "high country." A post office, saloon and boarding house once did business here. Later the Crystal River Railway constructed track just past this spot (in 1893). Janeway was always listed on the railway's depot list after that.

174

get around, however, he was always going somewhere and doing something. And when he rode horseback he used a sidesaddle. Some of the men who worked for him or logged independently were John and Sam Howard, Lou Rogan, Bob Bruce and Hank Southwick.

About fifty log or frame houses were built and the population of the town reached 185 residents. Strangely, however, no one filed on the land or surveyed a townsite and the area was never planted. There was no street arrangement, and the wagon road extended through the town and ended at the sawmill.

The town had a good school and the schoolhouse stood in a grove of tall pines across the stream from the town. A man named Rose taught the school in 1896 and a Professor H. H. Rhodes was a teacher in 1898. Other teachers were Miss Skinner (later Mrs. John McLaren), Miss Brooks, May Epperson, Jewell Greener, Miss Sanders.

Clem W. Mitchell and Rufus M. Deeds were early homesteaders; they filed on claims east of town. Mitchell didn't prove up on his land but Deeds did, receiving his patent title on October 12, 1900. Because of his manner of speech and dress he was called "Squire" Deeds. He had several horses which he raced in summertime and wintered in the vicinity of Basalt. Once he found a spring on his land, the water from which (so he said) tasted like vinegar. He tried to commercialize it but was unsuccessful.

93. Meredith, 1892.   The town of Meredith

Willow Park, once the main upper station of the Aspen & Western Railway, was only a short distance away from Colorado Coal & Iron Company's coal mine openings. The A&W trackage came up from the Crystal River along Thompson Creek, made a loop over the creek at Willow Park and looped sharply again on a steep grade, and entered a narrow stream drainage where the mines were located.

PHOTO BY MORRISON A. SMITH – COLLECTION OF JOHN W. MAXWELL

Crystal River & San Juan 4-6-0 Number 1 sizzles to herself in the Carbondale yard after doing her switching duties. This trim ten-wheeler was formerly the Denver & Rio Grande's Number 532 and was used in their passenger service prior to 1915.

was started about 1889 by a group of men who formed the Meredith Manufacturing Company. They quarried limestone and burned it in a kiln beside the Colorado Midland Railway track. That company built a long siding for their convenience. The town was named for one of their number, Professor Meredith. Whether the title was real or feigned is questionable, but he was always addressed as "Professor." According to Howard Dearhamer of Meredith, he was killed by a powder blast in the quarry and was buried about one-half mile east of the town. The grave is marked with a pile of stones.

About 1891 another group who called themselves the Miller Creek Lime & Lumber Company took over. The company manager was A. A. Beard and their bookkeeper was J. W. Saunders. The company erected a large house across the track from the kiln, which was used as an office, a commissary and a boarding-house.

Andrew A. Buck secured a post office which he opened as postmaster on January 25, 1893, in the company building. Beard was severely injured that

year when a carload of limestone ran over his foot.

In 1899 C. B. Anderson and R. F. Roberts of Leadville started a sawmill on Miller Creek. They shipped their lumber from Meredith. Anderson's daughter taught the first school. Other early settlers at or near the town were "Humpy" Miller, Paul Billow, A. J. Keifner, T. G. Takaman, A. J. Dearhamer, Fred Williams and Fred Jakeman. Miller and Jakeman Creeks are named for two of them.

E. T. Miltanberger and W. H. Gilstrap were prospectors on Miller Creek, and Robert Reed, Harvey Biglow and A. J. Dearhamer had another sawmill there. A. J. stayed in town to handle the commissary and to load the lumber. He built a small house and handled gloves, overalls, tobacco, whiskey and a few other things for the crew. In 1900 he built an addition to his house and started a small store. His stock was mainly groceries, hay, grain and the things that the lumberjacks and other workmen needed.

On July 28, 1905, Everett Myser was appointed postmaster but he declined the post and Isaac

176

A resident in Carbondale was using CR&SJ box car 101 in 1960 for a back yard shed. This car started its career on the Crystal River Railway in 1893, then went to work on the narrow gauge Coalbasin Branch of the Crystal River Railroad in 1899. The car is similar in size to other box cars used on other narrow gauge rail lines of the same era. About 1910 the car was fitted with standard gauge trucks—after the narrow gauge branch of the CRR was abandoned—so it could be operated on the mainline of the CR&SJ between Marble and Carbondale. Behind the box car the D&RGW depot can be seen—still in use by that company at the time the photograph was taken.

Watkins was appointed on October 4 of that year. About five years later he was supplanted by Mrs. Edith Dearhamer on June 20, 1910. A. J. moved the post office to his store where it still remains. Their son, Howard, now runs the post office and the store.

School District No. 11 built a school house in 1894, and two of the teachers were Lulu Thomson (later Mrs. Claude Crowley) and Margaret McHugh. When I lived in that locality in 1917, Minnete Miller was the teacher.

The town is now a popular hunting camp each fall.

94. Basalt, 1894. Owing to some conflict between the names Aspen, Aspen Junction, and Grand Junction the railroad company changed the name of Aspen Junction to Basalt in late 1894. The Post Office Department officially made the change in names on June 19, 1895. The name Basalt originated from the basaltic rock formation of Black Mountain which lay north of town. Later, it also took the name, Basalt.

Aspen Junction had one newspaper, the *Eagle County Examiner,* edited by W. H. Hildreth during 1894-96. Basalt had several papers: the *Basalt Tribune,* Basil L. Smith, publisher, 1896-98; the *Basalt Journal,* operated by the Basalt Journal Publishing Company from January 7, 1897, till sometime in 1910. It had several manager-editors, namely: R. H. Zimmerman, H. F. Kane, J. R. Newman, M. V. Crockett, Grant Ruland and W. H. Wildreth. The *Basalt Eagle* was published during 1909-12, first by Fred Stiffler and then by Daniel Barber. The *Frying Pan* was published by Roy Shadle (of Carbondale) during 1922-24.

On March 28, 1895, Basalt Lodge No. 93, I O O F, was instituted with nine charter members. The members built a hall on High Street at the location of the former Lupton Meat Market. It cost $2123 and an additional $528 for paraphenalia, and was opened on August 11. In 1899 there were sixty-four members and the lodge celebrated its fourth anniversary with a ball, which drew a large attendance.

A building boom occurred that year, and a Methodist Church and about twenty-five other buildings were constructed.

This magnificent panoramic view shows the towns of Carbondale (to the far left) and Satank (to the far right). The Crystal River rail line came into Carbondale from the canyon at the base of Mount Sopris and met the D&RGW at the wye. The D&RGW's Aspen Branch came through Carbondale and crossed the Roaring Fork River at the center fold. This branch

95. Wood's Lake, 1895. In the early 1890's Jim Woods, E. L. Peisar and Pete Engelbrecht (pronounced Engelbright) acquired land near the head of Lime Creek, northeast of Thomasville.

There was a large lake on the land, and the men built cabins and a lodge and started a resort which became known as Wood's Lake. Englebrecht eventually gained control of the property, enlarged the

formerly crossed over the Colorado Midland with the same bridge. The Midland is in view at the bottom of the scene—where their Carbondale depot was located. The never-completed Elk Mountain grade may be seen running along the hillside in the right-hand portion of the picture, disappearing near the base of Mount Sopris.

housing facilities and developed a thriving business which he operated for almost twenty-five years. He developed another lake and secured a post office which was called Troutville.

The resort still exists and it is operated by Clarence and Arthur Bowles, grandson and great-grandson of Samuel Bowles, one of the first settlers near Carbondale.

This photo presents much the same view of Mount Sopris with a powdering of new-fallen snow, while the valley below in late

afternoon sunshine.

Chapter XXVI

96. Basalt, 1898. About 1898 a large fire destroyed the west half of the business section of Basalt. A few homes were also burned. Jake Lucksinger, a lifelong resident of the town who remembers hundreds of details about the town's development, recalls the blaze and the tumult it aroused, but not the date of its occurrence. It started in a boarding-house which stood close to the site of the present Kelly Block and was caused by the explosion of a kerosene lamp.

According to reports, a train crew just off its run went into the place for coffee. The cook set the lamp on the stove and it suddenly went *Boom!* Then bedlam broke loose and the night was filled with confusion. A strong east wind fanned the flames into a halocaust which swiftly swept over that part of the town. Burning bits from the buildings were flung down the valley for two miles. Destroyed were the boarding-house, the Joe Tilletson building, the Kelly and Epperson saloons, the McCormac, Snell and Dooling homes.

Snell, who was an engineer, immediately rebuilt his home, using bricks this time so it wouldn't burn down so easily, he said. The present Kelly Block was built about 1900 and construction of the other buildings followed later.

Considerable building occurred in 1898. Mrs. Ella Tierney built a large brick building, 26 x 73 feet in size, on High Street and moved her mercantile business from Main Street. It was one of the better buildings of the town.

Other business at that time were John A. Smith, clothing; Lupton Brothers, meat market; Matt Hanson, shoe store owner; Pete Frison, cigar store proprietor; J. G. Ould, tonsorial parlors and baths; Auld & Dunn, carpenters; Home Restaurant, Mrs. Nell Smith; Ideal Restaurant, Mrs. O. B. Gaboury; Basalt Exchange, E. B. Kelly.

Also, a few names taken from the 1899 issue of the *Basalt Journal* were W. G. Fleming, railroad agent; who was succeeded by C. B. Carter and he by J. W. McKenna; P. F. Nott, manager of the Midland eating-house; replaced by L. C. Dettor; Fred Shehi, Walter White, John Genner, Charles Nelson, John May and J. K. Ikeler.

When the 78-day blockade of the Colorado Midland Railway occurred in January, 1899 (as described later), some 20-odd passengers marooned at Sellar and a few at other places, were brought back to Basalt and rerouted over the Denver & Rio Grande Railroad. Basalt was deprived of its regular mail and supplies, but mail soon came in via Emma. Coal ran short and the company released a few carloads en route to other places. The *Basalt Journal* ran out of newsprint and put out two editions—February 25 and March 4—on wrapping paper. Most of the news during the period of the blockade was about the fight to clear the tracks. There was much rejoicing when traffic was resumed on April 15.

Some of the engineers at that time were John Nelson, Andy Sebring, Jim Dooling, Jake Frison, Fred Stiffler, McCarty, Hall, Rieble, Dibble, Kissel, Rutherford and Jordan. Stiffler, Frison, Kissel, Rutherford and Jordan were pushing the big rotary plow when it broke down, and were snowbound at Ivanhoe from February 20 until early April. When they returned to Basalt, Stiffler told that he hadn't had his clothes off for thirty-eight days. He and the other engineers had slept in their engines and kept them alive with wood which had been sent in for that emergency. They had subsisted on lunches which had been sent in or on meals obtained at the section house at Ivanhoe.

During Basil Smith's term as a postmaster he housed the post office in his store. Later it was moved to Odd Fellows Hall on High Street and still later back to Main. On December 8, 1897, Mrs. Jennie Shryock replaced Smith as postmaster, and following her were John P. McMillen on March 26, 1898, and Mattie Stiffler, March 2, 1901.

97. Redstone, 1898. During the summer of 1899 I worked at Redstone on the construction crew of the Crystal River Railroad. Grading crews

COLLECTION OF THE AUTHOR

Main Street in Spring Gulch looked like this in 1908 as the author's wife pushed Cecil Shoemaker, their son, about town.

COLLECTION OF THE AUTHOR

The Colorado Supply Company store at Spring Gulch in 1908 was a favorite meeting place and on this day the store provided a free snack to customers. These stores provided nearly all the necessities of life for the coal camp workers and their families.

Candy Clark, a resident of Basalt, proudly shows her mount outside Carbondale. The Roaring Fork River is in the trees beyond, running beside the D&RGW trackage.

were then busy at the junction of the main line from Carbondale and the narrow-gauge branch to Coal Basin. Teamsters were hauling mine machinery to Placita, and laborers were clearing ground for the location of the coke ovens. James Leggett was the station agent and had the post office there. Paul Blout was John C. Osgood's surveying engineer and general manager.

In 1901 T. M. Gibb was superintendent, S. D. Blair was clerk, Dr. Angus Taylor was the company doctor, Mrs. Rose Wright and Miss Ira Freeman (later Mrs. Gibb) were the school teachers. During the next few years the company built 200 coke ovens, and developed a model camp for its employees. There were about 150 neat frame cottages, a fine hotel (the Elk Mountain Inn), a large schoolhouse, and a clubhouse which contained a library and a theatre.

That year the town had a population of 500 people; it had a brass band and a home talent group of actors who performed frequently in the theatre. At Christmastime a celebration was held at the Inn where the sponsors had set up a Christmas

tree laden with gifts for the children.

The Colorado Supply Company built and operated store No. 24 of its chain; it was opened on July 9, 1900. Frank X. Rickelman, James B. Bowen, Joseph H. Wilson, J. N. Graham, W. N. Young and T. C. McCullough were store managers during its existence. It was closed on March 19, 1910.

James Legett had been appointed postmaster on May 19, 1898, and had been succeeded by Alice B. Damon on March 13, 1900. Other postmasters who followed them were J. B. Bowen, December 18, 1900; Joseph B. Smith, June 15, 1906; J. H. Wilson, April 13, 1908; William R. Powell, June 6, 1910; Arizona F. Gibb, May 9, 1911; LeRoy Lyon, July 7, 1915; Joseph M. Snook, December 31, 1915; Ora M. Lehow, November 23, 1916; Fredia M. Bowles, March 30, 1918. The office was discontinued on September 30, 1918.

98. Placita, 1899. The Colorado Fuel & Iron Company constructed the main line of the Crystal River Railroad to Placita, a distance of four miles, in 1899, and completed its narrow-gauge branch to

184

These two photos show the upper camp and lower camp of Spring Gulch as they looked in 1906. The main entrance was located up the gulch in the top photo. Also shown are some of the Colorado Midland revenue cars near the end-of-track. The lower camp was for the more well-to-do families where homes were of more substantial wooden frame construction. The upper camp homes were constructed of logs and had sod roofs.

Not many of these Rocky Mountain "canaries" are in the mining areas now, since motor-driven vehicles have taken over nearly all of their work.

Coal Basin, a distance of twelve miles, in 1900. It opened a mine at Placita in 1899, but ran it only until 1901. R. S. Davis and B. L. Davis were mine superintendents. During 1899 the company worked thirty-five men and mined 6,500 tons of coal. Afterwards the mine was operated for several years by Rapini Brothers. A Colorado Supply Company store was opened in 1900. P. H. Smith was the store manager; Amborse Williams was his assistant. William H. Rees was appointed postmaster on October 25, 1899, then Smith was appointed on May 23, 1900.

Work on the mine was suspended in 1901 and Manager Smith and Superintendent B. L. Davis were transferred elsewhere. James L. Gardineer, the mine clerk and acting postmaster, was appointed postmaster on April 30, 1903, and served until the office was discontinued on November 19, 1903 (actually closed December 15, 1903).

Cardiff, on the Colorado Midland main-line, was one of the busier railroad towns along the railroad - and this was especially true once the Basalt division point was moved here late in 1907. At one time there was enough trackage in Cardiff to hold nearly 500 cars. The coke ovens in this photograph were supplied with coal from mines at Spring Gulch. The coal trestle in the center held the coal for loading into "larry" cars that ran out on top of the ovens. The coal was then lowered by chute into the top of the oven through a small opening. The Jerome Park Branch took off around the trestle.

Western Sunset.

Chapter XXVII

99. Colorado Midland Railroad, 1899.   In 1897 the new management of the Colorado Midland Railway Company, in an effort to evade payment of the fee to the Busk Tunnel Company, decided to reopen the high line through the Hagerman Tunnel. The cost of that job was over $65,000, for it included among other things the blasting of ice from the entire length of the tunnel.

However, the company put the road in usable condition and ran its trains over it for a period of fourteen months without much difficulty. Then disaster in the form of a long-continued and unusually terrific blizzard struck hard and knocked the company for a loop. Ordinarily it had been able to cope with the wintertime weather conditions but this time its tracks were snowed under despite all it could do to avert the tragedy. From January 27 to April 14, 1899, a period of seventy-eight days, all traffic was blocked by almost unceasing storms which swept across Hagerman Pass and piled up snow to unprecedented depths.

The blockade caused by the snow barrier was probably the most unusual event of its kind in the history of railroading in the Rocky Mountain Region. It was remarkable on account of the mighty effort put forth by every agency known to meet and combat the fierce elements. During the period the railway company used all of its manpower and equipment and hired or rented all other men and equipment that could be obtained. The fight never ceased except when the forces engaged, from sheer fatigue, had to retire for rest. When that occurred other men took their places and carried on. At one time some of the valiant workers continued forty-two hours without stopping. Two engine crews worked continuously for 624 hours.

Two great Jull Plows (augurs) and a powerful rotary plow, each backed by five great locomotives, were used. Each division was manned by complete crews—engineers, firemen, brakemen,

conductors and from twenty-five to 150 snow-shovelers. Each was provided with complete lodging and boarding outfits. Wood to fuel the engines was currently supplied.

Many trains were caught between Basalt and Hagerman Tunnel and the rotary plow was kept busy for several days liberating the many passengers that were marooned at the several section houses along the way. Somewhere above Ivanhoe the plow broke down and when eventually liberated by the Santa Fe Jull it had to be taken to Colorado City for repairs, via the Denver & Rio Grande Railroad. That road was sometimes blocked for short periods at Tennessee Pass, but managed to keep its tracks open most of the time.

In places below Hagerman tunnel the snow was banked to a depth of thirty-five feet. Once a big gang of men worked two hours to dig down to the top of a snowshed which covered the track. In many places it was necessary to tunnel the snow and blow up the overhead mass with dynamite.

The cost of the fight was great. It was estimated at that time by the managers of the combat force that the company spent $60,000. During February the expense of maintaining the army of workers amounted to $26,000. Sixteen engines were used and some of the engineers drew pay for twenty-four hours per day. The Julls, borrowed from other railroads, cost $40 per day. According to my brother, Will Shoemaker, who worked with the "snowbirds" for a 6-week period, over 1,000 snow shovels were used. In addition to the hired shovelers, almost every employee of the company shoveled snow when not otherwise needed.

Great was the joy of everyone concerned when at 4:30 p.m. on April 14, word was flashed over the wires that the track was clear. Thus ended one of the greatest battles with the god of storms that the railroads of the state, and probably the nation, have ever known.

Through the years several bad wrecks occurred on the railroad. Probably the most disastrous

The Hot Springs Lodge and Pool at Glenwood Springs is one of the most popular spots in Western Colorado. This is called the world's largest mineral hot springs swimming pool.

insofar as loss of life was concerned occurred at the Aspen Junction yards on July 12, 1891. A wild engine just in from its run was standing in the yards. Its brakes leaked and it ran down the siding and crashed into the Aspen-Glenwood Springs Saturday excursion train which happened to be passing at that moment. Nine persons were killed and as many more injured.

In September, 1902, I was riding on a passenger train down the Frying Pan canyon, when the engine struck a large bull. The carcass rolled under the engine and threw it off the rails and against the canyon-wall. It stopped so quickly that the cars never left the track. The engineer's cab and that side of the engine were demolished, but the engineer and fireman jumped to safety on the other side.

About 1900 a coal train on the Jerome Park branch line ran away on the steep grade below Pocahontas. When the engine left the track it struck the upper bank with such force that the engine cab was thrown about seventy feet onto the hillside above the track. All of the crew but one were killed.

During October, 1902, I worked with a bridge crew on that branch. Our crew of thirteen men were stationed at Cardiff and each morning we rode the upbound train to our job and pulled our hand-car behind the caboose. In the evening we coasted back to Cardiff, braking the car with a short pole. One day our brakeman broke the staff and the car ran away over the same road which the ill-fated coal train had covered. At a speed of about sixty miles per hour, it ran for three miles,

The Cardiff bridge across the Roaring Fork River originally was built over the Grand (Colorado) River in the 1880's.

Cardiff was the setting of this westbound freight train scene. Colorado Midland Number 39 was built by Schenectady Locomotive Works in 1889, the last in a series of 4-6-0's the Midland purchased.

One of the finest experiences in Glenwood Springs was to see these giant steam locomotives clank into town. This great D&RGW 2-8-8-2 articulated locomotive was eastbound on the main-line on June 17, 1944.

crossing several high, curved tressels en route. We finally stopped it near the place where the coal train had crashed. Not till then had we fully realized the horrible fate that had overtaken the train crew.

About 1907 a long train of freight cars, conducted by Harry Cline (on his initial run), stopped at Sellar. The crew set the air brakes and started switching cars. The air leaked and the train ran backward toward Nast for about two miles. When it left the rails it scattered cars and freight over a large area below the track. Two carloads of cattle were killed. A carload of canned goods was strewn over a large area. Fortunately, a lot of the cargo was coal which could be salvaged.

About 1908 an engine (No. 301) blew up in the Frying Pan canyon, and Engineer Jack Clegg and Fireman Clarence Augustine were killed. Details of the tragedy are lacking.

Several other railroad mishaps are recalled through Jake Lucksinger of Basalt, but the times of their occurrence is not known. A caboose broke loose from the train some distance above town and ran backward to Basalt. The yardmen were notified of its wild run and switched it into a carload of coal standing on the siding. The resulting collision was an exciting moment for the townspeople.

An engine blew up in the yards and scattered parts all over the downtown section. One day the engine No. 6, the evening passenger train, side-swiped a carload of oranges on the siding. The car was sadly damaged, but the bystanders who gathered-in the scattered fruit had a feast. The same thing occurred when a carload of oysters was wrecked below town. In a wreck above town, a carload of whiskey was smashed and began to leak. When the wrecker crew arrived at the wreck, they found the engineer of the wrecked train calmly collecting whiskey from one of the leaks. The wrecker crew immediately nicknamed him "Leaky" and the name stuck.

In 1900 the Colorado & Southern and the Rio Grande railroad companies negotiated for and took control of the Colorado Midland on July 2. However, over the years they met with so many reverses that they barely kept the road on its wheels. There was considerable legal controversy and the road was again forced into receivership. In February, 1917, Albert E. Carlton of Colorado Springs purchased the road for $1,425,000. The line from Colorado Springs to New Castle was 222 miles long, and there was an additional thirty-eight miles of branch line and siding.

In 1918 the railroad was closed down by order of Secretary MacAdoo of the U. S. Railway Administration as a War measure. The last train

191

Posed in the classic "grand manner" of railway photography, the Denver & Rio Grande Western's "California Zephyr" was unloading passengers when this scene was recorded at the Glenwood Springs depot in 1969. The Colorado River—flowing along beside the railroad—was once known as the Grand River, which caused confusion with the Rio Grande in the southern part of the state. The stainless steel train in this view still makes a thrice-weekly run through Glenwood Canyon and the heart of the Colorado Rockies, however, the D&RGW management wants to have the train eliminated from its system.

ran on August 14, 1918. On May 20, 1922, the Colorado Midland Railroad Company was dissolved by Carlton, acting for the road in bankruptcy. Soon afterward the rails were pulled up and sold with other equipment as junk.

Parts of the right-of-way are now used as roads and State Highway No. 82.

100. Thomasville, 1899. According to the *Basalt Journal* there was much activity at Thomasville in 1899. In one issue these items were given: C. A. Henning repaired and reopened some of the lime kilns. Swineford and Billow reopened and retimbered the Bessie Mine. Joe Stoddard

built a new cottage. George McLaren was working his tunnel. Mike Sweeny held a dance and entertained with a talking-machine. Nellie Noble gave a social dance at her home. Elijah Thompson was running his sawmill and Mrs. Thompson, the hotel. A masquerade ball, held at Alhambra Hall, was a successful affair; Mrs. Noble served the supper at her restaurant.

101. Coal Basin, 1900. W. D. Parry and G. D. Griffith discovered the coal seam at the site of the later developed Coal Basin Mine in 1881. They filed on a claim and sold it later to John C. Osgood for $500. A mine was opened in 1892 and the coal

This distant view of Glenwood Springs was taken at the turn of the century. The D&RG ran through town adjacent to the Colorado River (on the left) and its Aspen Branch curved out and under the Colorado Midland bridge that crossed the Roaring Fork River. The Midland's depot is just out of sight (to the right) and was served by trains either backing across the Roaring Fork or pulling in and backing out, as the main-line is on this bank.

proved to be the best coking coal that had been found in the state. When the railroad reached that point in 1900 the mine was reopened and operated by the Colorado Fuel & Iron Company until early 1909. During that time Dave Griffiths, James Stewart, John Shaw, Henry Funder, John Allen and William Manley were superintendents, and the mine produced 1,009,100 tons of coal.

The Colorado Supply Company started its store No. 26 on April 25, 1900, and ran it until January 12, 1909. Store managers who served during that time were C. O. Redd, L. A. Hanawald, E. T. Hind,

F. J. Young and E. O. Nordgren.

In 1905 the town had a population of 150 people. Thomas Hughes ran a hotel and O. F. Tracy, a saloon. John Shaw was mine superintendent, W. F. Julian, company doctor, and J. F. Young, station agent.

In November, 1908, during a drinking spree, Frank Buth killed Peter Niora. When the news reached Aspen, Sheriff Jim Begley and Coroner Irving Everett went over to the Basin and brought Niora's body to Redstone for burial, and Buth to Aspen for trial. His fate was not determined.

This elegant structure—built in 1906—stands today as one of the relatively few remaining operating depots on the D&RGW. The Glenwood Springs depot was built in a day when U.S. railroads put passenger service first—as it should be even today—and this building shows this obvious concern, both inside and out.

102. Carbondale, 1900. In the 1890's William H. Long operated a grocery and dry goods store in Carbondale. In the early 1900's his assistants were Elmer Long and W. Albert Witchey who had previously handled Dinkel's dry goods department.

A Methodist Church building was constructed in 1898. Up to that time religious services had been in the Schoolhouse. Some of the early pastors were the Reverends Bratton, Thompson, Law, Hollenback and Hole. In 1906 Augusta May Swigart and I were married in the church by the then resident pastor, the Rev. E. N. Mallory. A Christian church was built in the 1890's, but its services were soon discontinued.

On July 4, 1905, a fire which started in the Price Wycliffe saloon burned that and several other buildings. Merry-makers at the town pavillion nearby deserted the dance floor either to watch or to help suppress the blaze. The buildings which burned were replaced by others soon afterward.

For many years residents of the town got their water from the town ditch or from a water-wagoner who drove from door to door. In 1910 a survey was made to Nettle Creek, a distance of about eight miles, and a pipe-line and water mains were laid. A few years later a powerline was con-structed from Glenwood Springs, and electric lights were available.

103. Ruby, 1900. South Independence or Hurst's Camp was renamed Ruby when in the early 1900's the Ruby Mining & Development Company began operating there. It erected several large buildings, one of which housed a 50-ton concentrating plant equipped with crusher rolls, Huntington Mill and tables. It bored a long tunnel under Red Mountain, from which the name Ruby was derived.

A good wagon road was built from the Roaring Fork road to the camp in 1906, and considerable ore was hauled to Aspen and shipped to market. The project lasted until 1912 and intermittently for a few years afterwards. Barnes Brothers were the last operators; they mined many tons of ore which were hauled out by Billy Tagert of Aspen. However, the venture proved to be so unprofitable that the Barneses had to give it up and neither they nor Tagert derived much money for their labor.

Several old sourdoughs prospected there over the years, the last being Henry Foley and Al Morrow who were typical representatives of that old clan. They lived in the large boarding-house which had once housed fifty men, and were pleasant and congenial hosts who welcomed all visitors

194

This Colorado Midland train—bound for Colorado Springs (Colorado City)—was the overnight varnish. Locomotive Number 25 was waiting for orders here at Glenwood Springs with a baggage car, chair cars and a Pullman car.

warmly. One autumn day my wife and I arrived at their door, cold and wet after a long day in the saddle. While I unpacked and hobbled our horses, they took my wife inside, wrapped her in a quilt, pulled off her wet boots and proceeded to get supper. When she wanted to help, they strenuously objected. After the meal we visited with them until nearly midnight.

We still remember their good supper, but most of all we remember their kindness and hospitality. The next year when we inspected that range Mrs. Shoemaker took them a large chocolate cake as a token of appreciation and they were delighted.

Another resident of that locality at that time was "Rattlesnake Bill" Anderson, who lived at Anderson Lake, west of the camp. Someone dynamited the lake, and when I went to investigate the act Bill showed me a large pan full of 18-inch trout. Somewhat in jest, I asked him if he had dynamited the lake. He grabbed a large butcher-knife and angrily shouted, "If you accuse me, I cut your . . . . heart out!" I had to talk fast to get out of that situation. Incidentally, I couldn't find the

guilty person. Later, I restocked the lake.

104. Basalt, 1901. During the summer of 1901 the citizens of Basalt decided to incorporate.

President Theodore Roosevelt, on his trip to the West in March, 1903, arrived in the valley via the Colorado Midland Railway. He arrived at Basalt in the early morning and a large crowd was on hand to meet the bunting-bedecked train. But they were sorely disappointed for the President did not appear.

In March, 1905, an addition to the town jail was constructed. Although considerably smaller, it cost more than the original building. On May 1, W. W. Frey was elected mayor. About that time the railroad officials announced that they were going to move the division point to Cardiff and the board appointed a committee to discuss the matter with George W. Vallery, general manager of the company at Denver. The interview was held in June, but the company would not change its mind and the change was made soon thereafter.

After the Colorado Midland railroad was closed down in 1918, Basalt's mail, express and freight came in over the Denver & Rio Grande railroad to Emma. Individual contractors transported it to Basalt. The first of these was Ben Beaty and he was followed by Hotz Brothers and they by E. T. Gray.

105. Redstone, 1902. During the promotion and development of the Crystal River Railroad and his three coal camps, Redstone, Placita and Coal Basin, John C. Osgood used the name "Crystal River" repeatedly. He called the railroad "The Columbine Route" and had a large "CR" emblem on his engines. The repetition of the name soon resulted in the acceptance of it by the public.

In 1902 Osgood and his chief supporters, J. A. Kebler (for whom Kebler Pass is named), J. L. Jerome and A. C. Cass fought John W. Gates for control of the Colorado Fuel & Iron Company and won out. However, in 1903 the Gould-Rockefeller group defeated them, gained control of the company and took charge of its management.

Osgood retained control of Redstone, Cleveholm and the land thereabouts, but his ouster as president of the company doomed the project on which he had spent millions. When the company abandoned the mines at Placita and Coal Basin, those towns quickly folded up. Redstone, which was the most beautiful town I had ever seen, also declined. As its principal industry was the coking of the coal from those mines, its existence also seemed to be doomed. However, the renewal of work at Marble after World War I caused a slight revival at Redstone and Placita. The post office at each camp was reestablished and postmasters were appointed, to wit: Redstone—Charles R. Osgood, May 16, 1925; John M. Kenney, February 19, 1927. Placita—William Hughes, October 6, 1928; Mrs. Artelia Dawson, February 14, 1931.

Placita and Coal Basin are now ghosts; Redstone survived although many of its buildings were torn down. It is now an attractive resort with the Redstone Inn and Cleveholm serving as first-class hotels. All of the land and property thereabouts have been purchased recently by a man who proposes to develop a mammoth skiing and recreational resort there in the near future.

106. Sloss, 1903. One of the original sidings on the Colorado Midland Railway was called Sloane. The land there had been located by Otmar Lucksinger in the 1880's, but in 1903 S. Price Sloss of Basalt bought or otherwise secured title to it. He built a large brick house, a barn and other structures, and assisted by his sons, Alfred and Alvin, he conducted a cattle-raising business.

About 1907, according to Alvin Sloss of Glenwood Springs, he obtained a Sloss post office and the railroad company changed the name,

Sloane, to Sloss. Price was the postmaster until his death, then Alvin took over and ran the office until July 31, 1931, when it was discontinued.

Price was a fine old pioneer and a good friend when I worked there. He aided me in many ways and together we planned for and organized the Frying Pan Stockgrowers' Association. He was its president and led the movement to eradicate the giant larkspur menace to cattle in Lime Park. After two grubbings we reduced the death loss from thirty to two head of stock.

He liked to play practical jokes on his friends and acquaintances, and I was one of his easy victims. One of my first Forest Service jobs (in 1913) was to help the stockmen round up cattle and drive them to higher range in Lime Park. Supervisor John McLaren and Ranger Ben Beaty were also assisting. After we got started, Price and I followed the drags (end of the herd) and when we passed Thomasville he stopped and bought a quart of whiskey. He asked me to carry it which I did by wrapping it in my slicker.

A few miles farther on we stopped to rest the herd and Price asked me to pass the bottle that *I had bought* in Thomasville. As I hadn't bought it, didn't drink and didn't know where my boss stood on the question, I ignored his request. Whereupon he said, "If you won't pass your bottle I guess I'll have to pass mine." He went to his horse and got a bottle from his slicker and passed it. All of the men took a nip and when I refused he began to heckle me; he wondered why a man would buy whiskey if he didn't drink it or wouldn't share it with his friends. He kept badgering me till I was mad enough to pop, then Beaty broke into a hearty laugh and all of the men joined him. Too late I realized that I had been taken for a ride down the horsefly trail. Beaty told me later that Price and John had arranged the farce as a means of initiating me into the group. I later enjoyed and appreciated their friendship, and needless to say, I cherish the memory of that fun-loving pair.

107. Aspen, 1905. Aspen's population had decreased to about 4,000 in 1905 and its business economy had suffered accordingly. Some of its mines were still being worked, but the price of silver was so low that most of the operations were unprofitable.

On July 15, 1905, W. C. Tagert started a stage line to Ashcroft and ran it for several years. His first driver was Bob Johnson. His stage connected with one which plied between Ashcroft and Dorchester, a town in Taylor Park. Dorchester had a post office and was the supply base for the Taylor Park Mining Company, the name under which Thomas Goodale, an Eastern capitalist, was working the Enterprise Mine nearby. At that time Superintendent Alexander Forsyth had struck fairly good ore and was working about 150 men.

About 1910 Tagert contracted to carry the mail to Dorchester and extended his stage line to that town. Later the ore vein in the Enterprise played out, and the mine and the camp were deserted with the exception of two men—Alex Malmgreen, the postmaster, and one other.

Taking advantage of parcel post privileges, those men ordered all of their supplies sent in by mail. Their supplies included a weekly 20-pound bag of oats for their horse and ran into considerable weight. Tagert didn't mind that until snow blocked the road and his stage couldn't cross the Taylor Range. Bill Godfrey, his driver, after one trip on snowshoes, balked and Tagert was up against a real problem.

He took his troubles to a friend, George Folsom, who was then the deputy postmaster, and together they worked out a way to end the mail contract. They went to Dorchester and stayed overnight with Malmgreen and his companion. During the evening they played cards and enjoyed the liquor which they had taken along.

They retired at midnight and the Dorchester men were soon fast asleep, so Tagert and Folsom arose, gathered up all of the post office equipment and carried it over the range to Ashcroft. They delivered it to Dan McArthur, the postmaster there, went on home and waited for the inevitable postal inspection. Six weeks later a postal inspector arrived to investigate Malmgreen's complaint. He grimly listened to Tagert's and Folsom's explanation of what had been done, then said he would ask for a cancellation of the mail contract. And much to Billy's relief, the release came through a few weeks later.

About 1910 a movement was started to build a highway across Independence Pass between Aspen and Twin Lakes. In 1912 the U. S. Forest Service started the construction of a new road, beginning at the Cosseboom ranch about four miles above Aspen. Nothing more was done until 1915, when the State Highway Department said it might go ahead with the project. Governor E. M. Ammons had been requested to do something about it, and he had expressed a desire to go over the route with Engineer Ehrhart to size up the job. Consequently W. C. Tagert rigged up a 4-horse spring-wagon outfit and he and John Williams went over the Divide, picked up Ammons and Ehrhart at Twin Lakes, and brought them to Aspen. They

were entertained at the Hotel Jerome and before they returned to Denver they assured Aspen's citizens that the road would be built as fast as possible. Tagert thinks that his wagon was the last one to travel the old road which had been built in 1881.

The county, state and federal governments cooperated, and the road was completed in 1927, at a cost of $475,000. After the Colorado Midland's railroad was abandoned in 1918, its right-of-way from Aspen to Carbondale was acquired by the State and the two projects were linked to form State Highway No. 82.

When political machinations closed down the free coinage of silver and established the gold standard in 1892 and 1893, Aspen's economy collapsed, and it soon began its 50-year decline. Mines closed, banks and business ventures failed. People moved to other localities and eventually the town drowsed under the Western sun, a forlorn reminder of that once proud queen—the Crystal City of the Rockies.

After two decades had elapsed the town had a drab, half-deserted appearance, as many of its buildings fell into disuse and decay. Its most attractive features were the rows of large cottonwood trees which adorned its streets and the beautiful sweet peas and other flowers which grew in the yards or gardens of the remaining residents. The trees, planted in the 1880's by some nature-loving official, still add a charm to the town.

By 1920 the population had decreased to 1,265; it numbered 705 in 1930 and 769 in 1940. It stood at about that figure in 1945 when Walter Paepcke of Chicago came to see its skiing contests, saw its possibilities as a ski and recreational resort, and decided to do something about it. The rehabilitation of the community under his capable guidance is well known across the state and nation.

The town's revival during this decade is almost as marvelous, if not as spectacular as its rise in the 1880's. Already well-known as a skiing and cultural center, it seems destined to even greater greatness. Thousands of visitors follow the Maroon Lake Road (for whose construction I worked for many years) annually to the Elk Mountain region for rest or recreation. They find recreation, but seldom find rest because they are too busily running hither and yon in search of more recreation.

I lived there for more than sixteen years and have fond memories of the town and its people, my friends and associates. I would like to list all of their names, but the list would be too long. I can only say, "Crystal City of the Rockies! All Hail!"

Chapter XXVIII

108. **Spring Gulch, 1905.**   Spring Gulch was a thriving camp in 1905 and more than 250 miners were employed. Tim Tinsley was mine superintendent; Dick Malloy, pit boss; Pat Morgan and Jack Bickerton, shift bosses; John Nash, tipple boss; Sam Schwab, mine clerk; "Dad" Thomas, night watchman; "Doc" Foster, company doctor. In 1908 Newt Tenasse supplanted Schwab. John P. Thomas, who lived in Glenwood Springs, was division superintendent and made periodic inspections of the mine and camp.

Mrs. Pat (Winifred) Morgan, assisted by Miss Annie McKown, ran a boarding-house; Mrs. Buchanan and her daughter Joann ran another. Elizabeth Lamme was the school principal. Louis Neidermeyer had a barber shop. He also had a phonograph and nearly 2,000 records, and the machine was usually grinding out the tunes of the day. John Renstrom had a large saloon/pool-hall/dance-pavillion setup, and his barkeeper assistant was Otto Johnson. George Swigart ran a weekly supply wagon from Satank, and sold meat, vegetables and fresh fruit to the store.

Ambrose Williams was still the postmaster and store manager; Chester Hudson was meat cutter and John Williams was grocery clerk and deliveryman. He left the job in June, 1905, and I was hired to take his place. Because of the camp's peculiar location, there were no roads and all deliveries, of whatever kind, had to be packed in on burros. Two and later three jacks were used, and two or three trips were necessary each day.

A few of the miners were Tom Davis, Pete Moscon, Tom Oakley, Pete Gall, Tom and Pat Quinn, Vic Oprandi, August and Nick Pretti, Joe Ruggero, August and Jim Marchetti, and John Nardine. Arthur Gregory of Denver lived at the camp during the years 1907-18, inclusive, and worked first in the mine and later as tipple boss. He helped to organize, and played on, the baseball nine and the 27-piece band, and he remembers well the camp activities during that period.

During the winter of 1906-07 there were about 400 miners and the population was about 1,200 people. The company erected more houses, and my bride and I were glad to get one of them. Williams was transferred to the company's store at Crested Butte and Hudson was promoted to his job of manager and postmaster. I replaced him as meat cutter and Merino Moscon came on as clerk and deliveryman. Dr. Foster resigned and was replaced by Dr. A. E. Gill of Basalt.

After I went back to Spring Gulch from Marion, I was made cashier of that store and an incident connected with that job seems to be worth recounting. As there was no bank at the camp, the store and the saloon cashed the miner's checks each month. It now became my duty to go to Cardiff, accompanied by Dad Thomas, and bring back about $25,000 in gold for that purpose. A group of six young hoodlums of the lower valley, knowing of that practice, planned to hold up the train. They rode to the steep grade near Sunshine (where the train slowed to a crawl) and waited for the train to arrive. Fortunately for all concerned the train was two hours late that day, and before it reached the robber's roost their courage waned and they went home. In later years two of the group told my brother Will about the proposed holdup and gave sufficient evidence to convince him that their story was true.

Those coal mining camps contributed much to the economy of the valley. The amount and value of the coal from their mines were highly important to the success of the Colorado Midland Railway and the Colorado Fuel & Iron Company. The whole valley was benefitted by the fuel they furnished to its residents at low cost. Today the camps are merely names, yet even those names add a bit of glamour to the land where they once were.

109. **Nast, 1906.**   Arthur Hanthorn and James Morris started a tourist resort in the Frying Pan valley near Nast siding in the early 1900's. They

constructed a large lodge-hotel and other buildings and developed a thriving business. Hanthorn secured a post office and was appointed postmaster on May 4, 1909.

During the summer of 1914 I was stationed at Nast Ranger Station, and as Mrs. Hanthorn was very hospitable, we enjoyed many good times at the lodge.

Morris had two hogs which ran at large and foraged off the land. The boar, a large cantankerous beast, wanted to fight every time I chased him out of my barnyard. One morning I was riding swiftly toward Norrie when I almost ran over the hogs which were lying in the trail. They spooked and the sow plunged into the river that was then at floodtide. In dismay I watched the sow go tumbling downstream in that mighty torrent and all day and night I wondered how to tell Morris about the drowning of the sow.

Therefore, imagine my surprise when the next morning I found both hogs lying in my barnyard as they usually did. That the sow had escaped from the raging flood was almost beyond belief. But there she was, and believe it or not, she was suckling six little red pigs.

About two years later Ed Koch of Norrie, while out hunting, shot and killed the boar. He claimed that it had attacked him and he thought it was a wild animal.

When the Colorado Midland Railroad was about to be shut down, the post office was closed—on August 10, 1918. The resort is still being operated by other owners.

110. Norrie, 1906. In 1906 Harry G. Koch of Aspen acquired the Deeds land east of Norrie and built a large house there; he set up a large sawmill in Norrie and started a large timber operation. Norrie soon became the best timber camp in western Colorado, and thousands of carloads of timber products were shipped to Aspen and other markets annually.

111. Marble, 1906. Marble had a population of about 150 residents in 1905. It had a weekly newspaper, *The Marble Times,* which was published by Evan Williams. The Hoffman Smelter Company was operating a smelter, the only one in that part of the valley. Three small marble quarries were more or less active; the operators were Marble City Quarry Company, Yule Creek Marble Company, and J. C. Osgood.

A few other businesses and men were H. H. Williams, general supplies; Dr. E. W. Fuller, druggist, postmaster, justice of the peace; W. D. Parry, carpenter; W. W. Woods, real estate agent.

In 1906 the Colorado-Yule Marble Company was organized and started extensive operations under the direction of Colonel C. Frank Meek and A. J. Mitchell. They constructed 7.3 miles of new railroad between Placita and Marble which they called the Crystal River & San Juan. In December of 1910, the Crystal River & San Juan leased J. C. Osgood's Crystal River Railroad which operated between Placita and Carbondale, a distance of 20.6 miles. At Carbondale the Crystal River line interchanged with the Denver & Rio Grande, providing access to the outside world. They erected a huge finishing mill, 1,700 x 150 feet in size, and constructed a three-and-one-half-mile tram line to the marble deposits. Those beds of marble covered several hundreds acres and were 100 to 240 feet thick (and are said to be the largest in the world). The company opened new quarries, built a second tram line, cut, trammed and milled the marble, then shipped it to various markets.

By that time finished marble was being furnished to many markets. The most prominent buildings constructed of it were The First National Bank at Portland, Oregon, the Union Pacific railroad depot at Omaha, Nebraska, the Lincoln Memorial at Washington, D. C., the Postoffice Building and the Colorado National Bank at Denver, Colorado.

After 1926, when the Tomb of the Unknown Soldier was planned for Arlington Cemetery, a block of marble, weighing fifty-six tons, was shipped to an Eastern finishing mill. The finished stone was placed over the sarcophagus of the Unknown Soldier, who had been buried there on November 11, 1921. The tomb was designed and sculped by Thomas H. Jones. It was twelve feet high, fourteen feet long, and eight feet wide. At one end are emblematic figures signifying valor, victory and peace, and on the other end the words, "Here Rests in Honored Glory an American Soldier Known But to God." The Tomb and its approaches were finished in 1932. The residents of the valley may well be proud of that contribution to posterity.

The town, however, met with many misfortunes. On August 10, 1912, a tram train on which Colonel Meek was riding ran away and he jumped from it. He was so severely injured that he died on August 14. This was a regrettable loss to the community and would have been avoided if he had stayed with the train, for it reached the valley safely. However, a train did run away soon after that time and four persons were killed.

However, before those disasters occurred a greater one had damaged the mill. The concussion from a large avalanche, which ran on the slope opposite to the building, crushed much of the west wall, wrecked part of the interior and crippled its activity.

Two disastrous fires occured in the town. The first, in 1916, burned a large part of the business section and the second, in 1926, destroyed a part of the mill. The business houses destroyed were not rebuilt.

The mill was shut down during World War I, but was opened again in the early 1920's. However by that time the demand for marble products had diminished and the Colorado-Yule Marble Company abandoned the project shortly thereafter. The Vermont Marble Company revived the business in 1930, but they also shut down after a few years of operation.

In 1941 a flood which was caused by a heavy rainfall came down Carbonate Creek and destroyed a part of the residence section. All business ceased and most of the people moved to other localities. Thus ended the last town in that valley. Horace Williams died that year and John and Ambrose closed their store and the post office. In 1943, they moved to Phoenix, Arizona, but each year they return to Marble and spend the summer months there beside the crystal-clear stream where they spent so many years of their lives. A few other people do likewise.

The Crystal River & San Juan Railraod tracks have been dismantled and a highway occupies a part of their roadbeds and a part of the old Elk Mountain grade. The part of the highway below Placita is now State No. 133, which continues over McClure Pass to the North Fork of the Gunnison valley.

For a while a Glenwood Springs company exploited the waste marble from the old mill by turning it into a building material called marble chips.

112. Post Office Locations. Six post offices were located along the lines of the two railroads. They were Catherine, Watson, Snowmass, Woody Creek, Davies and Sherman.

Edward Stauffacher, a rancher who lived a few miles east of Carbondale, secured a post office in 1892, which was called Catherine. He was appointed its postmaster on November 23, and ran the office until he left that part of the country. He also constructed a cheese factory and ran it in connection with his ranch. He was a Dutchman and belonged to a group who called themselves The Sons of Herman. Annually he held a picnic in a cottonwood grove near his home, and the Colorado Midland Railway ran a special train from Aspen for the occasion. The people who attended danced, drank beer and usually fought with each other before the picnic ended.

Watson was a siding on the Colorado Midland about eight miles below Aspen. In 1889, Harvey W. Boyce applied for a post office to be located there and he was appointed its postmaster on May 31. He was replaced by James N. Ashby on July 24, 1891. On October 2, 1917, Auzel H. Gerbaz succeeded to the post, and, on June 14, 1918, he had the name changed to Gerbazdale. The office was closed on August 10, 1918, just before the railroad was shut down.

The local Grange (Farmer's Alliance No. 199) built an assembly hall there in the early 1900's. Later the building was used for dancing and other forms of recreation by the local people.

Snowmass was also a siding on the Colorado Midland. In the 1890's John H. Stewart ran a store there and was appointed postmaster on February 19, 1901. He was followed by John S. Stewart, who became the postmaster on October 7, 1904. John H. was appointed again on March 16, 1908, and ran the office until it was closed on December 27, 1913. (It actually ran until January 31, 1914.) The office was re-established on April 18, 1914, with Ena Mizer as postmaster, and Emma Bradshaw succeeded to the job on June 19, 1916.

Woody Creek was (and is) a siding on the Denver & Rio Grande Railroad. Someone started a store there and a post office was established when Frank O. Stevens was appointed postmaster on September 4, 1920. Ben M. Strawbridge of Aspen took over the setup as acting postmaster on March 22, 1922. He became postmaster on June 28 and ran the store. Jesse Bouge and Lee Jones were later incumbents.

The location of Davies post office is uncertain. It was established on January 7, 1895, with George E. Davies as postmaster, and it lasted only eight months, being discontinued on October 11. As its mail was then sent to Basalt (the closest post office) it is believed that it was a forerunner of Snowmass post office. A George Davis (or possibly Davies) lived near Snowmass at that time, according to a short item in the April 27, 1895, issue of the *Eagle County Examiner* of Basalt, to wit: "George Davis and a Frenchman named Arbaney, who live near the mouth of Snowmass Creek, quarreled and fought over the title to 40 acres of land which each claimed." This man could have been and probably was the postmaster.

An issue of the *Aspen Times* in 1890 stated: "A new post office called Sherman has been established on the Colorado Midland at Robinson's ranch." Robinson's ranch was H. B. Gillespie's El

Mount Sopris is seen in the distance in this view looking back on Glenwood Springs. The Salt Lake bound California Zephyr has just pulled past Funston Yards on the D&RGW here before the transcontinental highway forced the Rio Grande to rebuild the yards and main line on the far side of the Colorado River.

Jebel ranch below Basalt which was frequently referred to as "Robinson's" because a relative of Mrs. Gillespie (nee Sarah Robinson) had charge of the ranch in those days.

113. Valley Homesteaders. Very soon after the land within the valley was released to settlement on September 4, 1881, all arable land was located by the horde of immigrant settlers, many of whom had already squatted on desirable homesteads. At first these men held their claims by squatting on them and retaining their hold by right of possession. But eventually the land was surveyed and sectionized by government surveyors, a land office was set up at Glenwood Springs, and they were allowed to file legally on their claims.

Previously, in 1883, a telegraph line, which had been promoted and partially financed by H. B. Gillespie of Aspen, had been built to Aspen from Granite. That line was extended to Glenwood Springs, with agents in charge at the several towns. William Brown was the agent at Carbondale and George Swigart was employed as a courier by the government surveyors to carry messages from the line to the survey parties in the surrounding area.

Many claims were jumped and a few men were killed before all of the land was settled. One of those shooting frays was near Carbondale. Harry Burrows had located a homestead about one mile east of town and while temporarily absent, Mike Ryan, Dan Fenton and Charles Fuller took possession of it. When Burrows returned, he ordered them to leave, and when they refused he shot and killed Ryan and Fenton, and wounded Fuller. He was tried in Glenwood Springs, pleaded self-defense and was discharged when the jury brought in a verdict of justifiable homicide.

Mrs. Peers (Huberta) Coulter, who went to their Cattle Creek ranch as a bride in 1893, remembered the abundance of game there in the 1880's and 1890's. When it was less plentiful, Peers and his friends had to go down the Grand Valley to the Piceance country to get their venison. An interesting account of one of Peers' trips was given to me later by his daughter, Rosalee, of Glenwood Springs:

On that occasion Peers and his two companions found so many deer that each of them killed four instead of the two allowed by law. On their way home a local rancher told them that a game warden was inspecting all wagons which passed a ranch farther along the way. Consequently they stopped before they reached that ranch and during the night they packed their extra deer by a roundabout way to a point beyond the checking station.

The next morning they drove by that ranch, were duly inspected, and went on to where they had cached the extra carcasses. There they somewhat gleefully reloaded them and went on home. Peers and one companion got through Glenwood Springs safely but the man on the second wagon didn't. Before he reached the town he talked too freely to a man who had begged a ride with him. He laughingly told him how he had evaded the lawman, whereupon his hitch-hiker said, "Mister, you should be more careful when you talk to strangers. I am a game warden and you are under arrest."

However, the talkative hunter got off fairly easy; when haled into court, the justice leniently allowed him to keep his two lawfully killed deer.

114. U. S. Forest Service Administration. Following the trend made possible by the Congressional Act of March 3, 1891, all of the mountainous land within the boundaries of the valley became a part of the Holy Cross Forest Reserve on August 27, 1905. On that date President Theodore Roosevelt established that unit by presidential proclamation, and designated Glenwood Springs as its headquarters.

A few years later, on April 26, 1909, the southern part of the Holy Cross was cut off as another unit, and it was established as the Sopris National Forest by President William H. Taft. (The term "forest reserve" had been changed to "national forest" on March 4, 1907).

Shep N. Husted, as ranger-in-charge, first supervised the Holy Cross, then Harry H. French was appointed forest supervisor on November 1, 1906. He served in that capacity for about fifteen years. Some of his assistants before and after the division were Fred W. Morrell, Swift Berry, Jay Higgins, A. W. Miller, George Morrison and Peter Keplinger. Three of his early rangers (within the valley) were I. W. Foster, W. S. Cyphers and N. S. Ashlock.

When the forest was divided, John McLaren, who had been French's deputy, was made supervisor of the Sopris with headquarters at Aspen. He served as such until November 15, 1914, when he became District fire chief in the Denver office.

When the Colorado Midland Railroad quit operating, all of the timber business in the Frying Pan valley was soon discontinued. This led to a consolidation of the Sopris and Holy Cross National Forests on June 15, 1919, as a matter of economy. Arthur Upson was transferred to the Pike Forest and Harry French assumed charge of both areas. The union was officially confirmed by the executive order of President Woodrow Wilson on August 7, 1920.

The administration of the national forests was difficult in the early days because of the general opposition of the settlers to controlled use of the natural resources in them. The settlers had cut timber, grazed stock and in general had done whatever they pleased with the public lands. They resented the government interference and their resentment fell on the heads of the Forest Service employees who had to enforce its regulations.

Within the valley the activities of the Roaring Fork Stockgrowers' Association became so antagonistic that in Forest Service parlance the area was known as "the hotbed of the West." In 1907 Fred Light, a Sopris Creek stockman, tested the authority of the Forest Service regulations by purposely letting his cattle trespass on national forest lands. The trespass case which resulted was taken to the District and then to the Supreme Court. Each of those courts ruled that the regulations had the force of law and upheld the policies of the bureau in charging fees for the natural resources upon its lands.

The case was closed in 1911, but opposition to Federal control continued for many years. When I became district ranger at Aspen in 1918. "Cap" Dailey, editor of the *Aspen-Democrat Times,* was critical of everything that I or other officials did. However, ten years later he generously conceded: "I have changed my mind; the Forest Service is all right."

Even before that, the good that was being accomplished by protecting and preserving natural resources had been acknowledged by most of the settlers, and Federal control of the lands and resources had been accepted almost everywhere. Although there is some complaint by individuals occasionally, Forest Service administration is generally conceded to be "all right."

A few changes brought by the hand of Time are: Fred Morrell was promoted time after time and became eventually an Associate Forester in Washington, D. C. Upson was promoted to several high positions. Wehrly, Yarnall, Hunter and Richey died while in the Service; Keefe in World War I. Mountain peaks in the Elk Range have been named to honor the three last named.

My career in the Service dates back to May 25, 1913, when I accepted a six-months appointment as a forest guard. During that summer I was assistant to Ranger Ben Beaty at Norrie in the upper Frying Pan valley. I liked the work and on October 21 I took the Civil Service examination for assistant forest ranger. I passed the exam and was appointed on May 15, 1914. I was assigned to a station at Nast, four miles above Norrie, and

again acted as Beaty's assistant.

Thereafter my assignments were: Nast, May 15 to August 31, 1914; Woody Creek, to June 30, 1916; LWOP, to August 15, 1916; Aspen, to February 1, 1917; Thomasville, to April 1, 1918; Aspen, to June 20, 1928; LWOP, to October 1, 1928; Aspen, to August 10, 1934. On August 11 I was transferred to the Roosevelt National Forest, with headquarters at Boulder. (LWOP leave without-pay) was in both instances because of illness.

In addition to the administration of timber sales, the supervision of stock grazing and the suppression of forest fires (usually a ranger's heaviest activities), I maintained and constructed many improvements for our own and public convenience. One of the first of those was the construction of a telephone line to Lookout Mountain on the Woody-Frying Pan divide where a fire lookout was maintained for a few years. During those years I built, or bossed the construction of, about 300 miles of trails.

From the first day that I saw the beautiful Maroon Bells, I wanted a road constructed so that other people could drive up Maroon Creek to see them. Although it was outside my province as a ranger, I presistently urged the construction of the road to my superior officers. My plea fell on deaf ears for many moons, but in 1932 Ress Phillips of the Denver office advised me that the project had been approved. I was indeed jubilant when on August 30 I helped Surveyor Riley Cass run out the preliminary line for its construction.

I packed in and set up campground facilities at Snowmass Lake and several other recreational spots. I secured or helped to secure several rights-of-way through private land which were of great benefit to all. And in line with my instructions, I assigned names to many geographical features in that region. In those things, at least, people who live there may still see my footprints as I walked the highways and byways of that enchanting valley.

115. **Origin of Names.** The geographic names within any given area are usually as interesting as the story of its settlement and development. In many instances they show some of the names of the early settlers, or some of the quirks of their minds. Both are found in the names within the valley.

The origin of some of the names used herein have been shown in the text; in some cases they are obvious. Some of the other names and the sources from which they came are now added.

Henry Gannett, the leader of the topographic and geographic division of Dr. Hayden's Geological

Survey, and his geographer, W. D. Whitney, named many physical features in and around the Elk Mountain region. Among them were the six 14,000-foot peaks: Castle, Pyramid, Maroon, North Maroon, Snowmass and Capitol. Incidentally, they first called Pyramid, Black Pyramid; and

Each of those peaks was named for a distinctive characteristic: Castle for its castle-like turrets and spires, Pyramid for its shape, the Maroons for their color, Snowmass for the large snow-pack on its east face, Capitol for its dome-like crest. The three Maroons are now called, collectively, Maroon Bells, because of their shape. In the 1880's, according to Dan McArthur, the settlers called them First, Second and Third Maroon, as one sees them from the vicinity of Maroon Lake.

Gannett also named the creeks and lakes which bear similar names: Castle, Maroon, Snowmass and Capitol Creeks; Maroon, Snowmass and Capitol Lakes. He likewise named Roaring Fork River and Frying Pan Creek. It and Rock Creek, previously named by McGloughlin, qualified later as Frying Pan and Crystal rivers.

The same roar that caused the Utes to call the stream, "Thunder River," accounted for Gannett's use of the name, "Roaring Fork." As for his use of "Frying Pan," several stories exist. The indefinite tale about someone finding a frying pan hanging on a tree near the site of present Basalt seems to be the most logical one. Maybe one of Gannett's men found a pan that had been left by the mountain men, or fur trappers. The evolution of the name, "Crystal River," from Rock Creek, has already been told. Common usage brought about the change; no official action was taken.

Grizzly and Garfield Peaks on the Continental Divide were named by them; the former for the grizzled appearance of its north face, the latter

Lookout Mountain provides this view of Glenwood Springs, photographed shortly before a section of the Interstate Highway (I-70) was built through the town—next to the Colorado River (on the right). The Roaring Fork River comes in from the left. This scene looks west and shows the D&RGW grade crew at work on the original Colorado Midland right-of-way—relocating the main-line and freight yard. A D&RGW freight train is on the bridge crossing the Colorado River. (This bridge is now gone.) The historic Colorado Hotel dominates the scene to the left, near the Hot Springs Pool and Bath House. The elevation of Glenwoods Springs is 5,746-feet, population approximately 4,000.

PHOTO BY DAVID S. DIGERNESS

presumedly for President Garfield, although he wasn't President at that time. Grizzly is a magnificent, but awesome spectacle when viewed in June from the ridge between Independence and Grizzly Creeks. It is worth the climb from Highway 82 to the ridge.

Gannett named Mount Hayden for his leader, Dr. Hayden, and Cathedral Peak for its appearance—its large amphitheatric cirque. He could have done better by Dr. Hayden (and I think he should have) by naming one of the fourteeners for him.

The name, Taylor, attached to the Peak and Pass (and also to the river, park and lake outside the valley), was that of Jim Taylor, an old prospector-settler of that country who explored it in the 1860's. Also, Hunters Pass and Hunters Creek seem to be earlier names. Usage changed them to Independence Pass and Hunter Creek.

The early prospectors and settlers assigned names to many features. Pearl Pass and Pearl Mountain were named for Pearl Mine, one of the first there, according to McArthur. Others claim that it should be the other way around; that Gannett assigned the name to the mountain.

However, that same group undoubtedly named Crescent Mountain and creek nearby for their mine. Those old names, common in the 1880's, never gained recognition and the creek is now shown on the map as Cooper's Fork. It is actually a fork of Cooper Creek.

Early prospectors from Gothic named Treasure and Treasury Mountains at the head of Rock Creek. William Wood of Marble is accredited with the naming of Chair Mountain and Ragged Mountain.

Bowman Mountain and Pass were named for John Bowman, an early settler at Grandview on the Taylor Pass road. Grandview was changed later to Bowman, when he started and ran a large road-house there. He eventually moved to Aspen and ran a saloon for several years. His son, John Jr., later became Aspen's postmaster.

Traveler Peak (a spur of Castle) and Gulch were named for the Traveler Mine. Leo Pinger found gold there or nearby and made a stake; he then went to Aspen and started a grocery business. Later he was shot and killed by an unknown assailant as he walked homeward from the store (as previously related).

New York peaks, creek and pass were named for the New York Mine which was located on the creek. A government survey party assigned the name to the peaks and creek. It is believed that the name, "New York Peaks," has been approved by the U. S. Board of Geographic Names.

According to Jack Williams the mountain north of Independence Pass was named Belden Mountain, for Billy Belden (who discovered the mine), and the mountain south of the pass was named Doc Rice Mountain for Dr. Rice (who built the Independence Pass road) by the residents of Independence. Both men were prominent and well-liked citizens of that time.

Chicago Mountain and basin at the head of East Maroon Creek were named for the Chicago Mine, the location of which can still be seen on the mountain's steep face from the East Maroon Trail (the old Aspen-Gothic wagon road).

Smuggler and Red mountains near Aspen were named by the early prospectors. The name, Smuggler, as attached to the mountain and the mine it's ambiguous; no one seems to know which came first, the egg or the chick. Red Mountain was first called Phil Pratt Mountain and the name should have been retained for Phil was Aspen's staunchest pioneer. At the time of the Indian scare in 1897, he said, "I'm not going to leave my mine! I'll fight the whole . . . . Ute tribe if I have to!"

Coffee Pot Pass was named by the prospectors who first came to Highland in 1879. They found an old rusty pot on the pass, presumably a relic of the Hayden Survey party. Forest Supervisor John McLaren once told that the pot was still there in 1906. It was gone, however, when I looked for it in 1918. That party also named their town for Hayden's Highland triangulation station which lies westward on the Conundrum-Maroon divide.

Difficult Creek was named by two prospectors from Buena Vista who came over Taylor Range at Roaring Fork Pass and decided to go down the canyon instead of keeping to the ridge as most of the immigrants did. They found travel difficult along that route, so gave the stream that name.

Lost Man Creek was so-called because Billy Koch got lost there while going from Aspen to Leadville. He had followed the wrong fork of the creek. The miners at Independence tied the name to the creek after he had told them about being lost there. Lost Man Lake and pass naturally followed.

Cattle Creek was named by early homesteaders who found large herds of cattle there when they went in to locate claims. From various sources it is learned that Yule, Murray, Eames and other stockmen brought herds into Spring Valley and upper Cattle Creek basin from their Eagle River headquarters.

PHOTO BY H. H. BUCKWALTER – COURTESY OF FRED AND JO MAZZULLA

These beautifully painted refrigerator cars saw extensive use on the Colorado Midland after 1897. These were most unusual because of the Hanrahan refrigeration system containing center ice bunkers. These were painted bright yellow with tuscan red ends and featured a full-color Indian emblem, and had various colors in the lettering.

Threemile and Fourmile Creeks were so-called because they joined the Roaring Fork three and four miles above Glenwood Springs. The names are accredited to the railroad builders who constructed the Colorado Midland Railway.

Coal Creek was named by C. D. Griffith, one of the men who found coal seams at the site of Coal Basin, one of the Osgood coal camps.

Soon after I entered the employ of the U. S. Forest Service, rangers were instructed to assign names to unnamed geographic features. Consequently during 1918, 1919 and 1920, I assigned many names. I used them in my work and reports, and some of them got on the Forest Service map; many, however, never gained official recognition. Keefe and Hunter Peaks, on the Aspen District, and Richey Peak, on the Crystal River District,

were named for deceased forest officials. McArthur Mountain near Ashcroft was named for Dan McArthur, because of his long weather-station service. Those four names were officially approved by the U. S. Board of Geographic Names.

In the early 1920's I made up a list of the 130 peaks and mountains and the thirty-four mountain passes on the Aspen District, for the Aspen Chamber of Commerce. They proposed to use them in a brochure which would describe and extol the natural features of the region. Their committee approved the names, but unfortunately the brochure, because of a lack of funds, was not published. About one-half of the names on that list are officially recognized now.

About that time Harold Clark and others, through a petition to the Forest Service, named

The D&RGW's Aspen Branch junction in Glenwood Springs had this two-spout water tank when this view was made in 1933. Trains continue to use this branch line to serve the booming Aspen and Carbondale areas.

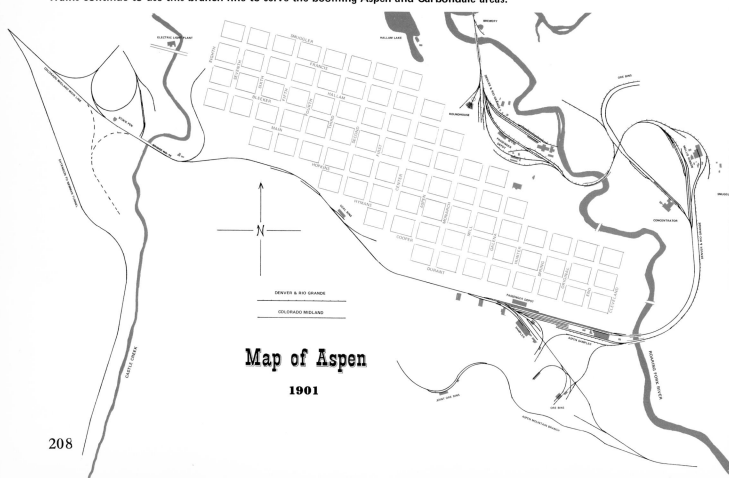

Map of Aspen

1901

208

This Glenwood Springs view—photographed in 1896—shows some of the construction that had taken place before the turn of the century. Denver & Rio Grande trackage can be seen running past the water tank and depot. The train on the wooden trestle crossing the Colorado River is on the westbound main-line. A small portion of the Colorado Midland main-line shows in the lower right-hand corner of the picture.

The Colorado Midland depot in Granite, shown here as it looked C. 1890, was an impressive two-story structure with a metal roof. A glimpse of the D&RG depot across the Arkansas River may be noticed to the right.

This view shows the D&RG depot in Granite. The photographer was looking toward the Arkansas River and the Midland grade. Notice the old-time order semaphore signal, mounted through the roof of the depot.

Back in 1890 the main street of Granite looked much like a motion picture set for a Western movie. The Roaring Fork area was very dependent on the business establishments in this village for their supplies of food, clothing, hardware and medicine.

Farview Peak and Roaring Fork Mountain, and they were approved. Likewise, Jack Leahy and others changed the name of Blue Lake to Cathedral Lake by the same procedure at a later date.

Some of my names which were accepted and put on the map were Casady, Sawmill, Wilbur, Spruce, Noname, Midway, Jack, Coleman, Ptarmagin, Brum, McFarlane, Sawyer, Sandy, Cataract and Brooklyn Creeks; Bald Knob, Geissler Mountain, Sievers Mountain, Crater Lake, Pierre Lakes and Kobey Park. Casady, Wilbur, Brum, McFarlane, Sawyer, Sandy, Geissler and Sievers were the names of settlers. Coleman was an engineer on the Independence Pass Highway.

Crater Lake had been called Upper Maroon and to get away from the duplication of names, Billy Taggert suggested the new name.

Ranger Harry Halleck named a tributary of Difficult, Columbia. Ranger Ben Beaty named two tributaries of the Frying Pan, Granite and Marten. He tried to have the name, South Fork of the Frying Pan, changed to Prospect Creek (the early prospector's name for it). The name Prospect was approved but the map-makers never got around to making the change. I had the same luck with the East and West Forks of Snowmass Creek. My new names for them, McKenzie and Pennell (both early settlers), were approved, but the changes were not made on the map. Ranger Floyd Chappel

211

This brids-eye view shows Granite, Colorado, at its peak, C. 1890. The trackage across the river belonged to the D&RG and was dual gauge at this time. The Colorado Midland depot is the two story fram building in the lower left corner. This settlement was of great importance to the prospectors of the Roaring Fork Valley before the D&RG and CM reached the area. Granite served as a railway connection to the outside world at that time. Prospectors would travel for days over Independence Pass to reach this town for supplies and trade.

secured approval to rename Little Snowmass Lake, Lake Geneva, but was unable to get the map-makers to cooperate. Recently, the name has been accepted and used.

I secured approval of the names, Triangle Peak and pass and Electric Peak and pass. Although not on the map, those names are used, especially the passes which have been crossed in late years by groups of trail riders. Triangle Peak resulted when I saw that three ridges converged there. When I was building the Panorama Trail across the Castle-Con-undrum divide in the 1920's, I got into some statical electricity on a peak, which was strong enough to knock me down three times before I could get out of it. After the third flop I sat on the ground, ran my fingers through my hair several times and got handfuls of live sparks. I got out of the predicament by rolling over and over down the mountainside until I got away from the current that was being generated on the top of the peak. I then and there named the spot Electric Peak. Afterwards, I learned that other people had had similar experiences and that some of Hayden's men had noticed the current at the time of their survey.

Buckskin Pass, on the Maroon-Snowmass divide, was named ''Buckskin'' twice, and that fact due wholly to coindidence will be interesting news to the many mountain climbers, trail riders and other vacationists who cross it each year. In 1922 I led a trail-blazing party of six from Maroon to Snowmass Lake to select a passable route for a trail. As we approached the pass someone wanted

212

PHOTO BY THE LATE JOHN B. SCHUTTE

Woody Creek tank on the Denver & Rio Grande Western looked like this during the last days of steam locomotive operations. Today the tank is gone and Woody Creek is the end of the line on the railroad's Aspen Branch.

to know its name. I told him it was not named. Soon afterward a large buck deer appeared and stood on the skyline. I called the attention of the group to the buck and suggested that we name the pass, Buckskin. The group accepted the name and thought it was a very appropriate designation.

In 1941 I found a hand-made map of that country in the Forest Service files which was dated December 1, 1915, and believe it or not, it showed the name Buckskin Pass at that identical spot. The source of that name was not known until recently, when it was found in the notes of Percy Hagerman. He and Harold Clark had crossed the pass in 1915 with saddle and pack animals, and one of the latter had rolled down the mountainside. Because of that trouble with the buckskin horse, they had named the pass, Buckskin. And incidentally, let me add that in my opinion the view from Buckskin Pass is the most beautiful of all the lovely landscapes in the valley.

213

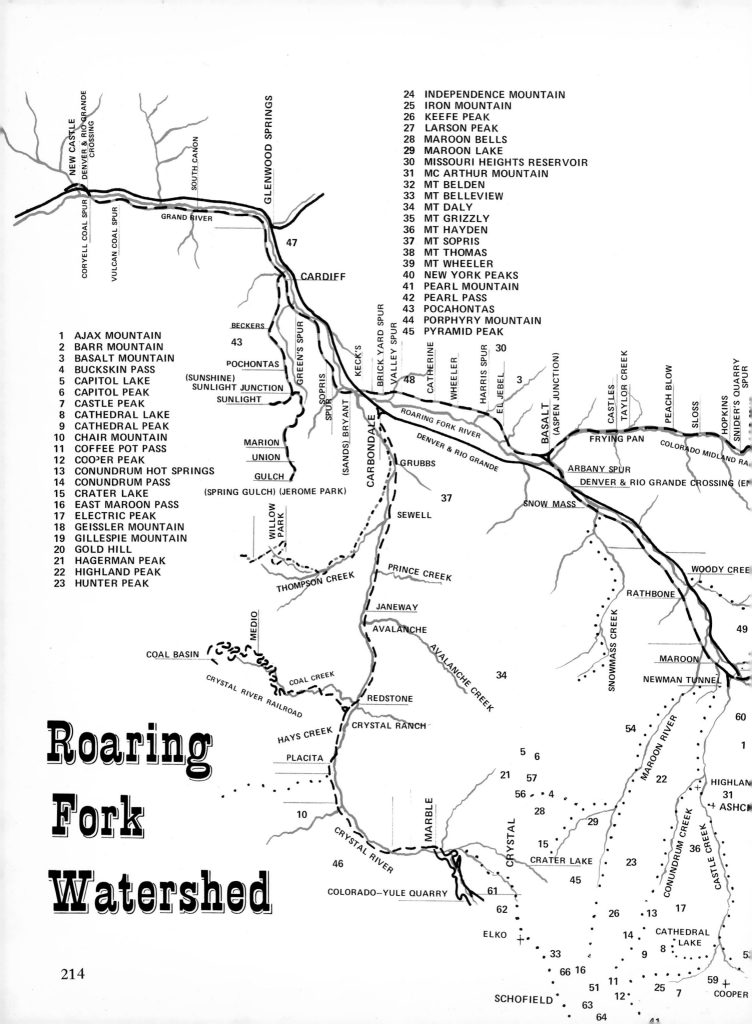

24 INDEPENDENCE MOUNTAIN
25 IRON MOUNTAIN
26 KEEFE PEAK
27 LARSON PEAK
28 MAROON BELLS
29 MAROON LAKE
30 MISSOURI HEIGHTS RESERVOIR
31 MC ARTHUR MOUNTAIN
32 MT BELDEN
33 MT BELLEVIEW
34 MT DALY
35 MT GRIZZLY
36 MT HAYDEN
37 MT SOPRIS
38 MT THOMAS
39 MT WHEELER
40 NEW YORK PEAKS
41 PEARL MOUNTAIN
42 PEARL PASS
43 POCAHONTAS
44 PORPHYRY MOUNTAIN
45 PYRAMID PEAK

1   AJAX MOUNTAIN
2   BARR MOUNTAIN
3   BASALT MOUNTAIN
4   BUCKSKIN PASS
5   CAPITOL LAKE
6   CAPITOL PEAK
7   CASTLE PEAK
8   CATHEDRAL LAKE
9   CATHEDRAL PEAK
10 CHAIR MOUNTAIN
11 COFFEE POT PASS
12 COOPER PEAK
13 CONUNDRUM HOT SPRINGS
14 CONUNDRUM PASS
15 CRATER LAKE
16 EAST MAROON PASS
17 ELECTRIC PEAK
18 GEISSLER MOUNTAIN
19 GILLESPIE MOUNTAIN
20 GOLD HILL
21 HAGERMAN PEAK
22 HIGHLAND PEAK
23 HUNTER PEAK

Roaring

Fork

Watershed

214

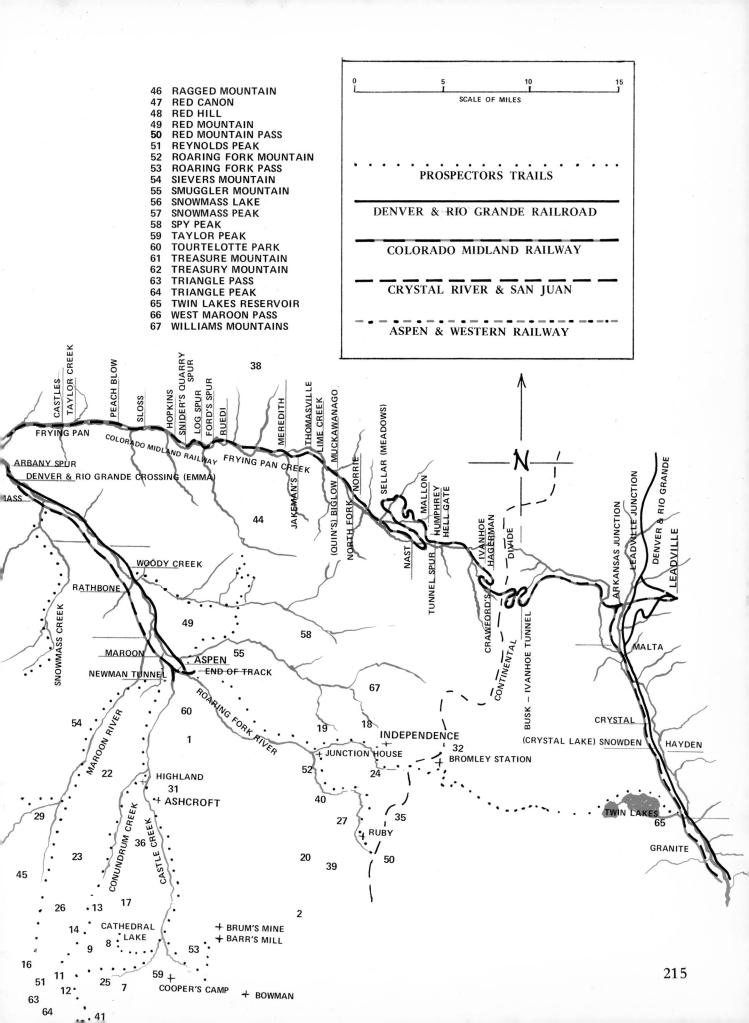

46 RAGGED MOUNTAIN
47 RED CANON
48 RED HILL
49 RED MOUNTAIN
50 RED MOUNTAIN PASS
51 REYNOLDS PEAK
52 ROARING FORK MOUNTAIN
53 ROARING FORK PASS
54 SIEVERS MOUNTAIN
55 SMUGGLER MOUNTAIN
56 SNOWMASS LAKE
57 SNOWMASS PEAK
58 SPY PEAK
59 TAYLOR PEAK
60 TOURTELOTTE PARK
61 TREASURE MOUNTAIN
62 TREASURY MOUNTAIN
63 TRIANGLE PASS
64 TRIANGLE PEAK
65 TWIN LAKES RESERVOIR
66 WEST MAROON PASS
67 WILLIAMS MOUNTAINS

SCALE OF MILES
0   5   10   15

· · · · · · · · · PROSPECTORS TRAILS

━━━━━━━━ DENVER & RIO GRANDE RAILROAD

━━━━━━━━ COLORADO MIDLAND RAILWAY

━ ━ ━ ━ CRYSTAL RIVER & SAN JUAN

━ ·━ ·━ ·━ ASPEN & WESTERN RAILWAY

215

INDEX